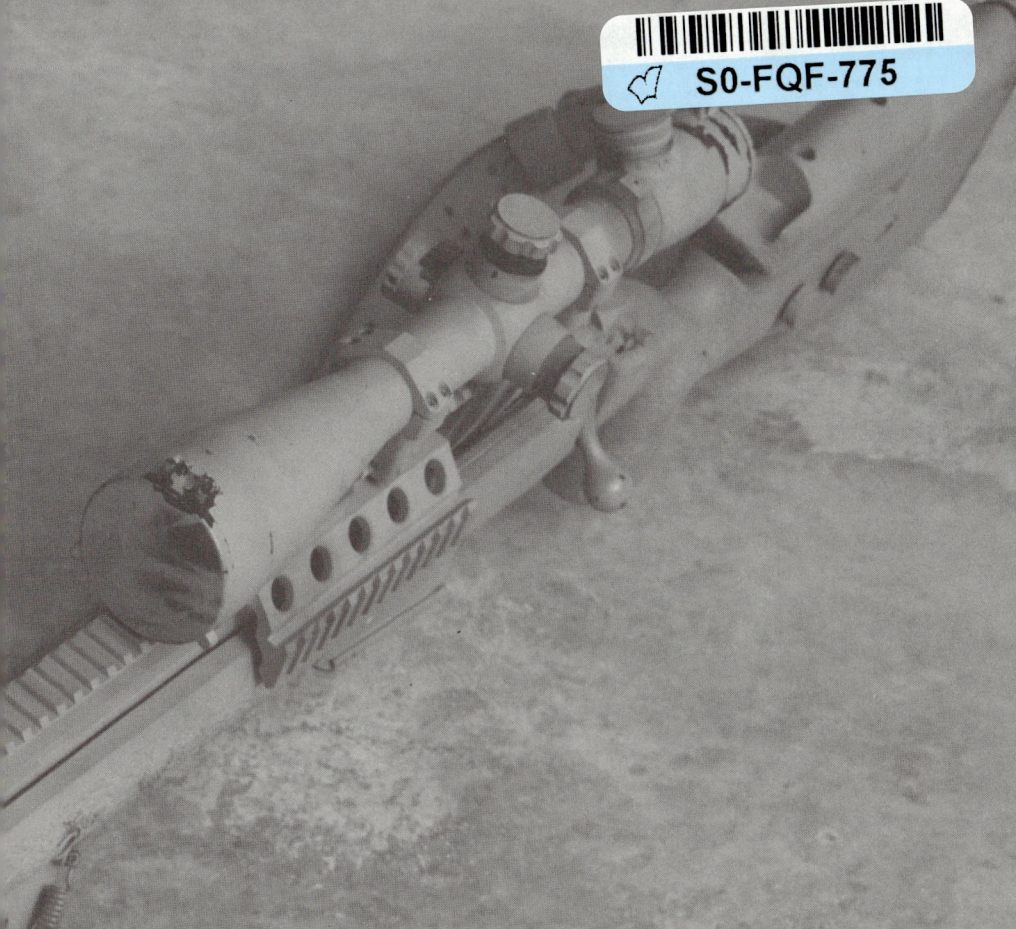

AMERICAN SNIPER

ALSO BY CHRIS KYLE

American Gun

AMERICAN SNIPER

★

MEMORIAL EDITION

★

THE AUTOBIOGRAPHY OF THE
MOST LETHAL SNIPER IN U.S.
MILITARY HISTORY

CHRIS KYLE

WITH JIM DeFELICE AND SCOTT McEWEN

WILLIAM MORROW
An Imprint of HarperCollinsPublishers

Map of Iraq on p. xi courtesy of the UN Cartographic Section.

AMERICAN SNIPER. Copyright © 2012, 2013 by CT Legacy, LLC. All rights reserved. Printed in the United States of America. No part of this book may be used or reproduced in any manner whatsoever without written permission except in the case of brief quotations embodied in critical articles and reviews. For information address HarperCollins Publishers, 10 East 53rd Street, New York, NY 10022.

HarperCollins books may be purchased for educational, business, or sales promotional use. For information e-mail the Special Markets Department at SPsales@harpercollins.com.

FIRST EDITION

Designed by Jamie Lynn Kerner

Library of Congress Cataloging-in-Publication Data has been applied for.

ISBN 978-0-06-229079-3
ISBN 978-0-06-231928-9 (Barnes & Noble signed edition)

13 14 15 16 17   OV/RRD   10 9 8 7 6 5 4 3 2 1

I dedicate this book to my wife, Taya, and my kids for sticking it out with me. Thanks for still being here when I got home.

I'd also like to dedicate it to the memory of my SEAL brothers Marc and Ryan, for their courageous service to our country and their undying friendship to me. I will bleed for their deaths the rest of my life.

CONTENTS

	Author's Note	ix
	Map of Iraq	xi
	Prologue: Evil in the Crosshairs	1
1.	Bustin' Broncs and Other Ways of Having Fun	7
2.	Jackhammered	22
3.	Takedowns	58
4.	Five Minutes to Live	74
5.	Sniper	92
6.	Dealing Death	117
7.	Down in the Shit	159
8.	Family Conflicts	201
9.	The Punishers	223
10.	The Devil of Ramadi	256
11.	Man Down	280
12.	Hard Times	303
13.	Mortality	332
14.	Home and Out	358
	Acknowledgments	380

CONTENTS

CHRIS KYLE, IN MEMORIAM	383
Introduction by Taya Kyle and Jim DeFelice	385
Wayne and Deby Kyle, Chris's mom and dad	388
Taya Kyle	392
Jeff Kyle, Chris's brother	398
Andrew Alexander, friend	403
Bo Pharr, friend	405
"W," writing on behalf of "the Teams"	407
Bryan Rury, lifelong friend	409
Marcus Luttrell, fellow SEAL, friend	411
Ashley Purvis Smith, family friend	413
Al Hemmle, principal, Midlothian High School	416
Glenn Beck, talk-show host	418
Jeff Burge, Dallas Police Department, friend	420
Dr. Karen Hanten, pediatrician, friend	421
Kelly Job, wife of Chris's SEAL teammate Ryan Job	423
"Dauber," fellow SEAL, friend	425
Kim and Kent Studebaker, Chris's parents-in-law	427
Anonymous, active-duty SEAL, friend	429
Kim Essary, neighbor, friend	431
Larry Toon, chairman of Elizabeth Toon Charities	434
Leanne Littlefield, friend	436
Marc Myers, businessman, ranch owner, friend	439
Mathew Bullinger, fellow Little League coach, friend	441
Omar Avila, wounded warrior, friend	443
Randy Cupp, businessman, friend	446
Rich Emberlin, Dallas Police Department, friend	450
Sarah and Ellyse Dyer, friends	453
Scott Brown, Musician, Marine, friend	455
Sergeant Vince Lee, Dallas Police Department, friend	458
Jim DeFelice, coauthor of *American Sniper*	460

AUTHOR'S NOTE

The events that happened in this book are true, recounted from the best of my memory. The Department of Defense, including high-ranking U.S.N. personnel, reviewed the text for accuracy and sensitive material. Even though they cleared the book for publication, this does not mean they like everything they read. But this is my story, not theirs. We've reconstructed dialogue from memory, which means that it may not be word for word. But the essence of what was said is accurate.

No classified information was used in the preparation of this book. The Pentagon's Office of Security Review and the Navy requested that certain changes be made for security reasons. Those requests were all honored.

Many of the people I served with are still active-duty SEALs. Others are working in different capacities for the government, protecting our nation. All may be considered enemies by our country's enemies, as am I. Because of that, I have not given their full identities in this book. They know who they are, and I hope they know they have my thanks.

—C.K.

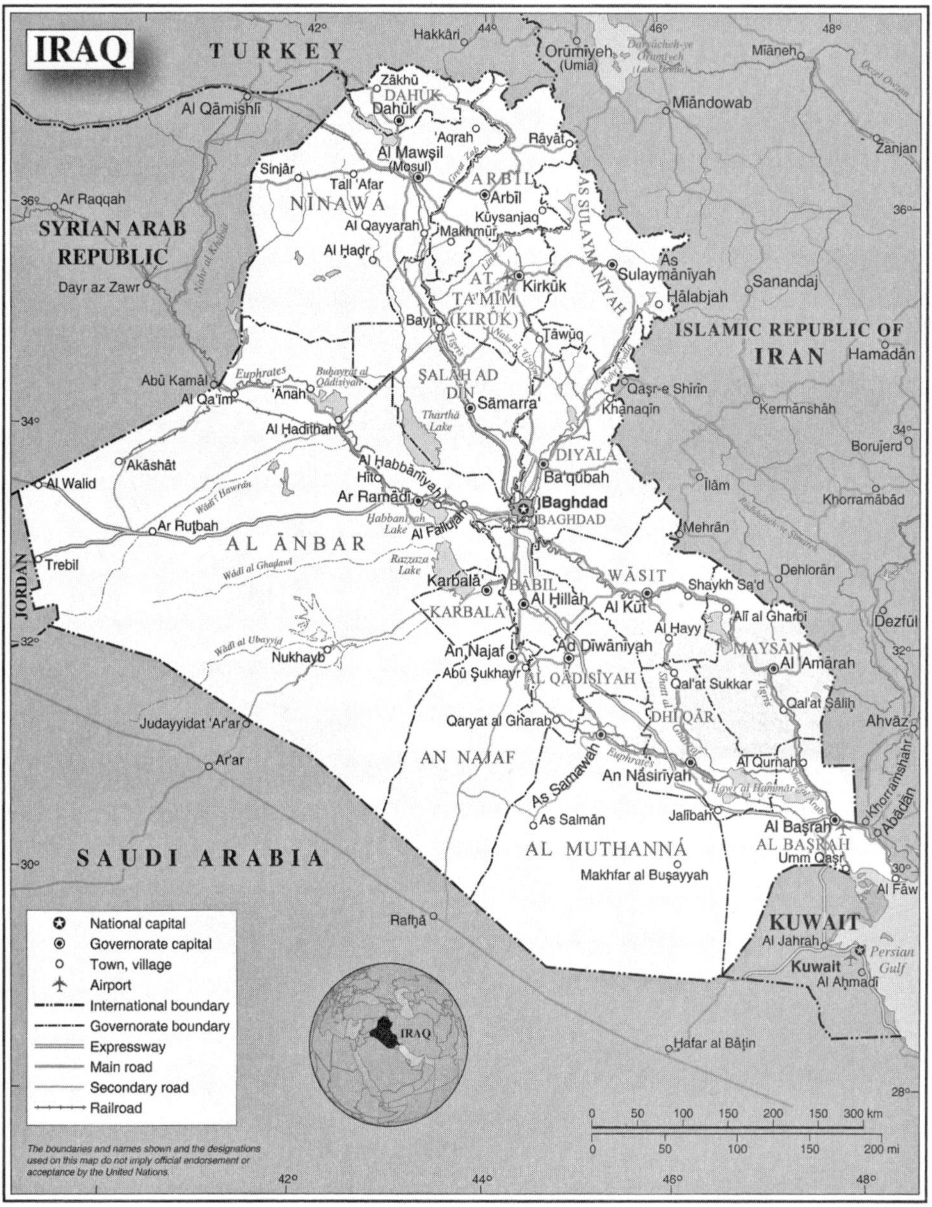

IRAQ
TURKEY
SYRIAN ARAB REPUBLIC
ISLAMIC REPUBLIC OF IRAN
SAUDI ARABIA
KUWAIT
JORDAN
Persian Gulf
NĪNAWÁ
DAHŪK
ARBĪL
AS SULAYMĀNĪYAH
AT TA'MĪM (KIRKŪK)
ŞALĀḨ AD DĪN
DIYĀLÁ
BAGHDAD
AL ĀNBAR
BĀBIL
KARBALĀ'
WĀSIT
MAYSĀN
AL QĀDISĪYAH
DHĪ QĀR
AN NAJAF
AL MUTHANNÁ
AL BAŞRAH
Baghdad
Zākhū
Dahūk
'Aqrah
Al Mawşil (Mosul)
Sinjār
Tall 'Afar
Arbīl
Kūysanjaq
Rāyāt
Al Qayyarah
Makhmūr
Al Ḩaḑr
Kirkūk
As Sulaymānīyah
Ḩalabjah
Bayjī
Ţāwūq
Sāmarrā'
Khānaqīn
Ba'qūbah
Abū Kamāl
Al Qā'im
'Ānah
Al Ḩadīthah
Ākāshāt
Al Walīd
Al Ḩabbānīyah
Hīt
Ar Ramādī
Al Fallūjah
Ar Ruţbah
Trebil
Karbalā'
Al Ḩillah
Al Kūt
Shaykh Sa'd
'Alī al Gharbī
Al Ḩayy
Ad Dīwānīyah
An Najaf
Abū Şukhayr
Qal'at Sukkar
Al 'Amārah
Qal'at Şāliḩ
Qaryat al Gharab
As Samawah
An Nāşirīyah
Al Qurnah
Jalībah
Al Başrah
Umm Qaşr
Al Fāw
As Salmān
Makhfar al Buşayyah
Nukhayb
Judayyidat 'Ar'ar
Ar'ar
Rafḩā
Ḩafar al Bāţin
Al Jahrah
Kuwait
Al Aḩmadī
Hakkâri
Al Qāmishlī
Ar Raqqah
Dayr az Zawr
Orūmīyeh (Umia)
Daryācheh-ye Orūmīyeh (Lake Urmia)
Mīāneh
Mīāndowab
Zanjan
Sanandaj
Hamadān
Qaşr-e Shīrīn
Kermānshāh
Borūjerd
Īlām
Khorramābād
Mehrān
Dehlorān
Dezfūl
Ahvāz
Khorramshahr
Ābādān
Euphrates
Tigris
Great Zab
Little Zab
Buḩayrat al Qādisīyah
Tharthār Lake
Ḩabbānīyah Lake
Razzaza Lake
Wādī Ḩawrān
Wādī al Ghadawī
Wādī al Ubayyid
Shaţţ al Gharraf
Hawr al Ḩammār
Shaţţ al 'Arab
Nahr al Khābūr
Nahr Diyālá
Nahr al 'Uzaym
42°
44°
46°
48°
36°
34°
32°
30°
28°
National capital
Governorate capital
Town, village
Airport
International boundary
Governorate boundary
Expressway
Main road
Secondary road
Railroad
0 50 100 150 200 250 300 km
0 50 100 150 200 mi
The boundaries and names shown and the designations used on this map do not imply official endorsement or acceptance by the United Nations.

PROLOGUE

EVIL IN THE CROSSHAIRS

LATE MARCH 2003. IN THE AREA OF NASIRIYA, IRAQ

I LOOKED THROUGH THE SCOPE OF THE SNIPER RIFLE, SCANning down the road of the tiny Iraqi town. Fifty yards away, a woman opened the door of a small house and stepped outside with her child.

The rest of the street was deserted. The local Iraqis had gone inside, most of them scared. A few curious souls peeked out from behind curtains, waiting. They could hear the rumble of the approaching American unit. The Marines were flooding up the road, marching north to liberate the country from Saddam Hussein.

It was my job to protect them. My platoon had taken over the building earlier in the day, sneaking into position to provide "overwatch"—prevent the enemy from ambushing the Marines as they came through.

It didn't seem like too difficult a task—if anything, I was glad the Marines were on my side. I'd seen the power of their weapons and I would've hated to have to fight them. The Iraq army didn't stand a chance. And, in fact, they appeared to have abandoned the area already.

The war had started roughly two weeks before. My platoon, "Charlie" (later "Cadillac") of SEAL Team 3, helped kick it off during the early morning of March 20. We landed on al-Faw Peninsula and secured the oil terminal there so Saddam couldn't set it ablaze as he had during the First Gulf War. Now we were tasked to assist the Marines as they marched north toward Baghdad.

I was a SEAL, a Navy commando trained in special operations. SEAL stands for "SEa, Air, Land," and it pretty much describes the wide ranges of places we operate. In this case, we were far inland, much farther than SEALs traditionally operated, though as the war against terror continued, this would become common. I'd spent nearly three years training and learning how to become a warrior; I was ready for this fight, or at least as ready as anyone can be.

The rifle I was holding was a .300 WinMag, a bolt-action, precision sniper weapon that belonged to my platoon chief. He'd been covering the street for a while and needed a break. He showed a great deal of confidence in me by choosing me to spot him and take the gun. I was still a new guy, a newbie or rookie in the Teams. By SEAL standards, I had yet to be fully tested.

I was also not yet trained as a SEAL sniper. I wanted to be one in the worst way, but I had a long way to go. Giving me the rifle that morning was the chief's way of testing me to see if I had the right stuff.

We were on the roof of an old rundown building at the edge of a town the Marines were going to pass through. The wind kicked dirt and papers across the battered road below us. The place smelled like a sewer—the stench of Iraq was one thing I'd never get used to.

"Marines are coming," said my chief as the building began to shake. "Keep watching."

I looked through the scope. The only people who were moving were the woman and maybe a child or two nearby.

I watched our troops pull up. Ten young, proud Marines in uniform got out of their vehicles and gathered for a foot patrol. As the Americans organized, the woman took something from beneath her clothes, and yanked at it.

She'd set a grenade. I didn't realize it at first.

"Looks yellow," I told the chief, describing what I saw as he watched himself. "It's yellow, the body—"

"She's got a grenade," said the chief. "That's a Chinese grenade."

"Shit."

"Take a shot."

"But—"

"Shoot. Get the grenade. The Marines—"

I hesitated. Someone was trying to get the Marines on the radio, but we couldn't reach them. They were coming down the street, heading toward the woman.

"Shoot!" said the chief.

I pushed my finger against the trigger. The bullet leapt out. I shot. The grenade dropped. I fired again as the grenade blew up.

It was the first time I'd killed anyone while I was on the sniper rifle. And the first time in Iraq—and the only time—I killed anyone other than a male combatant.

It was my duty to shoot, and I don't regret it. The woman was already dead. I was just making sure she didn't take any Marines with her.

It was clear that not only did she want to kill them, but she didn't care about anybody else nearby who would have been blown up by the grenade or killed in the firefight. Children on the street, people in the houses, maybe *her* child . . .

She was too blinded by evil to consider them. She just wanted Americans dead, no matter what.

My shots saved several Americans, whose lives were clearly worth more than that woman's twisted soul. I can stand before God with a clear conscience about doing my job. But I truly, deeply hated the evil that woman possessed. I hate it to this day.

SAVAGE, DESPICABLE EVIL. THAT'S WHAT WE WERE FIGHTING in Iraq. That's why a lot of people, myself included, called the enemy "savages." There really was no other way to describe what we encountered there.

People ask me all the time, "How many people have you killed?" My standard response is, "Does the answer make me less, or more, of a man?"

The number is not important to me. I only wish I had killed more. Not for bragging rights, but because I believe the world is a better place without savages out there taking American lives. Everyone I shot in Iraq was trying to harm Americans or Iraqis loyal to the new government.

I had a job to do as a SEAL. I killed the enemy—an enemy I saw day in and day out plotting to kill my fellow Americans. I'm haunted by the enemy's successes. They were few, but even a single American life is one too many lost.

I don't worry about what other people think of me. It's one of the things I most admired about my dad growing up. He didn't give a hoot what others thought. He was who he was. It's one of the qualities that has kept me most sane.

As this book goes to print, I'm still a bit uncomfortable with the idea of publishing my life story. First of all, I've always thought that if you want to know what life as a SEAL is like, you should go get your own Trident: earn our medal, the symbol of who we are. Go through our training, make the sacrifices, physical and mental. That's the only way you'll know.

Second of all, and more importantly, who cares about my life? I'm no different than anyone else.

I happen to have been in some pretty bad-ass situations. People have told me it's interesting. I don't see it. Other people are talking about writing books about my life, or about some of the things I've done. I find it strange, but I also feel it's my life and my story, and I guess I better be the one to get it on paper the way it actually happened.

Also, there are a lot of people who deserve credit, and if I don't write the story, they may be overlooked. I don't like the idea of that at all. My boys deserve to be praised more than I do.

The Navy credits me with more kills as a sniper than any other American service member, past or present. I guess that's true. They go back and forth on what the number is. One week, it's 160 (the "official" number as of this writing, for what that's worth), then it's way higher, then it's somewhere in between. If you want a number, ask the Navy—you may even get the truth if you catch them on the right day.

People always want a number. Even if the Navy would let me, I'm not going to give one. I'm not a numbers guy. SEALs are silent warriors, and I'm a SEAL down to my soul. If you want the whole story, get a Trident. If you want to check me out, ask a SEAL.

If you want what I am comfortable with sharing, and even some stuff I am reluctant to reveal, read on.

I've always said that I wasn't the best shot or even the best sniper ever. I'm not denigrating my skills. I certainly worked hard to hone them. I was blessed with some excellent instructors, who deserve a lot of credit. And my boys—the fellow SEALs and the Marines and the Army soldiers who fought with me and helped me do my job—were all a critical part of my success. But my high total and my so-called "legend" have much to do with the fact that I was in the shit a lot.

In other words, I had more opportunities than most. I served back-to-back deployments from right before the Iraq War kicked off until the time I got out in 2009. I was lucky enough to be positioned directly in the action.

There's another question people ask a lot: Did it bother you killing so many people in Iraq?

I tell them, "No."

And I mean it. The first time you shoot someone, you get a little nervous. You think, can I really shoot this guy? Is it really okay? But after you kill your enemy, you see it's okay. You say, *Great*.

You do it again. And again. You do it so the enemy won't kill you or your countrymen. You do it until there's no one left for you to kill.

That's what war is.

I loved what I did. I still do. If circumstances were different—if my family didn't need me—I'd be back in a heartbeat. I'm not lying or exaggerating to say it was fun. I had the time of my life being a SEAL.

People try to put me in a category as a bad-ass, a good ol' boy, asshole, sniper, SEAL, and probably other categories not appropriate for print. All might be true on any given day. In the end, my story, in Iraq and afterward, is about more than just killing people or even fighting for my country.

It's about being a man. And it's about love as well as hate.

1

BUSTIN' BRONCS AND OTHER WAYS OF HAVING FUN

JUST A COWBOY AT HEART

Every story has a beginning.

Mine starts in north-central Texas. I grew up in small towns where I learned the importance of family and traditional values, like patriotism, self-reliance, and watching out for your family and neighbors. I'm proud to say that I still try to live my life according to those values. I have a strong sense of justice. It's pretty much black-and-white. I don't see too much gray. I think it's important to protect others. I don't mind hard work. At the same time, I like to have fun. Life's too short not to.

I was raised with, and still believe in, the Christian faith. If I had to order my priorities, they would be God, Country, Family. There might be some debate on where those last two fall—these days I've come around to believing that Family may, under some circumstances, outrank Country. But it's a close race.

I've always loved guns, always loved hunting, and in a way I guess you could say I've always been a cowboy. I was riding horses from the time I could walk. I wouldn't call myself a true cowboy today, because it's been a long time since I've worked a ranch, and I've probably lost a lot of what I had in the saddle. Still, in my heart if I'm not a SEAL I'm a cowboy, or should be. Problem is, it's a hard way to make a living when you have a family.

I don't remember when I started hunting, but it would have been when I was very young. My family had a deer lease a few miles from our house, and we would hunt every winter. (For you Yankees: a deer lease is a property where the owner rents or leases hunting rights out for a certain amount of time; you pay your money and you get the right to go out and hunt. Y'all probably have different arrangements where you live, but this one is pretty common down here.) Besides deer, we'd hunt turkey, doves, quail—whatever was in season. "We" meant my mom, my dad, and my brother, who's four years younger than me. We'd spend the weekends in an old RV trailer. It wasn't very big, but we were a tight little family and we had a lot of fun.

My father worked for Southwestern Bell and AT&T—they split and then came back together over the length of his career. He was a manager, and as he'd get promoted we'd have to move every few years. So in a way I was raised all over Texas.

Even though he was successful, my father hated his job. Not the work, really, but what went along with it. The bureaucracy. The fact that he had to work in an office. He *really* hated having to wear a suit and tie every day.

"I don't care how much money you get," my dad used to tell me. "It's not worth it if you're not happy." That's the most valuable piece of advice he ever gave me: Do what you want in life. To this day I've tried to follow that philosophy.

In a lot of ways my father was my best friend growing up, but he was able at the same time to combine that with a good dose of fatherly discipline. There was a line and I never wanted to cross it. I got my share of whuppin's (you Yankees will call 'em spankings) when I deserved it, but not to excess and never in anger. If my dad was mad, he'd give himself a few minutes to calm down before administering a controlled whuppin'—followed by a hug.

To hear my brother tell it, he and I were at each other's throats most of the time. I don't know if that's true, but we did have our share of tussles. He was younger and smaller than me, but he could give as good he got, and he'd never give up. He's a tough character and one of my closest friends to this day. We gave each other hell, but we also had a lot of fun and always knew we had each other's back.

Our high school used to have a statue of a panther in the front lobby. We had a tradition each year where seniors would try and put incoming freshmen on the panther as a hazing ritual. Freshmen, naturally, resisted. I had graduated when my brother became a freshman, but I came back on his first day of school and offered a hundred dollars to anyone who could sit him on that statue.

I still have that hundred dollars.

WHILE I GOT INTO A LOT OF FIGHTS, I DIDN'T START MOST OF them. My dad made it clear I'd get a whuppin' if he found out I started a fight. We were supposed to be above that.

Defending myself was a different story. Protecting my brother was even better—if someone tried to pick on him, I'd lay them out. I was the only one allowed to whip him.

Somewhere along the way, I started sticking up for younger kids who were getting picked on. I felt I had to look out for them. It became my duty.

Maybe it began because I was looking for an excuse to fight without getting into trouble. I think there was more to it than that; I think my father's sense of justice and fair play influenced me more than I knew at the time, and even more than I can say as an adult. But whatever the reason, it sure gave me plenty of opportunities for getting into scrapes.

MY FAMILY HAD A DEEP FAITH IN GOD. MY DAD WAS A DEAcon, and my mom taught Sunday school. I remember a stretch when I was young when we would go to church every Sunday morning, Sunday night, and Wednesday evening. Still, we didn't consider ourselves overly religious, just good people who believed in God and were involved in our church. Truth is, back then I didn't like going a lot of the time.

My dad worked hard. I suspect it was in his blood—his father was a Kansas farmer, and those people worked hard. One job was never enough for my dad—he had a feed store for a bit when I was growing up, and we had a pretty modest-sized ranch we all worked to keep going. He's retired now, officially, but you can still find him working for a local veterinarian when he's not tending to things on his small ranch.

My mother was also a really hard worker. When my brother and I were old enough to be on our own, she went to work as a counselor at a juvenile detention center. It was a rough job, dealing with difficult kids all day long, and eventually she moved on. She's retired now, too, though she keeps herself busy with part-time work and her grandchildren.

Ranching helped fill out my school days. My brother and I would have our different chores after school and on the weekends: feed and look after the horses, ride through the cattle, inspect the fences.

Cattle always give you problems. I've been kicked in the leg, kicked in the chest, and yes, kicked where the sun doesn't shine. Never been kicked in the head, though. That might have set me straight.

Growing up, I raised steers and heifers for FFA, Future Farmers of America. (The name is now officially The National FFA Organization.) I loved FFA and spent a lot of time grooming and showing cattle, even though dealing with the animals could be frustrating. I'd get pissed off at them and think I was king of the world. When all else failed, I was known to whack 'em upside their huge hard heads to knock some sense into them. Twice I broke my hand.

Like I said, getting hit in the skull may have set me straight.

I kept my head when it came to guns, but I was still passionate about them. Like a lot of boys, my first "weapon" was a Daisy multi-pump BB rifle—the more you pumped, the more powerful your shot. Later on, I had a CO_2-powered revolver that looked like the old 1860 Peacemaker Colt model. I've been partial to Old West firearms ever since, and after getting out of the Navy, I've started collecting some very fine-looking replicas. My favorite is an 1861 Colt Navy Revolver replica manufactured on the old lathes.

I got my first real rifle when I was seven or eight years old. It was a bolt-action 30-06. It was a solid gun—so "grown-up" that it scared me to shoot at first. I came to love that gun, but as I recall what I *really* lusted after was my brother's Marlin 30-30. It was lever action, cowboy-style.

Yes, there was a theme there.

BRONCO BUSTIN'

YOU'RE NOT A COWBOY UNTIL YOU CAN BREAK A HORSE. I started learning when I was in high school; at first, I didn't know a whole heck of a lot. It was just: *Hop on them and ride until they quit bucking. Do your best to stay on.*

I learned much more as I got older, but most of my early education came on the job—or on the horse, so to speak. The horse would do something, and I would do something. Together, we came to an understanding. Probably the most important lesson was patience. I wasn't a patient person by nature. I had to develop that talent working with horses; it would end up being extremely valuable when I became a sniper—and even when I was courting my wife.

Unlike cattle, I never found a reason to smack a horse. Ride them till I wore them out, sure. Stay on them till they realized who was boss, absolutely. But hit a horse? Never saw a reason good enough. Horses are smarter than cattle. You can work a horse into cooperating if you give it enough time and patience.

I don't know if I exactly had a talent for breaking horses or not, but being around them fed my appetite for all things cowboy. So, looking back, it isn't very surprising that I got involved in rodeo competitions while still in school. I played sports in high school—baseball and football—but nothing compared with the excitement of the rodeo.

Every high school has its different cliques: jocks, nerds, and so on. The crew I was hanging out with were the "ropers." We had the boots and jeans, and in general looked and acted like cowboys.

I wasn't a *real* roper—I couldn't have lassoed a calf worth a lick at that point—but that didn't stop me from getting involved in rodeos around age sixteen.

I started out by riding bulls and horses at a small local place where you paid twenty bucks to ride as long as you could stay on. You would have to supply your own gear—spurs, chaps, your rigging. There was nothing fancy about it: you got on and fell off, and got on again. Gradually, I stayed on longer and longer, and finally got to the point where I felt confident enough to enter some small local rodeos.

Bustin' a bull is a little different than taming a horse. They buck forward, but their skin is so loose that when they're going forward, you not only go forward but you slip side to side. And bulls can really spin. Let me put it this way: staying on top of a bull is not an easy matter.

I rode bulls for about a year, without a ton of success. Wising up, I went to horses and ended up trying saddle bronc bustin'. This is the classic event where you not only have to stay on the horse for eight seconds, but also do so with style and finesse. For some reason, I did a lot better in this event than the others, and so I kept with it for quite a while, winning my share of belt buckles and more than one fancy saddle. Not that I was a champion, mind you, but I did well enough to spread some prize money around the bar.

I also got some attention from the buckle bunnies, rodeo's version of female groupies. It was all good. I enjoyed going from city to city, traveling, partying, and riding.

Call it the cowboy lifestyle.

I CONTINUED RIDING AFTER I GRADUATED HIGH SCHOOL IN 1992 and started going to college at Tarleton State University in

Stephenville, Texas. For those of you who don't know it, Tarleton was founded in 1899 and joined the Texas A&M University system in 1917. They're the third largest non-land-grant agriculture university in the country. The school has a reputation for turning out excellent ranch and farm managers as well as agricultural education teachers.

At the time, I was interested in becoming a ranch manager. Before enrolling, though, I had given some thought to the military. My mom's dad had been an Army Air Force pilot, and for a while I thought of becoming an aviator. Then I considered becoming a Marine—I wanted to see real action. I liked the idea of fighting. I also heard a bit about special operations, and thought about joining Marine Recon, which is the Corps' elite special warfare unit. But my family, Mom especially, wanted me to go to college. Eventually, I saw it their way: I decided I would go to school first, then join the military. Heck, the way I looked at it, doing that meant I could party for a while before getting down to business.

I was still doing rodeo, and getting fairly good at it. But my career ended abruptly around the end of my freshman year, when a bronco flipped over on me in a chute at a competition in Rendon, Texas. The guys watching me couldn't open up the chute because of the way the horse came down, so they had to pull him back over on top of me. I still had one foot in the stirrup, and was dragged and kicked so hard I lost consciousness. I woke up in a life-flight helicopter flying to the hospital. I ended up with pins in my wrists, a dislocated shoulder, broken ribs, and a bruised lung and kidney.

Probably the worst part of the recovery was the dang pins. They were actually big screws about a quarter-inch thick. They stuck out a few inches on either side of my wrists, just like on Frankenstein's monster. They itched and looked strange, but they held my hands together.

A few weeks after I was hurt, I decided it was time to call up a girl I'd been wanting to take out. I wasn't about to let the pins get in the way of a good time. We were driving along and one of the long metal screws kept hitting the signal indicator as I was driving. It pissed me off so bad I ended up breaking it off at the base close to my skin. I don't guess she was too impressed with that. The date ended early.

My rodeo career was over, but I continued partying like I was on tour. I ran through my money pretty quick, and so I started looking for work after school. I found a job in a lumberyard as a delivery guy, dropping off wood and other materials.

I was a decent worker, and I guess it showed. One day a fellow came in and started talking to me.

"I know a guy who owns a ranch and he's looking for a hired hand," he said. "I wonder if you'd be interested."

"Holy hell," I told him. "I'll go out there right now."

And so I became a ranch hand—a real cowboy—even though I was still going to school full-time.

LIFE AS A COWBOY

I WENT TO WORK FOR DAVID LANDRUM, IN HOOD COUNTY, Texas, and quickly found out I wasn't near as much of a cowboy as I thought I was. David took care of that. He taught me everything about working a ranch, and then some. He was a rough man. He would cuss you up one side and down the other. If you were doing good, he wouldn't say a word. But I ended up really liking the guy.

Working on a ranch is heaven.

It's a hard life, featuring plenty of hard work, and yet at the same time it's an easy life. You're outside all the time. Most days it's just you and the animals. You don't have to deal with people or offices or any petty bullshit. You just do your job.

David's spread ran ten thousand acres. It was a real ranch, very old-school—we even had a chuck wagon during the spring roundup season.

I want to tell you, this was a beautiful place, with gentle hills, a couple of creeks, and open land that made you feel alive every time you looked at it. The heart of the ranch was an old house that had probably been a way station—an "inn" in Yankee-speak—back in the nineteenth century. It was a majestic building, with screened porches front and back, nice-sized rooms inside, and a big fireplace that warmed the soul as well as the skin.

Of course, because I was a ranch hand, my quarters were a little more primitive. I had what we called a bunkhouse, which was barely big enough for an actual bunk. It might have measured six by twelve feet, and my bed took up most of that. There wasn't space for drawers—I had to hang all my clothes, including my underwear, on a pole.

The walls weren't insulated. Central Texas can be pretty cold in the winter, and even with the gas stove on high and an electric heater right next to the bed, I slept with my clothes on. But the worst thing about it was the fact that there wasn't a proper foundation under the floorboards. I was continually doing battle with raccoons and armadillos, who'd burrow in right under my bed. Those raccoons were ornery and audacious; I must've shot twenty of them before they finally got the message that they weren't welcome under my house.

I started out riding the tractors, planting wheat for the cattle in the wintertime. I moved on to sluffing feed to the cattle. Eventually, David determined I was likely to stick around and started giving me more responsibilities. He bumped my salary to $400 a month.

After my last class ended around one or two in the afternoon, I'd head over to the ranch. There I'd work until the sun went down, study a bit, then go to bed. First thing in the morning, I'd feed all the horses, then head to class. Summer was the best. I'd be on horseback at five o'clock in the morning until nine at night.

Eventually, I became the two-year man, training "cut horses" and getting them ready for auction. (Cutting horses—also called carving horses, sorting horses, whittlers—are trained to help cowboys "cut" cows from the herd. These working horses are important on a ranch, and a good one can be worth a good amount of money.)

This is really where I learned about dealing with horses, and became much more patient than I had been before. If you lose your temper with a horse, you can ruin it for life. I taught myself to take my time and be gentle with them.

Horses are extremely smart. They learn quickly—if you do it right. You show them something real small, then stop, and do it again. A horse will lick its lips when it's learning. That's what I looked for. You stop the lesson on a good note, and pick up the next day.

Of course, it took a while to learn all this. Anytime I messed up, my boss would let me know. Right away he'd cuss me out, tell me I was a worthless piece of shit. But I never got pissed at David. In my mind, I thought, *I'm better than that and I'll show you.*

As it happens, that's exactly the kind of attitude you need to become a SEAL.

AMERICAN SNIPER: MEMORIAL EDITION

"NO" FROM THE NAVY

OUT THERE ON THE RANGE, I HAD A LOT OF TIME AND SPACE to think about where I was headed. Studying and classes were not my thing. With my rodeo career ended, I decided that I would quit college, stop ranching, and go back to my original plan: join the military and become a soldier. Since that was what I really wanted to do, there was no sense waiting.

And so, one day in 1996, I made my way to the recruiters, determined to sign up.

This recruiting station was its own mini-mall. The Army, Navy, Marine, Air Force offices were all lined up in a little row. Each one watched as you came in. They were in competition with each other, and not necessarily a friendly competition, either.

I went to the Marine door first, but they were out to lunch. As I turned around to leave, the Army guy down the hall called over.

"Hey," he said. "Why don't you come on in here?"

No reason not to, I thought. So I did.

"What are you interested in doing in the military?" he asked.

I told him that I liked the idea of special operations, and that from what I'd heard of Army SF, I thought I'd like to serve in that branch—if I were to join the Army, that is. (Special Forces, or SF, is an elite unit in the Army charged with a number of special operations missions. The term "special forces" is sometimes used incorrectly to describe special operation troops in general, but when I use it, I mean the Army unit.)

At the time, you had to be an E5—a sergeant—before you could be considered for SF. I didn't like the idea of waiting all that time before getting to the good stuff. "You could be a Ranger," suggested the recruiter.

I didn't know too much about Rangers, but what he told me sounded pretty enticing—jumping out of airplanes, assaulting targets, becoming a small-arms expert. He opened my eyes to the possibilities, though he didn't quite close the sale.

"I'll think about it," I said, getting up to leave.

As I was on my way out, the Navy guy called to me from down the hall.

"Hey, you," he said. "Come on over here."

I walked over.

"What were you talking about in there?" he asked.

"I was thinking about going into SF," I said. "But you have to be an E5. So we were talking about the Rangers."

"Oh, yeah? Heard about the SEALs?"

At the time, the SEALs were still relatively unknown. I had heard a little about them, but I didn't know all that much. I think I shrugged.

"Why don't you come on in here," said the sailor. "I'll tell you all about 'em."

He started by telling me about BUD/S, or Basic Underwater Demolition/Scuba training, which is the preliminary school all SEALs must pass through. Nowadays, there are hundreds of books and movies on SEALs and BUD/S; there's even a pretty long entry on our training in Wikipedia. But back then, BUD/S was still a bit of a mystery, at least to me. When I heard how hard it was, how the instructors ran you and how less than 10 percent of the class would qualify to move on, I was impressed. Just to make it through the training, you had to be one tough motherfucker.

I liked that kind of challenge.

Then the recruiter started telling me about all the missions SEALs, and their predecessors, the UDTs, had completed. (UDTs were members of Underwater Demolition Teams, frogmen who scouted enemy beaches and undertook other special warfare assignments beginning in World War II.) There were stories about swimming between obstructions on Japanese-held beaches and gruesome fights behind the lines in Vietnam. It was all bad-ass stuff, and when I left there, I wanted to be a SEAL in the worst way.

MANY RECRUITERS, ESPECIALLY THE GOOD ONES, HAVE MORE than a little larceny in them, and this one was no different. When I came back and was about to sign the papers, he told me I had to turn down the signing bonus if I wanted to make sure I got the SEAL contract.

I did.

He was full of it, of course. Having me turn down the bonus made him look pretty good, I'm sure. I don't doubt he's got a great career ahead of him as a used-car salesman.

The Navy did not promise that I would be a SEAL; I had to earn that privilege. What they did guarantee, though, was that I would have a chance to try out. As far as I was concerned, that was good enough, because there was no way that I was going to fail.

The only problem was that I didn't even get a chance to fail.

The Navy disqualified me when my physical revealed that I had pins in my arm from the rodeo accident. I tried arguing, I tried pleading; nothing worked. I even offered to sign a waiver saying that I'd never make the Navy responsible for anything that happened to my arm.

They flat-out turned me down.

And that, I concluded, was the end of my military career.

THE CALL

WITH THE MILITARY RULED OUT, I FOCUSED ON MAKING A CAreer out of ranching and being a cowboy. Since I already had a good job on a ranch, I decided there was really no sense staying in school. I quit, even though I was less than sixty credits shy of graduating.

David doubled my pay and gave me more responsibilities. Larger offers eventually lured me to other ranches, though for different reasons I kept coming back to David's ranch. Eventually, just before the winter of 1997–98, I found my way out to Colorado.

I took the job sight-unseen, which turned out to be a big mistake. My thinking was, I'd been spending all my time in the Texas flatlands, and a move to the mountains would be a welcome change of scenery.

But wouldn't you know it: I got a job at a ranch in the only part of Colorado flatter than Texas. And a good deal colder. It wasn't long before I called up David and asked if he needed some help.

"Come on back," he told me.

I started to pack, but I didn't get very far. Before I finished making arrangements to move, I got a phone call from a Navy recruiter.

"Are you still interested in being a SEAL?" he asked.

"Why?"

"We want you," said the recruiter.

"Even with the pins in my arm?"

"Don't worry about that."

I didn't. I started working on the arrangements right away.

2

JACKHAMMERED

WELCOME TO BUD/S

"Drop! One hundred push-ups! NOW!"

Two hundred and twenty-some bodies hit the asphalt and started pumping. We were all in camis—camouflage BDUs, or battle-dress uniforms—with freshly painted green helmets. It was the start of BUD/S training. We were bold, excited, and nervous as hell.

We were about to get beat down, and we were loving it.

The instructor didn't even bother to come out of his office inside the building a short distance away. His deep voice, slightly sadistic, carried easily out the hall into the courtyard where we were gathered.

"*More push-ups! Give me forty! FOUR-TEEE!*"

My arms hadn't quite started to burn yet when I heard a strange hissing noise. I glanced up to see what was going on.

I was rewarded with a blast of water in my face. Some of the other instructors had appeared and were working us over with fire hoses. Anyone stupid enough to look up, got hosed.

Welcome to BUD/S.

"Flutter kicks! GO!"

BUD/S STANDS FOR BASIC UNDERWATER DEMOLITION/SEAL and it is the introductory course that all candidates must pass to become SEALs. It's currently given at the Naval Special Warfare Center in Coronado, California. It starts with "indoc" or indoctrination, which is designed to introduce candidates to what will be required. Three phases follow: physical training, diving, land warfare.

There have been a number of stories and documentaries over the years about BUD/S and how tough it is. Pretty much everything they've said on that score is true. (Or at least mostly true. The Navy and the instructors tone it down a bit for national consumption on TV reality shows and other broadcasts. Still, even the watered-down version is true enough.) Essentially, the instructors beat you down, then beat you down some more. When that's done, they kick your ass, and beat what's left down again.

You get the idea.

I loved it. Hated it, loathed it, cursed it . . . but loved it.

LAME AND LAMER

IT HAD TAKEN ME THE BETTER PART OF A YEAR TO REACH THAT point. I'd joined the Navy and reported for basic training in February 1999. Boot camp was pretty lame. I remember calling my dad at one point and saying that basic was easy compared to ranch work. That wasn't a good thing. I'd joined the Navy to be a SEAL and challenge myself. Instead I got fat and out of shape.

You see, boot camp is designed to prepare you to sit on a ship. They teach you a lot about the Navy, which is fine, but I wanted something more like the Marines' basic training—a physical challenge. My brother went into the Marines and came out of boot camp tough and in top condition. I came out and probably would have flunked BUD/S if I'd gone straight in. They have since changed the procedure. There's now a separate BUD/S boot camp, with more emphasis on getting and staying in shape.

Lasting over a half-year, BUD/S is extremely demanding physically and mentally; as I mentioned earlier, the dropout rate can top 90 percent. The most notorious part of BUD/S is Hell Week, 132 hours straight of exercise and physical activity. A few of the routines have changed and tested over the years, and I imagine they will continue to evolve. Hell Week has pretty much remained the most demanding physical test, and probably will continue to be one of the high points—or low points, depending on your perspective. When I was in, Hell Week came at the end of First Phase. But more about that later.

Fortunately, I didn't go directly to BUD/S. I had other training to get through first, and a shortage of instructors in the BUD/S classes would keep me (and many others) from being abused for quite a while.

According to Navy regs, I had to choose a specialty (or Military Occupation Specialty, or MOS, as it is known in the service) in case I didn't make it through BUD/S and qualify for the SEALs. I chose intelligence—I naively thought I'd end up like James Bond. Have your little laugh.

But it was during that training that I started working out more seriously. I spent three months learning the basics of the Navy's intelligence specialties, and, more importantly, getting my body into better shape. It happened that I saw a bunch of real SEALs on the base, and they inspired me to work out. I would go to the gym and hit every vital part of my body: legs, chest, triceps, biceps, etc. I also started running three times a week, from four to eight miles a day, jumping up two miles every session.

I hated running, but I was beginning to develop the right mindset: Do whatever it takes.

THIS WAS ALSO WHERE I LEARNED HOW TO SWIM, OR AT LEAST how to swim better.

The part of Texas I'm from is far from the water. Among other things, I had to master the sidestroke—a critical stroke for a SEAL.

When intel school ended, I was rounding into shape, but probably still not quite ready for BUD/S. Though I didn't think so at the time, I was lucky that there was a shortage of instructors for BUD/S, which caused a backlog of students. The Navy decided to assign me to help the SEAL detailers for a few weeks until there was an opening. (Detailers are the people in the military who handle various personnel tasks. They're similar to human resources people in large corporations.)

I'd work about half a day with them, either from eight to noon or noon to four. When I wasn't working, I trained up with other SEAL candidates. We'd do PT, or physical training—what old-school gym teachers call calisthenics—for two hours. You know the drill: crunches, push-ups, squats.

We stayed away from weight work. The idea was that you didn't want to get muscle-bound; you wanted to be strong but have maximum flexibility.

On Tuesdays and Thursdays, we'd do exhaustion swim—swim until you sink, basically. Fridays were long runs of ten and twelve miles. Tough, but in BUD/S you were expected to run a half-marathon.

My parents remember having a conversation with me around this time. I was trying to prepare them for what might lie ahead. They didn't know that much about SEALs; probably a good thing.

Someone had mentioned that my identity might be erased from official records. When I told them, I could see them grimace a little.

I asked if they were okay with it. Not that they would really have a choice, I suppose.

"It's okay," insisted my dad. My mom took it silently. They were both more than a little concerned, but they tried to hide it and never said anything to discourage me from going ahead.

Finally, after six months or so of waiting, working out, and waiting some more, my orders came through: Report to BUD/S.

GETTING MY ASS KICKED

I UNFOLDED MYSELF FROM THE BACKSEAT OF THE CAB AND straightened my dress uniform. Hoisting my bag out of the taxi, I took a deep breath and started up the path to the quarterdeck, the building where I was supposed to report. I was twenty-four years old, about to live my dream.

And get my ass kicked in the process.

It was dark, but not particularly late—somewhere past five or six in the evening. I half-expected I'd be jumped as soon as I walked in the door. You hear all these rumors about BUD/S and how tough it is, but you never get the full story. Anticipation makes things worse.

I spotted a guy sitting behind a desk. I walked over and introduced myself. He checked me in and got me squared away with a room and the other administrative BS that needed to be handled.

All the time, I was thinking: "This isn't too hard."

And: "I'm going to get attacked any second."

Naturally, I had trouble getting to sleep. I kept thinking the instructors were going to burst in and start whipping my ass. I was excited, and a little worried at the same time.

Morning came without the slightest disturbance. It was only then that I found out I wasn't really in BUD/S; not yet, not officially. I was in what is known as Indoc—or Indoctrination. Indoc is meant to prepare you for BUD/S. It's kind of like BUD/S with training wheels. If SEALs did training wheels.

Indoc lasted a month. They did yell at us some, but it was nothing like BUD/S. We spent a bit of time learning the basics of what would be expected of us, like how to run the obstacle course. The idea was that by the time things got serious, we'd have our safety down. We also spent a lot of time helping out in small ways as other classes went through the actual training.

Indoc was fun. I loved the physical aspect, pushing my body and honing my physical skills. At the same time, I saw how the candidates were being treated in BUD/S, and I thought, *Oh shit, I better get serious and work out more.*

And then, before I knew it, First Phase started. Now the training *was* for real, and my butt *was* being kicked. Regularly and with a great deal of feeling.

Which brings us up to the point where we started this chapter, with me getting hosed in the face while working out. I had been doing PT for months, and yet this was far harder. The funny thing is, even though I knew more or less what was going to happen, I didn't completely understand how difficult it was going to be. Until you actually experience something, you just don't know.

At some point that morning, I thought, *Holy shit, these guys are going to kill me. My arms are going to fall off and I'm going to disintegrate right into the pavement.*

Somehow I kept going.

The first time the water hit me, I turned my face away. That earned me a lot of attention—bad attention.

"Don't turn away!" shouted the instructor, adding a few choice words relating to my lack of character and ability. "Turn back and take it."

So I did. I don't know how many hundreds of push-ups or other exercises we did. I do know that I felt I was going to fail. That drove me—I did not want to fail.

I kept facing that fear, and coming to the same conclusion, every day, sometimes several times.

PEOPLE ASK ABOUT HOW TOUGH THE EXERCISES WERE, HOW many push-ups we had to do, how many sit-ups. To answer the first question, the number was a hundred each, but the numbers themselves were almost beside the point. As I recall, everyone could do a hundred push-ups or whatever. It was the repetition and constant stress, the abuse that came with the exercises, that made BUD/S so tough. I guess it's hard to explain if you haven't lived through it.

There's a common misunderstanding that SEALs are all huge guys in top physical condition. That last part is generally true—every SEAL in the Teams is in excellent shape. But SEALs come in all sizes. I was in the area of six foot two and 175 pounds; others who would serve with me ranged from five foot seven on up to six foot six. The thing we all had in common wasn't muscle; it was the will to do whatever it takes.

Getting through BUD/S and being a SEAL is more about mental toughness than anything else. Being stubborn and refusing to give in is the key to success. Somehow I'd stumbled onto the winning formula.

UNDER THE RADAR

THAT FIRST WEEK I TRIED TO BE AS FAR UNDER THE RADAR AS possible. Being noticed was a *bad* thing. Whether it was during PT or an exercise, or even just standing in line, the least little thing could make you the focus of attention. If you were slouching while in line, they fixed on you right away. If an instructor said to do something, I tried to be the first one to do it. If I did it right—and I sure tried to—they ignored me and went on to someone else.

I couldn't completely escape notice. Despite all my exercise, despite all the PT and everything else, I had a lot of trouble with pull-ups.

I'm sure you know the routine—you put your arms up on the bar and pull yourself up. Then you lower yourself. Repeat. Repeat. Repeat.

In BUD/S, we had to hang from the bar and wait there until the instructor told us to start. Well, the first time the class set up, he happened to be standing right close to me.

"Go!" he said.

"Ugghhhh," I moaned, pulling myself northward.

Big mistake. Right away I got tagged as being weak.

I couldn't do all that many pull-ups to begin with, maybe a half-dozen (which was actually the requirement). But now, with all the attention, I couldn't just slip by. I had to do *perfect* pull-ups. And many of them. The instructors singled me out, and started making me do more, and giving me a lot of extra exercise.

It had an effect. Pull-ups became one of my better exercises. I could top thirty without trouble. I didn't end up the best in the class, but I wasn't an embarrassment, either.

And swimming? All the work I'd done before getting to BUD/S paid off. Swimming actually became my *best* exercise. I was one of, if not *the* fastest, swimmers in the class

Again, minimum distances don't really tell the story. To qualify, you have to swim a thousand yards in the ocean. By the time you're done with BUD/S, a thousand yards is nothing. You swim all the time. Two-mile swims were routine. And then there was the time where we were taken out in boats and dropped off seven nautical miles from the beach.

"There's one way home, boys," said the instructors. "Start swimming."

MEAL TO MEAL

Probably everyone who's heard of SEALs has heard of Hell Week. It's five and a half days of continuous beat-down designed to see if you have the endurance and the will to become the ultimate warrior.

Every SEAL has a different Hell Week story. Mine actually begins a day or two before Hell Week, out in the surf, on some rocks. A group of us were in an IBS—"inflatable boat, small," your basic six-man rubber dinghy—and we had to bring it ashore past those rocks. I was point man, which meant it was my job to clamber out and hold the IBS tight while everyone else got off and picked it up.

Well, just as I was getting set, a huge wave came up in the surf and took the boat and put it down on my foot. It hurt like hell, and immediately got numb.

I ignored it as much as I could, and eventually wrapped it up. Later on, when we were finished for the day, I went with a buddy whose dad happened to be a doctor and had him check it out. He did an X-ray and found it was fractured.

Naturally, he wanted to put it in a cast, but I refused to let him. Showing up at BUD/S with a cast would mean I would have to put my training on hold. And if I did that before Hell Week, I'd have to go back to the very beginning—and no way I was going through everything I'd just been through again.

(Even during BUD/S, you're allowed to leave base with permission during your off time. And, obviously, I didn't go to a Navy doctor to get the foot checked out, because he would have sent me back—known as "roll back"—immediately.)

The night Hell Week was supposed to start, we were taken to a large room, fed pizza, and treated to a movie marathon—*Black Hawk Down, We Were Soldiers, Braveheart*. We were all relaxing in a non-relaxing kind of way, since we knew Hell Week was about to begin. It was like a party on the *Titanic*. The movies got us all psyched up, but we knew that iceberg was out there, looming in the dark.

Once more, my imagination got me nervous. I knew at some point an instructor was going to bust through that door with an M-60 machine gun shooting blanks, and I was going to have to run outside and form up on the grinder (asphalt workout area). But when?

Every minute that passed added to the churning in my stomach. I was sitting there saying to myself, "God." Over and over. Very eloquent and deep.

I tried to take a nap but I couldn't sleep. Finally, someone burst in and started shooting.

Thank God!

I don't think I've ever been so happy to be abused in my life. I ran outside. The instructors were throwing flash-crashes and had the hoses going full-blast. (Flash-crashes and flash-bang grenades give off an intense flash and make a very loud noise when they explode, but won't injure you. Technically, the terms are applied to different grenades used by the Army and Navy, but we generally use the names interchangeably.)

I was excited, ready for what some people think is the ultimate test for SEAL trainees. But at the same time, I was thinking, *What the hell is going on?* Because even though I knew all about Hell Week—or thought I did—never having experienced it, I really didn't understand it in my bones.

We were split up. They sent us to different stations and we began doing push-ups, flutter kicks, star jumpers . . .

After that, everything ran together. My foot? That was the least of the pain. We swam, we did PT, we took the boats out. Mostly, we just kept moving. One of the guys was so exhausted at one point, he thought a kayak coming to check on us in the boats was a shark and started yelling a warning. (It was actually our commander. I'm not sure if he took that as a compliment or not.)

Before BUD/S began, someone told me the best way to deal with it is to go meal-to-meal. Go as hard as you can until you get fed. They feed you every six hours, like clockwork. So I focused on that. Salvation was always no further than five hours and fifty-nine minutes away.

Still, there were several times I thought I wouldn't make it. I was tempted to get up and run over to the bell that would end my torture—if you ring this bell, you're taken in for coffee and a doughnut. And good-byes, since ringing the bell (or even standing up and saying "I quit") means the end of the program for you.

Believe it or not, my fractured foot gradually started to feel better as the week went on. Maybe I just became so used to the feeling that it became normal. What I couldn't stand was being cold. Lying out on the beach in the surf, stripped down, freezing my ass off—that was the worst. I'd lock arms with the guys on either side of me and "jackhammer," my body vibrating crazily with the chills. I prayed for someone to pee on me.

Everybody did, I'm sure. Urine was about the only warm thing available at that point. If you happen to look out on the surf during a BUD/S class and see a bunch of guys huddled together, it's because somebody out there is pissing and everybody is taking advantage of it.

If that bell was a little closer, I might have stood up and gone and rung it, gotten my warm coffee and doughnut. But I didn't.

Either I was too stubborn to quit, or just too lazy to get up. Take your pick.

I HAD ALL SORTS OF MOTIVATION TO KEEP ME GOING. I remembered every person who told me I'd flunk out of BUD/S. Sticking in was the same as sticking it to them. And seeing all the ships out off the coast was another incentive: I asked myself if I wanted to wind up out there.

Hell no.

Hell Week started on Sunday night. Come about Wednesday, I started feeling I was going to make it. By that point, my main goal was mostly to stay awake. (I got about two hours of sleep that whole time, and they weren't together.) A lot of the beating had gone away and it was more a mental challenge than anything else. Many instructors say Hell Week is 90 percent mental, and they're right. You need to show that you have the mental toughness to continue on with a mission even when you're exhausted. That's really what the idea is behind the test.

It's definitely an effective way of weeding out guys. I didn't see it at the time, to be honest. In combat, though, I understood. You can't just walk over and ring a bell to go home when you're being fired at. There's no saying, "Give me that cup of coffee and the doughnut you promised." If you quit, you die and some of your boys die.

My instructors in BUD/S were always saying things like, "You think this is bad? It's going to suck more once you get to the Teams. You'll be colder and more tired once you get there."

Lying in the surf, I thought they were full of shit. Little did I know that in a few years, I'd think Hell Week was a cakewalk.

BEING COLD BECAME MY NIGHTMARE.

I mean that literally. After Hell Week, I would wake up shivering all the time. I could be under all sorts of blankets and still be cold, because I was going through it all again in my mind.

So many books and videos have been done on Hell Week that I won't waste more of your time describing it. I will say one thing: going through it is far worse than reading about it.

ROLLED BACK

THE WEEK AFTER HELL WEEK IS A BRIEF RECOVERY PHASE called walk week. By then they've beaten you so bad your body feels permanently bruised and swollen. You wear tennis shoes and don't run—you just fast-walk everywhere. It's a concession that doesn't last for very long; after a few days, they start beating the hell out of you again.

"Okay, suck it up," the instructors yell. "You're over it."

They tell you when you're hurt and when you're not.

Having survived Hell Week, I thought I was home free. I traded my white shirt for brown and began part two of BUD/S, the dive phase. Unfortunately, somewhere along the way I'd gotten an infection. Not long after second phase started, I was in a dive tower, a special training apparatus that simulates a dive. In this particular exercise, I had to practice with a dive bell, making what is called a buoyant ascent while keeping the pressure in my inner and outer ears equalized. There are a few methods for doing that; one common one is to close your mouth, pinch your nostrils closed, and gently blow through your nose. If you don't or can't clear properly, there will be trouble . . .

I'd been told this, but because of the infection I couldn't seem to get it. Since I was in BUD/S and inexperienced, I decided to just suck it up and take a shot. That was the wrong thing to do: I went on down and ended up perforating my eardrum. I had blood coming out of my ears, nose, and eyes when I surfaced.

They gave me medical attention on the spot and then sent me to have my ears treated. Because of the medical problems, I was rolled back—assigned to join a later class once I healed.

When you're rolled back, you're in a sort of limbo. Since I had already made it through Hell Week, I didn't have to go all the way back to the start—there's no repeating Hell Week, thank God. I couldn't just lie on my butt until the next class caught up, though. As soon as I was able, I helped the instructors, did daily PT, and ran with a class of white shirts (first phase) as they got their asses busted.

ONE THING TO KNOW ABOUT ME IS THAT I LOVE DIPPING TO-bacco.

I have since I was a teen. My father caught me with chewing tobacco when I was in high school. He was opposed to it, and decided he'd break me of the habit once and for all. So he made me eat an entire can of wintergreen mint–flavored tobacco. To this day, I can't even use wintergreen toothpaste.

Other kinds of chew are a different story. These days, Copenhagen is my brand of choice.

You're not allowed to have tobacco as a candidate in BUD/S. But being a rollback, I guess I thought I could get away with it. One day I put some Copenhagen in my mouth and joined the formation for a run. I was deep enough in the pack that no one would be paying attention. Or so I thought.

Wouldn't you know, but one of the instructors came back and started talking to me. As soon as I answered, he saw I had some dip in my mouth.

"*Drop!*"

I fell out of formation and assumed the push-up position.

"Where's your can?" he demanded.

"In my sock."

"Get it."

I, of course, had to stay in my push-up position while I did that, so I reached back with one hand and took it out. He opened the can and put it down in front of me. "Eat it."

Every time I came down from a push-up, I had to take a big bite of Copenhagen and swallow it. I had been dipping from the time I was fifteen, and I already regularly swallowed my tobacco when I was done, so it wasn't as bad as you might think. It certainly wasn't as bad as my instructor wanted. Maybe if it had been wintergreen, it would have been a different story. It pissed him off that I wasn't throwing up. So he worked me for several hours with all these exercises and such. I *did* almost puke—not from the Copenhagen but exhaustion.

Finally, he let me be. After that, we got along pretty well. It turned out he was a dipper himself. He and another instructor from Texas took a liking to me toward the end of BUD/S, and I learned a ton from both men as the course went on.

A LOT OF PEOPLE ARE SURPRISED TO HEAR THAT INJURIES don't necessarily disqualify you from becoming a SEAL, unless they are so serious that they end your Navy career. It makes sense, though, since being a SEAL is more about mental toughness than physical prowess—if you have the psychological fortitude to come back from an injury and complete the program, you stand a decent chance of being a good SEAL. I personally know a SEAL who broke his hip so badly during training that it had to be replaced. He had to sit out for a year and a half, but he made it through BUD/S.

You hear guys talking about getting kicked out of BUD/S because they got into a fight with the instructor and beat the crap out of him. They're lying sacks of shit. No one fights with the instructors. You just don't. Believe me, if you did, they'd come together and whip your ass so fast you wouldn't ever walk again.

MARCUS

YOU GET CLOSE TO THE PEOPLE IN BUD/S, BUT YOU TRY NOT to get *too* close until after Hell Week. That's where the heaviest attrition is. We graduated two dozen guys out of our class; less than ten percent the number that started.

I was one of them. I'd started in class 231, but the rollback meant I graduated with 233.

After BUD/S, SEALs go to advance training—officially known as SQT or SEAL Qualifying Training. While I was there, I was reunited with a friend of mine I'd met while at BUD/S—Marcus Luttrell.

Marcus and I got along right away. It was only natural: we were a couple of Texas boys.

I don't suppose you'll understand that if you're not from Texas. There seems to be a special bond between people from the state. I don't know if it's shared experiences, or maybe it's something in the water—or maybe the beer. Texans tend to get on pretty well with each other, and in this case we formed an instant friendship. Maybe it's not that much of a mystery; after all, we had a lot of experiences in common, from growing up with a love of hunting to joining the Navy to toughing out BUD/S.

Marcus had graduated from BUD/S prior to me, then went off to do special advanced training before returning to SQT. Trained as a corpsman, he happened to check me over when I got my first O_2 hit while diving. (In layman's terms, an "O_2 hit" occurs when too much oxygen enters your bloodstream during a dive. It can be caused by a number of different factors and can be extremely serious. My case was very minor.)

Diving again. I always say I'm an " . . . L," not a SEAL. I'm a land guy; you can keep air and sea for someone else.

The day my incident occurred, I was swimming with a lieutenant, and we were determined to get the day's golden fin—an award for the best shit-hot dive of the day. The exercise involved swimming under a ship and planting limpet mines. (A limpet mine is a special charge that is placed against the hull of a ship. Generally, it will have a timed charge.)

We were doing extremely well when suddenly, while I was underneath the hull of the ship, I experienced vertigo and my brain turned into a vegetable. I managed to grab hold of a pylon and hug it. The lieutenant tried handing me a mine, then tried signaling to me when I wouldn't take it. I stared blankly into the ocean. Finally, my head cleared, and I was able to get out and continue.

No golden fin for us that day. By the time I got back to the surface, I was all right, and both Marcus and the instructors cleared me.

Though we ended up in different Teams, Marcus and I kept in touch as the years went by. It seemed like every time I was coming back from a combat deployment, he was coming in to relieve me. We'd have lunch together and trade informal intel back and forth.

TOWARD THE END OF SQT, WE GOT ORDERS TELLING US WHICH SEAL Team we were about to join. Even though we had graduated BUD/S, we didn't consider ourselves real SEALs yet; it was only when we joined a Team that we would get our Tridents—and even then we'd have to prove ourselves first. (The SEAL Tridents—also known as a Budweiser—is a metal "device" or badge worn by SEALs. Besides Neptune's trident, the symbol includes an eagle and an anchor.) At the time, there were six Teams, meaning three choices on each coast, East and West; my top pick was Seal Team 3, which was based out of Coronado, California. I chose it because that team had seen action in the Middle East and was likely to return. I wanted to get into the heat if I could. I think all of us did.

My next two choices were for Teams based on the East Coast, because I'd been in Virginia, where they are headquartered. I'm not a big fan of Virginia, but I liked it a lot better than California. San Diego—the city near Coronado—has beautiful weather, but

Southern California is the land of nuts. I wanted to live somewhere with a little more sanity.

I'd been told by the detailer I worked for that he would make sure I got my top choice. I wasn't 100 percent sure that was going to happen, but at that point I would have accepted whatever assignment I got—obviously, since I had no real say in the matter.

Getting the actual assignment was the opposite of dramatic. They brought us into a big classroom and handed out paper with our orders. I got my top choice: Team 3.

LOVE

Something else happened to me that spring that had an enormous impact not just on my military career, but on my life.

I fell in love.

I don't know if you believe in love at first sight; I don't think I did before the night in April of 2001 when I saw Taya standing at a bar in a San Diego club, talking with one of my friends. She had a way of making black leather pants look smokin' hot *and* classy. The combination suited me fine.

I'd just joined Team 3. We hadn't started training yet, and I was enjoying what amounted to a week of vacation before getting down to the serious business of becoming a SEAL and earning my place on a Team.

Taya was working for a pharmaceutical company as a drug rep when we met. Originally from Oregon, she'd gone to college in Wisconsin and moved out to the coast a couple years before we met. My first impression was that she was beautiful, even if she looked pissed off about something. When we started talking, I also found out she was smart, and had a good sense of humor. I sensed right away she was someone who could keep up with me.

But maybe she should tell the story; her version sounds better than mine:

Taya:

I remember the night we met—some of it, at least. I wasn't going to go out. This was all during a low spot in my life. My days were spent in a job I didn't like. I was fairly new in town and still looking for some solid female friendships. And I was casually dating guys, with not much success. Over the years I'd had some decent relationships and a couple of bad ones, with a few dates in between. I remember literally praying to God before I met Chris to just send me a nice guy. Nothing else mattered, I thought. I just prayed for someone who was inherently good and nice.

A girlfriend called and wanted to go down to San Diego. I was living in Long Beach at the time, about ninety miles away. I wasn't going to go but somehow she talked me into it.

We were walking around that night and we passed a bar named Maloney's. They were blaring "Land Down Under" by Men at Work. My friend wanted to go in but they had an outrageous cover charge, something like ten or fifteen bucks.

"I'm not doing that," I told her. "Not for a bar that's playing Men at Work."

"Oh, shut up," my girlfriend said. She paid the cover and in we went.

We were at the bar. I was drinking and irritable. This tall, good-looking guy came over and started talking to me. I'd been talking to one of his friends, who seemed like a jerk. My mood was still pretty bad, though he had a certain air about him. He told me his name—Chris—and I told him mine.

"What do you do?" I asked.

"I drive an ice cream truck."

"You're full of shit," I told him. "Obviously you're military."

"No, no," he protested. He told me a bunch of other things. SEALs almost never admit to strangers what they really do, and Chris had some of the best BS stories ever. One of the better ones was dolphin waxer: he claimed that dolphins in captivity need to be waxed so their skin didn't disintegrate. It's a pretty convincing story—if you're a young, naive, and tipsy girl.

Fortunately, he didn't try that particular one on me—I hope because he could tell I wouldn't fall for it. He's also convinced girls that he mans an ATM machine, sitting inside and doling out money when people put their cards in. I wasn't anywhere near that naive, or drunk, for him to try that story.

One look at him and I could have told he was military. He was ripped and had short hair, and had an accent that said "not from here."

Finally, he admitted he was in the service.

"So what do you do in the military?" I asked.

He said a bunch of other things and finally I got the truth: "I just graduated from BUD/S."

I was like, okay, so you're a SEAL.

"Yeah."

"I know all about you guys," I told him. You see, my sister had just divorced her husband. My brother-in-

law had wanted to be a SEAL—he'd gone through some of the training—and so I knew (or thought I did) what SEALs were all about.

So I told Chris.

"You're arrogant, self-centered, and glory-seeking," I said. "You lie and think you can do whatever you want."

Yes, I was at my charming best.

What was intriguing was how he responded. He didn't smirk or get clever or even act offended. He seemed truly . . . puzzled.

"Why would you say that?" he asked, very innocently and genuine.

I told him about my brother-in-law.

"I would lay down my life for my country," he answered. "How is that self-centered? That's the opposite."

He was so idealistic and romantic about things like patriotism and serving the country that I couldn't help but believe him.

We talked for a while more, then my friend came over and I turned my attention to her. Chris said something like he was going to go home.

"Why?" I asked.

"Well, you were saying about how you never would date a SEAL or go out with one."

"Oh no, I said I would never marry one. I didn't say I wouldn't go out with one."

His face lit up.

"In that case," he said, with that sly little smile he has, "I guess I'll get your phone number."

> *He hung around. I hung around. We were still there at last call. As I got up with the crowd to go, I was pushed against him. He was all hard and muscle-y and smelled good, so I gave him a little kiss on his neck. We went out and he walked us to the parking lot . . . and I started puking my brains out from all the Scotch on the rocks I'd been drinking.*

How can you *not* love a girl who loses it the first time you meet? I knew from the start that this was someone I wanted to spend a lot of time with. But at first, it was impossible to do that. I called her the morning after we met to make sure she was okay. We talked and laughed a bit. After that, I'd call her and leave messages. She didn't call back.

The other guys on the Team started ribbing me about it. They were betting about whether she'd ever call me on her own. You see, we talked a few times, when she would actually answer the phone—maybe thinking it was someone else. After a while, it was obvious even to me that she never initiated.

Then, something changed. I remember the first time she called *me*. We were on the East Coast, training.

When we were done talking, I ran inside and started jumping on my teammates' beds. I took the call as a sign she was *really* interested. I was happy to share that fact with all the naysayers.

Taya:

> *Chris was always very aware of my feelings. He is extremely observant in general and it is the same with his awareness of my emotions. He doesn't have to say much. A simple question or easy way of bringing something to light reveals that he is 100 percent aware of my feelings. He*

doesn't necessarily enjoy talking about feelings, but he has a sense of when it is appropriate or necessary to bring things out that I may have been intent on keeping in.

I noticed it early on in our relationship. We would be talking on the phone and he was very caring.

We are, in many ways, opposites. Still, we seemed to click. One day on the phone he was asking what I thought made us compatible. I decided to tell him some of the things that drew me to him.

"I think you're a really good guy," I told him, "really nice. And sensitive."

"Sensitive?!?" He was shocked, and sounded offended. "What do you mean?"

"You don't know what sensitive means?"

"You mean like I go around crying at movies and stuff?"

I laughed. I explained that I meant that he seemed to pick up on how I was feeling, sometimes before I did. And he let me express that emotion, and, importantly, gave me space.

I don't think that's the image most people have of SEALs, but it was and is accurate, at least of this one.

SEPTEMBER 11, 2001

AS OUR RELATIONSHIP GOT CLOSER AND CLOSER, TAYA AND I started spending more time with each other. Finally, we'd spend nights at each other's apartment, either in Long Beach or San Diego.

I woke up one morning to her yelling. "Chris! Chris! Wake up! You've got to see this!"

I stumbled into the living room. Taya had turned on the television and jacked the volume. I saw smoke pouring out of the World Trade Center in New York.

I didn't understand what-all was happening. Part of me was still sleeping.

Then as we watched, an airplane flew right into the side of the second tower.

"Motherfuckers!" I muttered.

I stared at the screen, angry and confused, not entirely sure it was real.

Suddenly I remembered that I left my cell phone off. I grabbed it, and saw I'd missed a bunch of messages. The sum total of them was this:

Kyle, get your ass back to base. Now!

I grabbed Taya's SUV—it had plenty of gas and my truck didn't—and hauled down to base. I don't know exactly how fast I was going—it might have been three digits—but it was certainly a high rate of speed.

Down around San Juan Capistrano, I glanced in the rearview mirror and saw a set of red lights flashing.

I pulled over. The cop who came up to the truck was pissed.

"Is there any reason you're going so fast?" he demanded.

"Yes, sir," I told him. "I apologize. I'm in the military and I just got recalled. I understand you got to write me a ticket. I know I was in the wrong but with all due respect can you just hurry and give me the ticket so I can get back to base?"

"What branch are you in?"

Motherfucker, I thought. *I just told you I have to report. Can't you just give me the damn ticket?* But I kept my cool.

"I'm in the Navy," I told him.

"What do you do in the Navy?" he asked.

By now I was pretty annoyed. "I'm a SEAL."

He closed his ticket book.

"I'll take you to the city line," he told me. "Go get some fuckin' payback."

He put his lights on and pulled in front of me. We went a bit slower than I'd been going when he nabbed me, but it was still well past the limit. He took me as far as his jurisdiction went, maybe a little farther, then waved me on.

TRAINING

WE WERE PUT ON IMMEDIATE STANDBY, BUT IT WOULD TURN out that we weren't needed in Afghanistan or anywhere else at that moment. My platoon would have to wait roughly a year before we got into action, and when we did, it would be against Saddam Hussein, not Osama bin Laden.

There's a lot of confusion in the civilian world about SEALs and our mission. Most people think we're strictly sea-based commandos, meaning that we always operate off ships, and hit targets on the water or the immediate coastline.

Admittedly, a fair amount of our work involves things at sea—we are in the Navy, after all. And from a historical perspective, as briefly mentioned earlier, SEALs trace their origins to the Navy's Underwater Demolition Teams, or UDTs. Established during World War II, UDT frogmen were responsible for reconning beaches before they were hit, and they trained for a variety of other waterborne tasks, such as infiltrating harbors and planting limpet mines on enemy ships. They were the mean, bad-ass combat divers of World War II and the postwar era, and SEALs are proud to carry on in their wake.

But as the UDT mission expanded, the Navy recognized that

the need for special operations didn't end at the beach line. As new units called SEALs were formed and trained for this expanded mission, they came to replace the older UDT units.

While "land" may be the final word in the SEAL acronym, it's hardly the last thing we do. Every special operations unit in the U.S. military has its own specialty. There's a lot of overlap in our training, and the range of our missions is similar in many respects. But each branch has its own expertise. Army Special Forces—also known as SF—does an excellent job training foreign forces, both in conventional and unconventional warfare. Army Rangers are a big assault force—if you want a large target, say an airfield, taken down, that's their thing. Air Force special operators—parajumpers—excel at pulling people out of the shit.

Among our specialties are DAs.

DA stands for "direct action." A direct-action mission is a very short, quick strike against a small but high-value target. You might think of it as a surgical strike against the enemy. In a practical sense, it could range from anything like an attack on a key bridge behind enemy lines to a raid on a terrorist hideout to arrest a bomb maker—a "snatch and grab," as some call it. While those are very different missions, the idea is the same: strike hard and fast before the enemy knows what's going on.

After 9/11, SEALs began training to deal with the places Islamic terrorists were most likely to be located—Afghanistan number one, and then the Middle East and Africa. We still did all the things a SEAL is supposed to do—diving, jumping out of planes, taking down ships, etc. But there was more emphasis on land warfare during our workup than there traditionally had been in the past.

There was debate about this shift far above my pay grade. Some people wanted to limit SEALs to ten miles inland. Nobody asked my opinion, but as far as I'm concerned, there shouldn't be any limits. Personally, I'm just as happy to stay out of the water, but that's beside the point. Let me do what I'm trained to do wherever it needs to be done.

The training, most of it anyway, was fun, even when it was a kick in the balls. We dove, we went into the desert, we worked in the mountains. We even got water-boarded and gassed.

Everybody gets water-boarded during training. The idea is to prepare you in case you're captured. The instructors tortured us as hard as they could, tying us up and pounding on us, just short of permanently damaging us. They say each of us has a breaking point, and that prisoners eventually give in. But I would have done my best to make them kill me before I gave up secrets.

Gas training was another kick. Basically, you get hit with CS gas and have to fight through it. CS gas is "captor spray" or tear gas—the active ingredient is 2-chlorobenzalmalononitrile, for all of you chemistry majors. We thought of it as "cough and spit," because that's the best way to deal with it. You learn during training to let your eyes run; the worst thing to do is rub them. You're going to get snotty and you're going to be coughing and crying, but you can still shoot your weapon and fight through it. That's the point of the exercise.

We went up to Kodiak, Alaska, where we did a land navigation course. It wasn't the height of winter, but there was still so much snow on the ground that we had to put on snowshoes. We started with basic instruction on keeping warm—layering up, etc.—and learned about things like snow shelters. One of the important points of this training, which applied everywhere, was learning how to conserve weight in the field. You have to figure out whether it's more important to be lighter and more mobile, or to have more ammunition and body armor.

I prefer lightness and speed. I count ounces when we go out, not pounds. The lighter you are, the more mobile you become. The little bastards out there are faster than hell; you need every advantage you can get on them.

The training was pretty competitive. We found out at one point that the best platoon in the Team would be shipped out to Afghanistan. Training picked up from that point on. It was a fierce competition, and not just out on the training range. The officers were backstabbing each other. They'd go to the CO and dime each other out:

Did you see what those guys did on the range? They're no good...

The competition came down to us and one other platoon. We came in second. They went to war; we stayed home.

That's about the worst fate a SEAL can imagine.

WITH THE CONFLICT IN IRAQ LOOMING ON THE HORIZON, OUR emphasis shifted. We practiced fighting in the desert; we practiced fighting in cities. We worked hard, but there were always lighter moments.

I remember one time when we were on a RUT (real urban training). Our command would find a municipality that was willing to have us come in and take down an actual building—an empty warehouse, say, or a house—something a little more authentic than you would find on a base. On this one exercise, we were working at a house. Everything had been carefully arranged with the local police department. A few "actors" had been recruited to play parts during the exercise.

My role was to pull security outside. I blocked out traffic, waving vehicles away as some of the local cops watched from the sidelines.

While I was standing there, gun out, not looking particularly friendly, this guy walked down the block toward me.

I started going through the drill. First I waved him off; he kept coming. Then I shined my light on him; he kept coming. I put my laser dot on him; he kept coming.

Of course, the closer he got, the more convinced I was that he was a role-player, sent to test me. I mentally reviewed my ROEs ("rules of engagement"), which covered how I was supposed to act.

"What are you, the popo?" he asked, sticking his face out toward mine.

"Popo" (a thug's term for police) wasn't in the ROEs, but I figured he was ad-libbing. The next thing on my list was to throw him down. So I did. He started to resist, and reached under his jacket for what I assumed was a weapon, which is exactly what a SEAL playing a bad guy would do. So I reacted in kind, giving a good SEAL response as I wrestled him into the dirt and busted him up a bit.

Whatever was under his jacket broke and liquid went everywhere. He was cussing and carrying on, but I didn't take the time to think about all that just then. As the fight ran out of him, I cuffed him and looked around.

The cops, seated in their patrol car nearby, were just about doubled over laughing. I went over to see what was up.

"That's so-and-so," they told me. "One of the biggest drug dealers in the city. We wish we could have beat him like you just did."

Apparently, Mr. Popo ignored all the signs and wandered into the training exercise figuring he'd carry on business as usual. There are idiots everywhere—but I guess that explains how he got into that line of work in the first place.

HAZED AND HITCHED

FOR MONTHS, THE UNITED NATIONS SECURITY COUNCIL pressured Iraq to comply fully with U.N. resolutions, especially those requiring inspections of suspected weapons of mass destruction and related sites. War wasn't a foregone conclusion—Saddam Hussein could have complied and shown inspectors everything they wanted to see. But most of us knew he wouldn't. So when we got the word that we were shipping out to Kuwait, we were excited. We figured we were going to war.

One way or the other, there was plenty to do out there. Besides watching Iraq's borders and protecting the Kurdish minority, who Saddam had gassed and massacred in the past, U.S. troops were enforcing no-fly zones in the north and south. Saddam was smuggling oil and other items both into and out of his country, in violation of the U.N. sanctions. The U.S. and other allies were stepping up operations to stop that.

Before we deployed, Taya and I chose to get married. The decision surprised both of us. One day we started talking in the car, and we both came to the conclusion that we should get married.

The decision stunned me, even as I made it. I agreed with it. It was completely logical. We were definitely in love. I knew she was the woman I wanted to spend my life with. And yet, for some reason, I didn't think the marriage would last.

We both knew that there is an extremely high divorce rate in the SEALs. As a matter of fact, I've heard marriage counselors claim that it is close to 95 percent, and I believe it. So maybe that was what worried me. Perhaps part of me wasn't really ready to think about a lifetime commitment. And of course I understood how demanding my job was going to be once we went to war. I can't explain the contradictions.

But I do know that I was absolutely in love, and that she loved me. And so, for better or worse, make that peace or war, marriage was our next step together. Happily, we've survived it all.

ONE THING YOU OUGHT TO KNOW ABOUT SEALs: WHEN you're new to the Teams, you get hazed. The platoons are very tight-knit groups. Newcomers—always called "new guys"—are treated like hell until they prove they belong. That usually doesn't happen until well into their first deployment, if then. New guys get the shit jobs. They're constantly tested. They're always beat on.

It's a kind of an extended hazing that takes many forms. For example: on a training exercise, you work hard. The instructors kick your ass all day long. Then, when you're done, the platoon will go out and party. When we're out on a training mission, we usually drive around in large, twelve-passenger vans. A new guy always drives. Which, of course, means he can't drink when we hit the bars, at least not to SEAL standards.

That's the mildest form of hazing. In fact, it's so mild it's not really hazing.

Choking him out while he's driving—that's hazing.

One night soon after I joined my platoon, we were out partying after a training mission. When we left the bar, all the older guys piled into the back. I wasn't driving, but I had no problem with that—I like to sit up front. We were speeding along for a while and all of a sudden I heard, "One-two-three-four, I declare a van war."

The next thing I knew, I was pummeled. "Van war" meant it was open season on the new guys. I came out of that one with bruised ribs and a black eye, maybe two. I must have gotten my lip busted a dozen times during hazing.

I should say that van wars are separate from bar fights, another SEAL staple. SEALs are pretty notorious for getting into bar scrapes, and I was no exception. I've been arrested more than once through the years, though as a general rule the charges were either never filed or quickly dismissed.

Why do SEALs fight so much?

I haven't made a scientific study of it, but I think a lot is owed to pent-up aggression. We're trained to go out and kill people. And then, at the same time, we're also being taught to think of ourselves as invincible bad-asses. That's a pretty potent combination.

When you go into a bar, you'll always have someone who will poke a shoulder into you or otherwise imply you should fuck off. Happens in every bar across the world. Most people just ignore things like that.

If someone does that to a SEAL, we're going to turn and knock you out.

But at the same time, I have to say that while SEALs *end* a lot of fights, we usually don't start many. In a lot of cases, the fights are the result of some sort of stupid jealousy or the need for a dumbass to test his own manhood and earn bragging rights for fighting a SEAL.

When we go into bars, we don't just cower down in the corner or lay low. We go in extremely confident. Maybe we're loud. And, with us being mostly young and in great shape, people take notice. Girls gravitate toward a group of SEALs, and maybe that makes their boyfriends jealous. Or guys want to prove something for some other reason. Either way, things escalate and fights happen.

BUT I WASN'T TALKING ABOUT BAR FIGHTS; I WAS TALKING about hazing. And my wedding.

We were in the Nevada mountains; it was cold—so cold that it was snowing. I had gotten a few days leave to get married; I was due to take off in the morning. The rest of the platoon still had some work to do.

We got back that night to our temporary base and went inside to the mission-planning room. The chief told everybody that we'd relax and have a few beers while we mapped out the next day's operation. Then he turned to me.

"Hey, new guy," he told me. "Go grab the beer and the booze out of the van and bring it in here."

I hopped to.

When I came back in, everyone was sitting in chairs. There was only one left, and it was kind of in the middle of a circle of the others. I didn't think too much about it as I sat down.

"All right, this is what we're going to do," my chief said, standing in front of dry-erase board at the front of the room. "The operation will be an ambush. The target will be in the center. We will completely encircle it."

That doesn't sound too smart, I thought. *If we come in from every direction, we'll be shooting each other.* Usually our ambushes are planned in an L-shape to avoid that.

I looked at the chief. The chief looked at me. Suddenly, his serious expression gave way to a shit-ass grin.

With that, the rest of the platoon bum-rushed me.

I hit the floor a second later. They cuffed me to a chair, and then began my kangaroo court.

There were a lot of charges against me. The first was the fact that I had let it be known that I wanted to become a sniper.

"This new guy is ungrateful!" thundered the prosecutor. "He does not want to do his job. He thinks he is better than the rest of us."

I tried to protest, but the judge—none other than the chief himself—quickly ruled me out of order. I turned to my defense attorney.

"What do you expect?" he said. "He's only got a third-grade edu-Kay-shun."

"Guilty!" declared the judge. "Next charge!"

"Your Honor, the defendant is disrespectful," said the prosecutor. "He told the CO to fuck off."

"Objection!" said my lawyer. "He told the *OIC* to fuck off."

The CO is the commanding officer of the Team; the OIC is the officer in charge of the platoon. A pretty big difference, except in this case.

"Guilty! Next charge!"

For every offense I was found guilty of—which meant anything and everything they could make up—I had to take a drink of Jack Daniels and Coke, followed by a shooter of Jack.

They got me pretty wasted before we even got to the felonies. At some point, they stripped me down and put ice down my drawers. Finally I passed out.

Then they spray-painted me, and for good measure, drew Playboy bunnies on my chest and back with a marker. Just the sort of body art you want for your honeymoon.

At some point, my friends apparently became concerned about my health. So they taped me to a spine board completely naked, took me outside, and stood me up in the snow. They left me for a while until I regained some amount of consciousness. By then I was jackhammering hard enough to put a hole through a bunker roof. They gave me an IV—the saline helps cut down the alcohol in your system—and finally took me back to the hotel, still taped to the spine board.

All I remember from the rest of the night is being lifted up a bunch of stairs, apparently to my motel room. There must have been a few spectators, because the boys were yelling, "Nothing to see here, nothing to see!" as they carried me in.

TAYA WASHED OFF MOST OF THE PAINT AND THE BUNNIES when I met up with her the next day. But a few were still visible under my shirt. I kept my jacket tightly buttoned for the ceremony.

By then, the swelling in my face was almost completely gone. The stitches in my eyebrow (from a friendly fight among teammates a few weeks early) were healing nicely. The cut on my lip (from a training exercise) was also healing pretty well. It's probably not every bride's dream to have a spray-painted, beat-up groom, but Taya seemed happy enough.

The amount of time we had for our honeymoon, though, was a sore point. The Team was gracious enough to give me three days to get hitched and honeymoon. As a new guy, I was appreciative of the brief leave. My new wife wasn't quite as understanding, and made that clear. Nonetheless, we married and honeymooned quickly. Then I got back to work.

3

TAKEDOWNS

GUN READY

"Wake up. We got a tanker."

I roused myself from the side of the boat where I'd been catching some rest despite the cold wind and choppy waters. I was soaked from the spray. Despite the fact that I was a new guy on my first deployment, I'd already mastered the art of sleeping in all sorts of conditions—an unheralded but critical SEAL skill.

An oil tanker loomed ahead. A helicopter had spotted it trying to sneak down the Gulf after loading up illegally in Iraq. Our job was to get aboard her, inspect her papers, and if, as suspected, she was violating the U.N. sanctions, turn her over to the Marines or other authorities for processing.

I scrambled to get ready. Our RHIB (rigid hulled inflatable boat, used for a variety of SEAL tasks) looked like a cross between a rubber life raft and an open speedboat with two monster motors

TAKEDOWNS

in the back. Thirty-six feet long, it held eight SEALs and hit upward of forty-five knots on a calm sea.

The exhaust from the twin motors wafted over the boat, mixing with the spray as we gathered speed. We were hauling at a good pace, riding the wake of the tanker where radar couldn't pick us up. I went to work, taking a long pole from the deck of the boat. Our speed dropped as our RHIB cut alongside the tanker, until we were just about matching its pace. The Iranian ship's engines pulsed in the water, so loud our own motors were drowned out.

As we pushed alongside the tanker, I extended the pole upward, trying to angle the grappling hook at the top onto the ship's rail. Once the hook caught, I jerked the pole down.

Gotcha.

A bungee cord connected the hook to the pole. A steel cable ladder was connected to the hook. Someone grabbed hold of the bottom and held it while the lead man began climbing up the side of the ship.

A loaded oil tanker can sit fairly low in the water, so low, in fact, that you sometimes can just grab the rail and hop over. That wasn't the case here—the railing was quite a bit higher than our little boat. I'm not a fan of heights, but as long as I didn't think too much about what I was doing, I was fine.

The ladder rocked with the ship and the wind; I pulled myself upward as quickly as I could go, my muscles remembering all those pull-ups in BUD/S. By the time I reached the deck, the lead guys were already headed toward the wheelhouse and bridge of the ship. I ran to catch up.

Suddenly the tanker began gaining speed. The captain, belatedly realizing he was being boarded, was trying to head for Iranian waters. If he reached them, we'd have to jump off—our orders strictly forbade taking any ship outside of international waters.

I caught up to the head of the team just as they reached the door to the bridge. One of the crew got there at roughly the same time, and tried to lock it. He wasn't fast enough, or strong enough—one of the boarding party threw himself against the door and bashed it open.

I ran through, gun ready.

We'd done dozens of these operations over the past few days, and rarely had anyone even hinted of resistance. But the captain of this ship had some fight in him, and even though he was unarmed, he wasn't ready to surrender.

He made a run at me.

Pretty stupid. First of all, I'm not only bigger than him, but I was wearing full body armor. Not to mention the fact that I had a submachine gun in my hand.

I took the muzzle of my gun and struck the idiot in his chest. He went right down.

Somehow, I managed to slip as well. My elbow flew out and landed straight on his face.

A couple of times.

That pretty much took the fight out of him. I rolled him over and cuffed him.

BOARDING AND SEARCHING SHIPS—OFFICIALLY KNOWN AS VBSS, for Visit, Board, Search, Seize—is a standard SEAL mission. While the "regular" Navy has specially trained sailors to handle the job in peacetime, we're trained to handle the searches in places where resistance is likely. And in the lead-up to war during the winter of 2002–03, that meant the Persian Gulf off Iraq. The U.N. later estimated that, in violation of international sanctions, billions of dollars of oil and other items were smuggled out of Iraq and into the pockets of Saddam's regime.

Smuggling took all sorts of forms. You'd find oil being carried in wheat carriers, hidden in barrels. More commonly, tankers took on thousands and thousands of gallons in excess of what they were permitted in the U.N. Oil-for-Food program.

It wasn't just oil. One of the biggest contraband shipments we came across that winter were dates. Apparently they could fetch a decent price on the world market.

IT WAS DURING THOSE FIRST MONTHS OF MY FIRST DEPLOYment that I became acquainted with the Polish *Wojskowa Formacja Specjalna GROM im. Cichociemnych Spadochroniarzy Armii Krajowej*—Special Military Formation GROM of the Dark and Silent Parachutists of the Polish Army—better known as GROM. They're the Polish version of the Special Forces, with an excellent reputation in special operations, and they worked on the takedowns with us.

Generally, we worked off a big ship, which we used as kind of a floating home port for our RHIBs. Half of the platoon would go out for one twenty-four-hour period. We would sail to a designated spot and drift in the night, waiting. With luck, a helo or a ship would radio intel about a ship coming out of Iraq sailing pretty low in the water. Anything that had a cargo would be boarded and inspected. We'd go out and take it down.

A few times we worked with an Mk-V boat. The Mk-V is a special operations craft that some people have compared to World War II–era PT boats. The craft looks like an armored speedboat, and its job is to get SEALs into harm's way as quickly as possible. Built out of aluminum, it can haul serious ass—the boats are said to hit sixty-five knots. But what we liked about them were their flat decks behind the superstructure. Ordinarily, we would load two Zodiacs back there. But since the Zodiacs weren't needed, the whole company would board from the RHIBs and stretch out to grab some sleep until ships were spotted. That beat leaning across the seat or twisting yourself around to rest on the gunwale.

Taking down ships in the Gulf quickly became routine. We could take dozens in a night. But our biggest takedown didn't come off Iraq; it was some fifteen hundred miles away, off the coast of Africa.

SCUDS

IN LATE FALL, A SEAL PLATOON IN THE PHILIPPINES SNUCK alongside a freighter. From that point on, the North Korean ship was literally a marked vessel.

The 3,500-ton freighter had an interesting history of transporting items to and from North Korea. According to one rumor, she had transported chemicals that could be used to create nerve weapons. In this case, though, the ship's papers declared that she was carrying cement.

What she was really carrying were Scud missiles.

The ship was tracked around the Horn of Africa while the Bush administration decided what to do about it. Finally, the President ordered that the ship be boarded and searched: just the sort of job SEALs excel at.

We had a platoon in Djibouti, which was a hell of a lot closer to the craft than we were. But because of the way the chain of command and assignments worked—the unit happened to be working for the Marines while we were directly under a Navy command—we were tasked to take down the freighter.

You can imagine how happy our sister platoon was to see us when we landed in Djibouti. Not only had we "stolen" a mission they considered theirs, they had to suffer the indignity of helping us offload and get ready for action.

As soon as I got off the plane, I spotted a buddy.

"Hey!" I shouted.

"Fuck off," he answered.

"What's up?"

"Fuck you."

That was the extent of his welcome. I couldn't blame him; in his place, I'd have been pissed myself. He and the others eventually came around—they weren't mad at us; they were mad at the situation. Grudgingly, they helped us prepare for the mission, then got us aboard a mail-and-resupply helicopter from the USS *Nassau*, an amphibious assault ship out in the Indian Ocean.

Amphibs, as they're called, are large assault ships that carry troops and helicopters, and occasionally Marine Harrier attack aircraft. They look like old-fashioned aircraft carriers with a straight-through flight deck. They're fairly large, and have command and control facilities that can be used as forward planning and command posts during assault operations.

There are several ways to take down a ship, depending on the conditions and the target. While we could have used helicopters to get to the North Korean freighter, looking at photos of the ship we noticed that there were a number of wires running above the deck. Those wires would have to be removed before we could land, which would add time to the operation.

Knowing we'd lose the element of surprise if we went in with helos, we opted to use RHIBs instead. We started doing practice runs off the side of the *Nassau* with boats that had been brought out there by a Special Boat Unit. (Special Boat Units are the SEALs' dedicated taxi service. They run the RHIBs, Mk-Vs, and other SEAL-related vessels. Among other things, the units are equipped and trained to make combat insertions, braving fire to get SEALs in and out of trouble.)

The freighter, meanwhile, continued sailing toward us. We geared up as it came within range, preparing to hit it. But before we could board the boats, we got a call telling us to stand by—the Spaniards had moved in.

What?

The Spanish frigate *Navarra* had confronted the North Korean ship, which had been fooling exactly nobody by sailing without a flag and with her name covered up. According to later reports, Spanish spec-op troops went in after the freighter failed to comply with the frigate's orders to stop. Of course, they used helicopters, and just as we had thought, were delayed by having to shoot out the wires. From what I've heard, that delay would have given the captain aboard the vessel time to get rid of incriminating paperwork and other evidence, that's what I think happened.

OBVIOUSLY, THERE WAS A LOT GOING ON BEHIND THE SCENES that we weren't aware of.

Whatever.

Our mission was quickly changed from taking down the ship to going aboard and securing it—and uncovering the Scud missiles.

You wouldn't think missiles would be hard to find. But in this case, they were nowhere to be seen. The ship's hold was full of bags of cement—eighty-pound bags. There must have been hundreds of thousands.

There was only one place the Scuds could be. We started moving cement. Bag after bag. That was our job for twenty-four hours. No sleep, just move bags of cement. I must have moved thousands myself. It was miserable. I was covered with dust. God knows what my lungs looked like. Finally, we found shipping containers underneath. Out came our torches and saws.

I worked one of the quickie saws. Also known as a cut-off saw, it looks like a chain saw with a circular blade on the front. It cuts through just about anything, including Scud containers.

Fifteen Scud missiles lay under the cement. I'd never seen a Scud up close before, and to be honest, I thought they were kind of cool-looking. We took pictures, then waved the EOD guys—"explosive ordinance disposal," or bomb disposal experts—in to make sure they were inert.

By that point, the entire platoon was completely covered with cement dust. A few guys went over the side to clean off. Not me. Given my history with dives, I wasn't taking any chances. That much cement, who the hell knows what happens when it touches the water?

WE HANDED THE FREIGHTER OVER TO THE MARINES AND went back aboard the *Nassau*. Command sent word that we would be pulled out and returned to Kuwait in "the same expedient fashion you were brought in."

Of course, they were full of shit. We stayed on the *Nassau* for two weeks. For some reason, the Navy couldn't figure out how to free up one of the umpteen helicopters they had sitting on the flight deck to get us back to Djibouti. So we played video games and pumped iron, waiting. That and slept.

Unfortunately, the only video game we had with us was Madden Football. I got pretty good at it. Up until that time, I hadn't been much for playing video games. Now I'm an expert—especially at Madden. That was probably where I got hooked. I think my wife still cusses my two weeks aboard the *Nassau* to this very day.

A FOOTNOTE ON THE SCUDS: THE MISSILES WERE BOUND FOR Yemen. Or at least that's what Yemen said. There have been rumors that they were part of some sort of a deal with Libya involving a payoff to take Saddam Hussein into exile, but I have no idea whether that's true or not. In any event, the Scuds were released and went on to Yemen, Saddam stayed in Iraq, and we went back to Kuwait to get ready for war.

CHRISTMAS

THAT DECEMBER WAS THE FIRST CHRISTMAS I'D EVER BEEN away from my family, and it felt a little depressing. The day kind of came and went without a memorable celebration.

I do remember the presents Taya's folks sent that year, though: remote-control Hummers.

They were small, radio-controlled toys that were just a blast to drive around. Some of the Iraqis working on base had apparently never seen anything like them before. I'd drive a vehicle toward them and they would scream and bolt away. I don't know if they thought it was some sort of guided missile or what. Their high-pitched screams, coupled with sprints in the opposite direction, had me doubled over. Cheap thrills in Iraq were priceless.

Some of the people we had working for us were not exactly the best of the best, nor were all of them particularly fond of Americans.

They caught one jerking off into our food.

He was quickly escorted from the base. The head shed—our commanding officers—knew that as soon as everyone found out what he'd done, someone would probably try and kill him.

We stayed at two different camps in Kuwait: Ali al-Salem and Doha. Our facilities at both were relatively bare-bones.

Doha was a large U.S. Army base, and played important roles in both the First and what would be the Second Gulf War. We were given a warehouse there and framed-out rooms with the help of some Seabees, the Navy combat engineers. We'd come to rely on the Seabees for similar support in the future.

Ali al-Salem was even more primitive, at least for us. There we got a tent and some shelving units; that was about it. I guess the powers-that-be figured SEALs don't need much.

I was in Kuwait when I saw my first desert sandstorm. The day suddenly became night. Sand swirled everywhere. From the distance, you can see a vast orange-brown cloud moving toward you. Then, suddenly, it's black and you feel like you're in the middle of swirling mineshaft, or maybe the rinse cycle in a bizarre washing machine that uses sand instead of water.

I remember being in an airplane hangar, and even though the doors were closed, the amount of dust in the air was unbelievable. The sand was a fine grit that you never wanted to get in your eyes, because it would never come out. We quickly learned to wear goggles to protect them; sunglasses wouldn't do.

60 GUNNER

Being a new guy, I was the 60 gunner.

As I'm sure many of you know, "60" refers to the M-60 general-purpose machine gun, a belt-fed weapon that has served the U.S. military in a number of versions for several decades.

The M-60 was developed in the 1950s. It fires 7.62-mm bullets; the design is so flexible that it can be used as the basis for a coaxial machine gun in armored vehicles and helicopters, and a light, man-carried squad-level weapon. It was a workhorse in the Vietnam War, where grunts called it "the Pig" and occasionally cursed over the hot barrel, which required an asbestos glove to change after firing a few hundred rounds—not particularly convenient in combat.

The Navy made substantial improvements to the weapon over the years, and it remains a potent gun. The newest version is so improved, in fact, that it rates a different designation: the Navy calls it an Mk-43 Mod 0. (Some contend it should be considered a completely separate weapon; I'm not going to wade into that debate.) It's comparatively light—in the area of twenty-three pounds—and has a relatively short barrel. It also has a rail system, which allows scopes and the like to be attached.

Also currently in service are M-240s, M-249s, and the Mk-46, a variant of the M-249.

As a general rule, the machine guns carried by shooters in my platoons were always called *60s*, even when they were actually something else, like the Mk-48. We used more Mk-48s as time went on during my days in Iraq, but unless it's significant for some reason, I refer to any squad-level machine gun as a 60 and leave others to sort out the fine print.

The old "Pig" nickname for the 60 survives, which leads a lot of 60 gunners to be called Pigs, or a creative variation; in our platoon, a friend of mine named Bob got tagged with it.

It never applied to me. My nickname was "Tex," which was one of the more socially acceptable things people called me.

TAKEDOWNS

WITH WAR BECOMING INEVITABLE, WE BEGAN PATROLLING the border across Kuwait, making sure that the Iraqis weren't going to try and sneak across in a preemptory strike. We also began training for a role in the upcoming fight.

That meant spending quality time in DPVs, also known as SEAL dune buggies.

DPVs ("Desert Patrol Vehicles") look extremely cool from the distance, and they are far better equipped than your average ATV. There's a .50-caliber machine gun and an Mk-19 grenade launcher on the front, and an M-60 on the back. Then there are the LAW rockets, one-shot anti-tank weapons that are the spiritual descendants of World War II bazookas and Panzerfausts. The rockets are mounted in special brackets on the tubular upper frame. Adding to the coolness factor is the sat radio antenna on the very top of the vehicle, with a donkey-dick radio antenna next to it.

Practically every picture you see of a DPV has the sucker flying over a sand dune and popping a wheelie. It is an exceedingly bad-ass image.

Unfortunately, it is just that—an image. Not a reality.

From what I understand, the DPVs were based on a design that had been used in the Baja races. Stripped down, they were undoubtedly mean mothers. The problem is, we didn't drive them stripped down. All that ordnance we carried added considerable weight. Then there were our rucks, and the water and food you need to survive in a desert for a few days. Extra gas. Not to mention three fully equipped SEALs—driver, navigator, and Pig gunner.

And, in our case, a Texas flag flying off the rear. Both my chief and I were Texans, which made that a mandatory accessory.

The load added up quickly. The DPVs used a small Volkswagen engine that was, in my experience, a piece of junk. It was probably fine in a car, or maybe a dune buggy that didn't see combat. But if we took the vehicle out for two or three days, we'd almost always end up working on it for the same amount of time when we got back. Inevitably, there was some sort of bearing or bushing failing. We had to do our own maintenance. Luckily for us, my platoon included an ASCE-certified mechanic, and he took charge of keeping the vehicles running.

But by far their biggest drawback was the fact that they were two-wheel drive. This was a huge problem if the ground was in the least bit soft. As long as we kept going we were usually okay, but if we stopped we ended up in trouble. We were constantly digging them out of the sand in Kuwait.

They were a blast when they worked. Being the gunner, I had the elevated seat behind the driver and navigator, who sat side by side below me. Geared up with tactical ballistic goggles and a helicopter-type helmet, I strapped myself in with a five-point restraint and held on as we raced across the desert. We'd do seventy miles an hour. I'd let off a few bursts with the .50-cal, then pull the lever up on the side of the seat and swivel around toward the back. There I'd grab the M-60 and shoot some more. If we were simulating an attack from the side while we were moving, I could grab the M-4 I was carrying and shoot in that direction.

Shooting the big machine gun was *fun*!

Aiming that sucker while the vehicle was bounding up and down across the desert was something else again. You can move the gun up and down to keep it on target, but you're never going to be particularly precise—at best, you lay down enough fire so you can get the hell out of there.

Besides our four three-seat DPVs, we had two six-seaters. The six-seater was the plain-vanilla version—three rows of two seats, with the only weapon the 60 on the front. We used it as the command-and-control wagon. Very boring ride. It was kind of like riding in a station wagon with Mom when Dad's got the sports car.

We practiced for a few weeks. We did a lot of land navigation, built hide sights, and did SR ("surveillance and reconnaissance") along the border. We'd dig in, cover the vehicles with netting, and try and make them disappear in the middle of the desert. Not easy for a DPV: usually it ended up looking like a DPV trying to hide in the middle of the desert. We also practiced deploying the DPVs out of helicopters, riding out the back when they touched down: a rodeo on wheels.

As January neared its end, we started getting worried, not that the war was going to break out, but that it would start without us. The usual SEAL deployment at the time was six months. We'd shipped out in September, and were due to rotate back to the States within a few weeks.

I wanted to fight. I wanted to do what I'd been trained for. American taxpayers had invested considerable dollars in my education as a SEAL. I wanted to defend my country, do my duty, and do my job.

I wanted, more than anything, to experience the thrill of battle.

Taya saw things a lot differently.

Taya:

I was terrified the whole time as the buildup continued toward war. Even though the war hadn't officially started, I knew they were working dangerous ops. When SEALs work, there's always some risk involved. Chris tried to play things down to me so I wouldn't worry, but I wasn't oblivious and I could read between the lines. My anxiety came out in different ways. I was jumpy. I'd see things out of the corner of my eye that weren't there. I couldn't sleep without all the lights on; I'd read every night until my eyes closed involuntarily. I did everything I could to avoid being alone or having too much time to think.

Chris called twice with stories about helicopter accidents that he'd been in. Both were extremely minor, but he was worried that they would be reported and that I would hear about them and worry.

"I just want you to know, in case you hear it on the news," he'd say. "The helo was in a minor bang-up and I'm okay."

One day he told me he had to go out on another helicopter exercise. The next morning, I was watching the news and they reported that a helicopter had gone down near the border and everyone had died. The newscaster said it had been filled with special-forces soldiers.

In the military, "Special Forces" refers to Army special-operations troops, but the newscasters had a tendency to use the term for SEALs. Immediately, I jumped to conclusions.

I didn't hear from him that day, even though he had promised he'd call.

I told myself, I'm not going to panic. It wasn't him.

I poured myself into my work. That night, with still no call, I started to feel a little more anxious. . . . Then a little freaked out. I couldn't sleep, though I was exhausted from working and holding back the tears that kept threatening to overtake any sense of calm I was faking.

Finally, around one o'clock, I was starting to crack. The phone rang. I jumped to answer it.

"Hey, babe!" he said, as cheerful as ever.

I started bawling.

Chris kept asking what was wrong. I couldn't even choke out the words to explain. My fear and relief came out as unintelligible sobs.

After that, I vowed to stop watching the news.

4

FIVE MINUTES TO LIVE

DUNE BUGGIES AND MUD DON'T MIX

Geared up and strapped in, I sat vibrating in the gunner's chair of the DPV shortly after nightfall March 20, 2003, as an Air Force MH-53 lifted off the runway in Kuwait. The vehicle had been loaded into the rear of the PAVE-Low aircraft, and we were en route toward the mission we'd spent the past several weeks rehearsing. The waiting was about to come to an end; Operation Iraqi Freedom was underway.

My war was finally here.

I was sweating, and not just with excitement. Not knowing exactly what Saddam might have in store, we'd been ordered to wear full MOPP gear ("Mission Oriented Protective Posture," or spacesuits to some). The suits protect against chemical attacks, but they're about as comfortable as rubber pajamas, and the gas mask that comes with them is twice as bad.

"Feet wet!" said someone over the radio.

I checked my guns. They were ready, including the 50. All I had to do was pull back the charging handle and load.

We were pointed straight toward the back of the helicopter. The rear ramp was not all the way up, so I could see out into the night. Suddenly, the black strip I was watching above the ramp speckled with red—the Iraqis had kicked on anti-aircraft radars and weapons that intel had claimed didn't exist, and the chopper pilots began shooting off decoy flares and chaff to confuse them.

Then came the tracers, streams of bullets arcing across the narrow rectangle of black.

Damn, I thought. *We're going to get shot down before I even get a chance to smoke someone.*

Somehow, the Iraqis managed to miss us. The helicopter kept moving, swooping toward land.

"Feet dry!" said someone over the radio. We were now over land.

All hell was breaking loose. We were part of a team tasked to hit Iraqi oil resources before the Iraqis could blow them up or set them on fire as they had during Desert Storm in 1991. SEALs and GROM were hitting gas and oil platforms (GOPLATs) in the Gulf, as well as on-shore oil refinery and port areas.

Twelve of us were tasked to hit farther inland, at the al-Faw oil refinery area. The few extra minutes it took translated into a hell of a lot of gunfire, and by the time the helicopter touched down, we were in the shit.

The ramp dropped and our driver hit the gas. I locked and loaded, ready to fire as we sped down the ramp. The DPV careened onto the soft dirt . . . and promptly got stuck.

Son of a bitch!

The driver started revving the engine and slapping the transmission back and forth, trying to budge us free. At least we were out of the helicopter—one of the other DPVs got stuck half on and half off the ramp. His 53 jerked up and down, trying desperately to free him—pilots hate like hell to get fired at, and they wanted out.

By this time I could hear the different DPV units checking in over the radio. Just about everybody was stuck in the oil-soaked mud. The intel specialist advising us had claimed that the ground would be hard-packed where we were going to land. Of course, she and her colleagues had also claimed that the Iraqis didn't have anti-aircraft weapons. Like they say, military intelligence is an oxymoron.

"We're stuck!" said our chief.

"Yeah, we're stuck too," said the lieutenant.

"We're stuck," said somebody else.

"Fuck, we got to get out of here."

"All right, everybody get out of your vehicles and go to your positions," said the chief.

I undid the five-point harness, grabbed the 60 off the back, and humped in the direction of the fence that blocked off the oil facility. Our job was to secure the gate, and just because we didn't have wheels to do it with didn't mean it wasn't getting done.

I found a pile of rubble in sight of the gate and set up the 60. A guy came up next to me with a Carl Gustav. Technically a recoilless rifle, the weapon fires a bad-ass rocket that can take out a tank or poke a hole in a building. Nothing was getting through that gate without our say-so.

The Iraqis had set up a defensive perimeter outside the refinery. Their only problem was that we had landed inside. We were now between them and the refinery—in other words, behind their positions.

They didn't like that all that much. They turned around and started firing at us.

As soon as I realized that we weren't getting gassed, I threw off my gas mask. Returning fire with the 60, I had plenty of targets—too many, in fact. We were heavily outnumbered. But that was not a real problem. We began calling in air support. Within minutes, all sorts of aircraft were overhead: F/A-18s, F-16s, A-10As, even an AC-130 gunship.

The Air Force A-10s, better known as Warthogs, were awesome. They're slow-moving jets, but that's intentional—they're designed to fly low and slow so they can put a maximum amount of gunfire on ground targets. Besides bombs and missiles, they're equipped with a 30-mm Gatling cannon. Those Gatlings chewed the hell out of the enemy that night. The Iraqis rolled armor out of the city to get us, but they never got close. It got to the point where the Iraqis realized they were fucked and tried to flee.

Big mistake. That just made them easier to see. The planes kept coming, nailing them. They had them zeroed in, and zeroed them out. You'd hear the rounds coming past you in the air—*errrrrrrrr*—then you'd hear the echo—*erhrhrrhrh*, followed closely by secondary explosions and whatever other havoc the bullets caused.

Fuck, I thought to myself, *this is great. I fucking love this. It's nerve-wracking and exciting and I fucking love it.*

GASSED

A BRITISH UNIT FLEW IN IN THE MORNING. BY THEN, THE BATTLE was over. Of course, we couldn't resist needling them about it.

"Come on in. The fight's over," we said. "It's safe for you."

I don't think they thought it was funny, but it was hard to tell. They speak English funny. Exhausted, we moved back inside the gate to a house that had been almost completely destroyed during the firefight. We went into the ruins, dropped down between the rubble, and fell asleep.

A few hours later, I got up. Most of the other guys in my company were stirring as well. We went outside and started checking the perimeter of the oil fields. While we were out, we spotted some of the air defenses the Iraqis didn't have. But the intel reports didn't have to be updated—those defenses were now in no shape to bother anyone.

There were dead bodies everywhere. We saw one guy who'd literally had his ass blown off. He'd bled to death, but not before he tried to drag himself away from the planes. You could see the blood trail in the dirt.

While we were sorting things out, I spotted a Toyota pickup in the distance. It drove up on the road and stopped a little more than a mile away.

White civilian pickup trucks were used by the Iraqis as military vehicles throughout the war. Usually they were some version of the Toyota Hilux, the compact pickup built in a variety of styles. (In the States, the Hilux was often called the SR5; the model was eventually discontinued here, though it continued to be sold overseas.) Not sure what was going on, we stared at the truck for a few moments until we heard a *whup*.

Something went *splat* a few yards from us. The Iraqis had fired a mortar round from the rear bed. It sank harmlessly into the oily mud.

"Thank God that thing didn't blow up," somebody said. "We'd be dead."

White smoke started pouring out of the hole where the projectile had landed.

"Gas!" yelled someone.

We started running as fast as we could back to the gate. But just before we reached it, the British guards slammed it shut and refused to open up.

"You can't come in!" one of them yelled. "You've just been gassed."

While Marine Cobras flew in overhead to take care of the mortar trucks, we tried to figure out if we were going to die.

When we were still breathing a few minutes later, we realized the smoke had been just that—smoke. Maybe it was steam from the mud. Whatever. It was all sizzle, no boom, no gas.

Which was a relief.

SHATT AL-ARAB

WITH AL-FAW SECURED, WE RIGGED UP TWO OF OUR DPVs and hit the road, driving north to Shatt al-Arab, the river that separates Iran and Iraq as it flows out to the Gulf. Our job was to look for suicide boats and mine layers that might be coming down the river to the Gulf. We found an old border station abandoned by the Iraqis and set up an observation post.

Our ROEs when the war kicked off were pretty simple: *If you see anyone from about sixteen to sixty-five and they're male, shoot 'em. Kill every male you see.*

That wasn't the official language, but that was the idea. Now that we were watching Iran, however, we were under strict orders *not* to fire, at least not at Iran.

Every night someone on the other side of the river would stand up and take a shot at us. We would dutifully call it in and ask for permission to return fire. The answer was always a very distinct, "NO!" Very loud and clear.

Looking back, this made a lot of sense. Our heaviest weapons were a Carl Gustav and two 60s. The Iranians had plenty of artillery, and they had the position dialed in. It wouldn't have taken anything for them to hit us. And, in fact, what they were probably trying to do was suck us into a fight so they could kill us.

It did piss us off, though. Somebody shoots at you, you want to shoot back.

After the high of the start of the war, our spirits sagged. We were just sitting around doing nothing. One of the guys had a video camera and we made a video poking fun at it. There wasn't much else to do. We found a few Iraqi weapons and gathered them in a pile to be blown up. But that was it. The Iraqis weren't sending boats our way, and the Iranians would only fire a single shot then duck and wait for us to react. About the most entertaining thing we could do was wade into the water and piss in their direction.

For a week we took turns on watch—two guys on, four guys off—monitored the radio and watched the water. Finally, we were relieved by another set of SEALs and headed back to Kuwait.

THE RACE TO BAGHDAD

BY NOW, THE SO-CALLED RACE TO BAGHDAD HAD BEGUN. American and allied units were streaming across the border, making large advances every day.

We spent a few days hanging around our camp back in Kuwait, waiting for an assignment. As frustrating as our stay at the border station was, this was worse. We wanted to be in action. There were any number of missions we could have accomplished—eliminating some of those "nonexistent" air defenses farther into Iraq, for example—but the command didn't seem to want to use us.

Our deployment had been extended so that we could take part in the beginning of the war. But now the rumor was that we would be rotated back to the States and replaced by Team 5. No one wanted to leave Iraq now that the action was getting hot. Morale hit rock bottom. We were all pissed off.

TO TOP THINGS OFF, THE IRAQIS HAD SENT SOME SCUDS OVER just before the war started. Most had been taken care of by Patriot missiles, but one got through. Wouldn't you know it took out the Starbucks where we'd hung out during our prewar training?

That's low, hitting a coffee place. It could have been worse, I guess. It could have been a Dunkin' Donuts.

The joke was that President Bush only declared war when the Starbucks was hit. You can mess with the U.N. all you want, but when you start interfering with the right to get caffeinated, someone has to pay.

WE STAYED FOR THREE OR FOUR DAYS, GROUSING AND DEpressed the whole time. Then, finally, we joined the Marine push in the area of Nasiriya. We were back in the war.

NEAR NASIRIYA

NASIRIYA IS A CITY ON THE EUPHRATES RIVER IN SOUTHERN Iraq, about 125 miles northwest of Kuwait. The city itself was taken by the Marines on March 31, but action in the area continued for quite some time, as small groups of Iraqi soldiers and Fedayeen continued to resist and attack Americans. It was near Nasiriya that

Jessica Lynch was captured and held during the first few days of the war.

Some historians believe that the fighting in the area was the fiercest the Marines encountered during the war, comparing it with the most ferocious firefights in Vietnam and later in Fallujah. Besides the city itself, the Marines took Jalibah Airfield, several bridges over the Euphrates, and highways and towns that secured the passage to Baghdad during the early stages of the war. Along the way, they began encountering the sort of fanatical insurgency that would characterize the war after Baghdad fell.

We had an extremely small part in the conflict there. We got into some very intense battles, but the bulk of the action was by Marines. Obviously, I can't write about most of that; what I saw of the overall battle was like looking at an enormous landscape painting through a tiny straw.

When you're working with Army and Marine Corps units, you immediately notice a difference. The Army is pretty tough, but their performance can depend on the individual unit. Some are excellent, filled with hoorah and first-class warriors. A few are absolutely horrible; most are somewhere in between.

In my experience, Marines are gung ho no matter what. They will all fight to the death. Every one of them just wants to get out there and kill. They are bad-ass, hard-charging mothers.

We inserted into the desert in the middle of the night, with two three-seat DPVs, driving off the back of a 53. The ground was firm enough that no one got stuck.

FIVE MINUTES TO LIVE

We were behind the tip of the U.S. advance, and there were no enemy units in the area. We drove up through the desert until we came to an Army base camp. We rested a few hours with them, then took off to scout for the Marines ahead of their advance.

The desert wasn't entirely empty. While there were long stretches of wilderness, there were also towns and very small settlements strung out in the distance. We mostly skirted the towns, observing them from the distance. Our job was to get an idea of where the enemy strongpoints were, radioing them back so the Marines could decide whether to attack or bypass them. Every so often we'd reach high ground, stop for a while, and take a scan.

We had only one significant contact that day. We were skirting by a city. We obviously got too close, because they started engaging us. I fired the .50-cal, then swung around to the 60 as we hauled ass out of there.

We must have traveled hundreds of miles that day. We lay up for a while in late afternoon, got some rest, then took off again after nightfall. When we started attracting fire that night, our orders were changed. The head shed called us back and arranged for the helicopters to come back and pick us up.

You might think that our job was to attract fire, since that revealed where the enemy was. You might think that the fact that we were close enough to get the enemy to fire meant we had discovered a significant force that was previously unknown. You might think that meant we were doing well.

You might be right. But to our CO, it was all wrong. He wanted us *not* to get contacted. He didn't want to risk any casualties, even if that meant we couldn't do our mission properly. (And I should add that, despite the gunfire and the earlier contact, we had not taken any casualties.)

We were pissed. We went out expecting to be scouting for a week. We had plenty of fuel, water, and food, and had already figured out how to get resupplied if we needed to. Hell, we could have gone all the way to Baghdad, which at the moment was still in Iraqi hands.

We reported back to base, dejected.

THAT WASN'T THE END OF THE WAR FOR US, BUT IT WAS A BAD sign of what lay ahead.

You have to understand: no SEAL *wants* to die. The purpose of war, as Patton put it, is to make the other dumb bastard die. But we also want to fight.

Part of it is personal. It's the same way for athletes: an athlete wants to be in a big game, wants to compete on the field or in the ring. But another part, a bigger part I think, is patriotism.

It's the sort of thing that if it has to be explained, you're not going to understand. But maybe this will help:

One night a little later on, we were in an exhausting firefight. Ten of us spent roughly forty-eight hours in the second story of an old, abandoned brick building, fighting in hundred-degree-plus heat wearing full armor. Bullets flew in, demolishing the walls around us practically nonstop. The only break we took was to reload.

Finally, as the sun came up in the morning, the sound of gunfire and bullets hitting brick stopped. The fight was over. It became eerily quiet.

When the Marines came in to relieve us, they found every man in the room either slumped against a wall or collapsed on the floor, dressing wounds or just soaking in the situation.

One of the Marines outside took an American flag and hoisted it over the position. Someone else played the National Anthem—I have no idea where the music came from, but the symbolism and the way it spoke to the soul was overwhelming; it remains one of my most powerful memories.

Every battle-weary man rose, went to the window, and saluted. The words of the music echoed in each of us as we watched the Stars and Stripes wave literally in dawn's early light. The reminder of what we were fighting for caused tears as well as blood and sweat to run freely from all of us.

I've lived the literal meaning of the "land of the free" and "home of the brave." It's not corny for me. I feel it in my heart. I feel it in my chest. Even at a ball game, when someone talks during the anthem or doesn't take off his hat, it pisses me off. I'm not one to be quiet about it, either.

For myself and the SEALs I was with, patriotism and getting into the heat of the battle were deeply connected. But how much a unit like ours can fight depends a lot on leadership. Much of it is up to the head shed, the officers who lead us. SEAL officers are a real mix. Some are good, some are bad. And some are just pussies.

Oh, they may be tough individuals, but it takes more than *personal* toughness to be good leaders. The methods and goals have to contribute to the toughness.

Our top command wanted us to achieve 100 percent success, and to do it with 0 casualties. That may sound admirable—who doesn't want to succeed, and who wants anyone to get hurt? But in war those are incompatible and unrealistic. If 100 percent success, 0 casualties are your goal, you're going to conduct very few operations. You will never take any risks, realistic or otherwise.

Ideally, we could have done sniper overwatches and undertaken scouting missions for the Marines all around Nasiriya. We could have been a much bigger part of the Marines' drive. We might have saved some of their lives.

We wanted to go out at night and hit the next big city or town the Marine Corps was going to pass through. We'd soften the target for them, killing off as many bad guys as we could. We did do a few missions like that, but it was certainly a lot less than we could have done.

EVIL

I HAD NEVER KNOWN THAT MUCH ABOUT ISLAM. RAISED AS A Christian, obviously I knew there had been religious conflicts for centuries. I knew about the Crusades, and I knew that there had been fighting and atrocities forever.

But I also knew that Christianity had evolved from the Middle Ages. We don't kill people because they're a different religion.

The people we were fighting in Iraq, after Saddam's army fled or was defeated, were fanatics. They hated us because we weren't Muslim. They wanted to kill us, even though we'd just booted out their dictator, because we practiced a different religion than they did.

Isn't religion supposed to teach tolerance?

PEOPLE SAY YOU HAVE TO DISTANCE YOURSELF FROM YOUR enemy to kill him. If that's true, in Iraq, the insurgents made it really easy. My story earlier about what the mother did to her child by pulling the pin on the grenade was only one gruesome example.

The fanatics we fought valued nothing but their twisted interpretation of religion. And half the time they just *claimed* they valued their religion—most didn't even pray. Quite a number were drugged up so they could fight us.

Many of the insurgents were cowards. They routinely used drugs to stoke their courage. Without them, alone, they were nothing. I have a tape somewhere showing a father and a girl in a house that was being searched. They were downstairs; for some reason, a flash-bang went off upstairs.

On the video, the father hides behind the girl, afraid that he's going to be killed and ready to sacrifice his daughter.

HIDDEN BODIES

THEY MAY HAVE BEEN COWARDS, BUT THEY COULD CERTAINLY kill people. The insurgents didn't worry about ROEs or court-martials. If they had the advantage, they would kill any Westerner they could find, whether they were soldiers or not.

One day we were sent to a house where we had heard there might be U.S. prisoners. We didn't find anyone in the building. But in the basement, there were obvious signs that the dirt had been disturbed. So we set up lights and started digging.

It wasn't long before I saw a pants leg, then a body, freshly buried.

An American soldier. Army.

Next to him was another. Then another man, this one wearing Marine camis.

My brother had joined the Marines a little before 9/11. I hadn't heard from him, and I thought that he had deployed to Iraq.

For some reason, as I helped pull the dead body up, I was sure it was my brother.

It wasn't. I said a silent prayer and we kept digging.

Another body, another Marine. I bent over and forced myself to look.

Not him.

But now, with each man we pulled out of that grave—and there were a bunch—I was more and more convinced I was going to see my brother. My stomach tightened. I kept digging. I wanted to puke.

Finally, we were done. He wasn't there.

I felt a moment of relief, even elation—none of them were my brother. Then I felt tremendous sadness for the murdered young men whose bodies we had pulled out.

When I finally heard from my brother, I found out that even though he was in Iraq, he hadn't been anywhere near where I'd seen those bodies. He'd had his own scares and hard times, I'm sure, but hearing his voice just made me feel a lot better.

I was still big brother, hoping to protect him. Hell, he didn't need me to watch over him; he was a Marine, and a tough one. But somehow those old instincts never go away.

At another location, we found barrels of chemical material that was intended for use as biochemical weapons. Everyone talks about there being no weapons of mass destruction in Iraq, but they seem to be referring to completed nuclear bombs, not the many deadly chemical weapons or precursors that Saddam had stockpiled.

Maybe the reason is that the writing on the barrels showed that the chemicals came from France and Germany, our supposed Western allies.

The thing I always wonder about is how much Saddam was able to hide before we actually invaded. We'd given so much warning before we came in, that he surely had time to move and bury tons of material. Where it went, where it will turn up, what it will poison—I think those are pretty good questions that have never been answered.

ONE DAY WE SAW SOME THINGS IN THE DESERT AND THOUGHT they were buried IEDs. We called the bomb-disposal people and they came out. Lo and behold, what they found wasn't a bomb—it was an airplane.

Saddam had buried a bunch of his fighters in the desert. He had them covered with plastic and then tried to hide them. Probably he figured we'd come through like we did in Desert Storm, hit quick and then leave.

He was wrong about that.

"WE'RE GOING TO DIE"

WE CONTINUED WORKING WITH THE MARINES AS THEY marched north. Our missions would typically take us out ahead of their advance, scouting for knots of defenders. Although we had intel that there were some enemy soldiers in the area, there weren't supposed to be any large units.

By this time, we were working with the entire platoon; all sixteen of us. We came up to a small building compound at the edge of a town. Once we were there, we began taking fire.

The firefight quickly ratcheted up, and within a few minutes we realized we were surrounded, our escape cut off by a force of several hundred Iraqis.

I started killing a lot of Iraqis—we all were—but for everyone we shot, four or five seemed to materialize to take their place. This went on for hours, with the fighting stoking up, then dying down.

Most firefights in Iraq were sporadic. They might be very intense for a few minutes, perhaps even an hour or more, but eventually the Iraqis would withdraw. Or we would.

That didn't happen here. The fight continued in waves all through the night. The Iraqis knew they had us outnumbered and surrounded and they weren't quitting. Little by little, they started getting closer and closer, until it became obvious that they were going to overrun us.

We were done. We were going to die. Or worse, we'd be captured and made prisoners. I thought about my family and how horrible that would all be. I determined I was dying first.

I fired off more of my rounds, but now the fight was getting closer. I was starting to think about what I would do if they charged us. I'd use my pistol, my knife, my hands—anything.

And then I would die. I thought of Taya, and how much I loved her. I tried not to get distracted by anything, tried concentrating on the fight.

The Iraqis kept coming. We estimated we had five minutes to live. I started counting it off in my head.

I hadn't gotten very far when the company radio squeaked with a transmission: "We're coming up on your six."

Friendlies were approaching our position.

The cavalry.

The Marines, actually. We weren't going to die. Not in five minutes anyway.

Thank God!

OUT OF THE FIGHT

THAT ACTION TURNED OUT TO BE OUR LAST SIGNIFICANT ENcounter during that deployment. The CO pulled us back to base.

It was a waste. The Marines were going into Nasiriya every night, trying to clear the place out as the insurgency stoked up. They could have given us our own section that we could patrol. We could have rolled in and taken out the bad guys—but the CO vetoed it.

We heard it at the forward bases and camps where we were sitting around waiting for something real to do. The GROM—the Polish special forces—were going out and doing jobs. They told us we were lions led by dogs.

The Marines were blunter. They'd come back every night and bust on us:

"*How many did y'all get tonight? Oh, that's right—y'all didn't go out.*"

Ballbusters. But I couldn't blame them. I thought our head shed was a bunch of pussies.

We had started training to take down Mukarayin Dam northeast of Baghdad. The dam was important not only because it provided hydroelectric power, but because if it were allowed to flood it could have slowed military forces attacking Iraqis in the area. But the mission was continually postponed, and finally given to SEAL Team 5 when they rotated into the Gulf toward the end of our stay. (The mission, which followed our basic plan, was a success.)

There were many things we could have done. How much of an impact on the war they would have had, I have no idea. We certainly could have saved a few lives here and there, maybe shortened some conflicts by a day or more. Instead, we were told to get ready to go home. Our deployment was over.

I sat back at base for a couple of weeks with nothing to do. I felt like a little fucking coward, playing video games and waiting to ship out.

I was pretty pissed. In fact, I was so mad I wanted to leave the Navy, and give up being a SEAL.

5

SNIPER

Taya:
 The first time Chris came home, he was really disgusted with everything. With America, especially.
 In the car on the way back to our house, we listened to the radio. People weren't talking about the war; life went on as if nothing was happening in Iraq.
 "People are talking about bullshit," he said. "We're fighting for the country, and no one gives a shit."
 He'd been really disappointed when the war began. He was back in Kuwait and had seen something on television that was negative about the troops. He called and said, "You know what? If that's what they think, fuck them. I'm out here ready to give my life and they're doing bullshit."
 I had to tell him there were a lot of people who cared,

not just for the troops in general, but for him. He had me, he had friends in San Diego and Texas, and family.

But the adjustment to being home was hard. He'd wake up punching. He'd always been jumpy, but now, when I got up in the middle of the night, I'd stop and say his name before I got back into bed. I had to wake him up before coming back to bed to ensure I wasn't hit with his basic reflex.

One time I woke up to him grabbing my arm with both of his hands. One hand was on the forearm and one just slightly above my elbow. He was sound asleep and appeared to be ready to snap my arm in half. I stayed as still as possible and kept repeating his name, getting louder each time so as not to startle him, but also to stop the impending damage to my arm. Finally, he woke and let go.

Slowly, we settled into some new habits, and adjusted.

SCARES

I DIDN'T QUIT THE SEALs.

I might have, if my contract hadn't still had a lot of time to run. Maybe I would have gone to the Marines. But it wasn't an option.

I had some reason for hope. When you come home and the Team returns from a deployment, there's a reshuffling at the top and you get new leadership. There was always a chance our new head shed would be better.

I talked to Taya and told her how pissed off I was. Of course, she had a different perspective: she was just happy that I was alive and home in one piece. Meanwhile, the brass got huge promotions and congratulations for their part in the war. They got the glory.

Bullshit glory.

Bullshit glory for a war they didn't fight and the cowardly stance they took. Their cowardice ended lives we could have saved if they would have let us do our jobs. But that's politics for you: a bunch of game-players sitting around congratulating each other in safety while real lives are getting screwed up.

EVERY TIME I RETURNED HOME FROM DEPLOYMENT, STARTING then, I wouldn't leave the house for about a week. I'd just stay there. Generally, we'd get about a month off after unloading and sorting our gear and stuff. That first week I'd always stay home with Taya and keep to myself. Only after that would I start seeing family and friends.

I didn't have flashbacks of battle or anything dramatic like that; I just needed to be alone.

I do remember once, after the first deployment, when I had something *like* a flashback, though it only lasted a few seconds. I was sitting in the room we used as an office in our house in Alpine near San Diego. We had a burglar alarm system, and for some reason, Taya set it off accidentally when she came home.

It scared the ever-living shit out of me. I just immediately went right back to Kuwait. I dove under the desk. I thought it was a Scud attack.

We laugh about it now—but for those few seconds I was truly scared, more scared even than I had been in Kuwait when the Scuds actually did fly over.

I'VE HAD MORE FUN WITH BURGLAR ALARMS THAN I CAN RE-
count. One day I woke up after Taya had left for work. As soon as I
got out of bed, the alarm went off. This one was in voice mode, so
it alerted me with a computerized voice:

"*Intruder alert! Intruder in the house! Intruder alert!*"

I grabbed my pistol and went to confront the criminal. No son
of a bitch was breaking into my house and living to tell about it.

"*Intruder: living room!*"

I carefully proceeded to the living room and used all of my
SEAL skills to clear the living room.

Vacant. Smart criminal.

I moved down the hall.

"*Intruder: kitchen!*"

The kitchen was also clear. The son of a bitch was running
from me.

"*Intruder: hall!*"

Motherfucker!

I can't tell you how long it took before I realized *I* was the intruder: the system was tracking me. Taya had set the alarm to a
setting that assumed the house was vacant, turning on the motion
detectors.

Y'all feel free to laugh. With me, not at me, right?

I ALWAYS SEEMED MORE VULNERABLE AT HOME. AFTER EVERY
deployment, something would happen to me, usually during training. I broke a toe, a finger, all sorts of little injuries. Overseas, on
deployment, in the war, I seemed invincible.

"You take your superhero cape off every time you come home
from deployment," Taya used to joke.

After a while, I figured it was true.

My parents had been nervous the entire time I was away. They wanted to see me as soon as I got home, and I think my need to keep to myself at first probably hurt them more than they'll say. When we finally did get together, though, it was a pretty happy day.

My dad took my deployment especially hard, outwardly showing his anxiousness a lot more than my mother. It's funny—sometimes the strongest individuals feel the worst when events are out of their control, and they can't really be there for the people they love. I've felt it myself.

It was a pattern that would repeat itself every time I went overseas. My mom carried on like the stoic one; my otherwise stoic dad became the family worrier.

SCHOOLED

I gave up part of my vacation and came back from leave a week early to go to sniper school. I would have given up much more than that for the chance.

Marine snipers have justifiably gotten a lot of attention over the years, and their training program is still regarded as one of the world's best. In fact, SEAL snipers used to be trained there. But we've gone ahead and started our own school, adapting a lot of what the Marines do but adding a number of things to prepare SEAL snipers for our mission. The SEAL school takes a little more than twice as long to complete because of that.

Next to BUD/S, sniper training was the hardest school I ever went through. They were constantly messing with our heads. We had late nights and early mornings. We were always running or being stressed in some way.

That was a key part of the instruction. Since they can't shoot at you, they put as much pressure on you as they can manage in every other way. From what I've heard, only 50 percent of the SEALs who take the school make it through. I can believe it.

The first classes teach SEALs how to use the computers and cameras that are part of our job. SEAL snipers aren't just shooters. In fact, shooting is only a small part of the job. It's an important, vital part, but it's far from everything.

A SEAL sniper is trained to observe. It's a foundation skill. He may find himself out ahead of a main force, tasked to discover everything he can about the enemy. Even if he's assigned to get into position to take out a high-value target, the first thing he has to be able to do is observe the area. He needs to be able to use modern navigational skills and tools like GPS, and at the same time present the information he's gathered. So that's where we start.

The next part of the course, and in a lot of ways the hardest, is stalking. That's the part where most guys fall out. Stalking means sneaking into a position without being seen: easier said than done. It's moving slowly and carefully to the exact right spot for the mission. It's not patience, or at least that's not all it is. It's professional discipline.

I'm not a patient person, but I learned that to succeed as a stalker I need to take my time. If I know I'm going to kill someone, I will wait a day, a week, two weeks.

Make that, I *have* waited.

I will do whatever it takes. And let's just say there are no bathroom breaks, either.

For one of the exercises, we had to sneak through a hay field. I took hours arranging the grass and hay in my ghillie suit. The ghillie suit is made of burlap and is a kind of camouflage base for a sniper on a stalking mission. The suit allows you to add hay or grass or whatever, so you can blend in with your surroundings. The burlap adds depth, so it doesn't look like a guy with hay sticking out of your butt as you cross a field. You look like a bush.

But the suits are hot and sweaty. And they don't make you invisible. When you come to another piece of terrain, you have to stop and rearrange your camouflage. You have to look like whatever it is you're crossing.

I remember one time I was making my way s-l-o-w-l-y across a field when I heard the distinct rattle of a snake nearby. A rattler had taken a particular liking to the piece of real estate I had to cross. Willing it away didn't work. Not wanting to give away my position to the instructor grading me, I crept slowly to the side, altering my course. Some enemies aren't worth fighting.

DURING THE STALKING PORTION OF OUR TRAINING, YOU'RE not graded on your first shot. You're graded on your second. In other words, once you've fired, can you be seen?

Hopefully, no. Because not only is there a good possibility you'll have to take more shots, but you have to get out of there, too. And it would be nice to do that alive.

It's important to remember that perfect circles do not exist in nature, and that means you have to do what you can to camouflage your scope and rifle barrel. I would take tape and put it over my barrel, then spray-paint the tape up to camouflage it further. I'd keep some vegetation in front of my scope as well as my barrel—you don't need to see everything, just your target.

For me, stalking was the hardest part of the course. I nearly failed because of a lack of patience.

It was only after we mastered stalking that we moved on to shooting.

GUNS

PEOPLE ASK A LOT ABOUT WEAPONS, WHAT I USED AS A SNIPER, what I learned on, what I prefer. In the field, I matched the weapon to the job and the situation. At sniper school, I learned the basics of a range of weapons, so I was prepared not only to use them all, but also to choose the right one for the job.

I used four basic weapons at sniper school. Two were magazine-fed semiautomatics: the Mk-12, a 5.56 sniper rifle; and the Mk-11, a 7.62 sniper rifle. (When I talk about a gun, I often just mention the caliber, so the Mk-12 is the 5.56. Oh, and there's no "point" in front of the numbers; it's understood.)

Then there was my .300 Win Mag. That was magazine-fed, but it was bolt-action. Like the other two, it was suppressed. Which means that it has a device on the end of the barrel that suppresses muzzle flash and reduces the sound of bullet as it leaves the gun, much like a muffler on a car. (It's not actually a silencer, though some think of it that way. Without getting too technical, the suppressor works by letting gas out of the barrel as the bullet discharges. Generally speaking, there are two types, one that attaches to the barrel of the weapon and another that's integrated with the barrel itself. Among the practical effects of the suppressor on a sniper rifle is that it tends to reduce the amount of "kick" the shooter experiences. This helps make it more accurate.)

I also had a .50 caliber, which was not suppressed.

Let's talk about each weapon individually.

Mk-12

Officially, the United States Navy Mk-12 Special Purpose Rifle, this gun has a sixteen-inch barrel, but is otherwise the same platform as an M-4. It fires a 5.56 × 45 mm round from a thirty-round magazine. (It can also be fitted with a twenty-round box.)

Derived from what became known as the .223 cartridge and therefore smaller and lighter than most earlier military rounds, the 5.56 is not a preferred bullet to shoot someone with. It can take a few shots to put someone down, especially the drugged-up crazies we were dealing with in Iraq, unless you hit him in the head. And contrary to what you're probably thinking, not all sniper shots, certainly not mine, take the bad guys in the head. Usually I went for center mass—a nice fat target somewhere in the middle of the body, giving me plenty of room to work with.

The gun was super-easy to handle, and was virtually interchangeable with the M-4, which, though not a sniper weapon, is still a valuable combat tool. As a matter of fact, when I got back to my platoon, I took the lower receiver off my M-4 and put it on the upper receiver of my Mk-12. That gave me a collapsible stock and allowed me to go full-auto. (I see now that some Mk-12s are being equipped with the collapsible stock.)

On patrol, I like to use a shorter stock. It's quicker to get up to my shoulder and get a bead on somebody. It's also better for working inside and in tight quarters.

Another note on my personal configuration: I never used full auto on the rifle. The only time you really want full auto is to keep someone's head down—spewing bullets doesn't make for an accurate course of fire. But since there might be a circumstance where it would come in handy, I always wanted to have that option in case I needed it.

Mk-11

Officially called the Mk-11 Mod X Special Purpose Rifle and also known as the SR25, this is an extremely versatile weapon. I particularly like the idea of the Mk-11 because I could patrol with it (in place of an M-4) and still use it as a sniper rifle. It didn't have a collapsible stock, but that was its only drawback. I would tie the suppressor onto my kit, leaving it off during the start of a patrol. If I needed to take a sniper shot, I would put it on. But if I was on the street or moving on foot, I could shoot back right away. It was semiautomatic, so I could get a lot of bullets on a target, and it fired 7.62 × .51 mm bullets from a twenty-round box. Those had more stopping power than the smaller 5.56 NATO rounds. I could shoot a guy once and put him down.

Our rounds were match-grade ammo bought from Black Hills, which makes probably the best sniper ammo around.

The Mk-11 had a bad reputation in the field because it would often jam. We wouldn't have jams that much in training, but overseas was a different story. We eventually figured out that something to do with the dust cover on the rifle was causing a double feed; we solved a lot of the problem by leaving the dustcover down. There were other issues with the weapon, however, and personally it was never one of my favorites.

.300 Win Mag

The .300 is in another class entirely.

As I'm sure many readers know, .300 Win Mag (pronounced "three hundred win mag") refers to the bullet the rifle fires, the .300 Winchester Magnum round (7.62 × 67 mm). It's an excellent all-around cartridge, whose performance allows for superb accuracy as well as stopping power.

Other services fire the round from different (or slightly different) guns; arguably, the most famous is the Army's M-24 Sniper Weapon System, which is based on the Remington 700 rifle. (Yes, that is the same rifle civilians can purchase for hunting.) In our case, we started out with MacMillan stocks, customized the barrels, and used 700 action. These were nice rifles.

In my third platoon—the one that went to Ramadi—we got all new .300s. These used Accuracy International stocks, with a brand-new barrel and action. The AI version had a shorter barrel and a folding stock. They were bad-ass.

The .300 is a little heavier gun by design. It shoots like a laser. Anything from a thousand yards and out, you're just plain nailing it. And on closer targets, you don't have to worry about too much correction for your come-ups. You can dial in your five-hundred-yard dope and still hit a target from one hundred to seven hundred yards without worrying too much about making minute adjustments.

I used a .300 Win Mag for most of my kills.

.50 Caliber

The fifty is huge, extremely heavy, and I just don't like it. I never used one in Iraq.

There's a certain amount of hype and even romance for these weapons, which shoot a 12.7 × 99 mm round. There are a few different specific rifles and variations in service with the U.S. military and other armies around the world. You've probably heard of the Barrett M-82 or the M-107, developed by Barrett Firearms Manufacturing. They have enormous ranges and in the right application are certainly good weapons. I just didn't like them all that much. (The one .50 I do like is the Accuracy International model, which has a more compact, collapsible stock and a little more accuracy; it wasn't available to us at the time.)

Everyone says that the .50 is a perfect anti-vehicle gun. But the truth is that if you shoot the .50 through a vehicle's engine block, you're not actually going to stop the vehicle. Not right away. The fluids will leak out and eventually it will stop moving. But it's not instant by any means. A .338 and even a .300 will do the same thing. No, the best way to stop a vehicle is to shoot the driver. And that you can do with a number of weapons.

.338

We didn't have .338s in training; we started getting them later on during the war. Again, the name refers to the bullet; there are a number of different manufacturers, including MacMillan and Accuracy International. The bullet shoots farther and flatter than a .50 caliber, weighs less, costs less, and will do just as much damage. They are awesome weapons.

I used a .338 on my last deployment. I would have used it more if I'd had it. The only drawback for me was my model's lack of a suppressor. When you're shooting inside a building, the concussion is strong enough that it's a pain—literally. My ears would hurt after a few shots.

SINCE I'M TALKING ABOUT GUNS, I'LL MENTION THAT MY CURrent favorites are the weapons systems made by GA Precision, a very small company started in 1999 by George Gardner. He and his staff pay close attention to every detail, and his weapons are just awesome. I didn't get a chance to try one until I got out of the service, but now they're what I use.

SCOPES ARE AN IMPORTANT PART OF THE WEAPON SYSTEM. Overseas, I used a 32-power scope. (The powers on a scope refer to the magnification of the focal length. Without getting too technical, the higher the power, the better a shooter can see at a distance. But there are tradeoffs, depending on the situation and the scope. Scopes should be chosen with a mind toward the situation they'll be used in; to give an obvious example, a 32-power scope would be wildly inappropriate on a shotgun.) Additionally, depending on the circumstances, I had an infrared and visible red laser, as well as night vision for the scope.

As a SEAL, I used Nightforce scopes. They have very clear glass, and they're extremely durable under terrible conditions. They always held their zero for me. On deployments, I used a Leica range finder to determine how far I was from a target.

Most of the stocks on my guns used adjustable cheek-pieces. Sometimes called a comb (technically, the comb is the top piece of the stock, but the terms are sometimes interchanged), the extension let me keep my eye in position when sighting through the scope. On older weapons, we would adapt a piece of hard-packed foam and raise the stock to the right height. (As scope rings have gotten larger and more varied in size, the ability to change the stock height has become more important.)

I used a two-pound trigger on my rifles. That's a fairly light pull. I want the trigger to surprise me every time; I don't want to jerk the gun as I fire. I want no resistance:

Get set, get ready, put my finger and gently start squeezing, and it goes off.

AS A HUNTER, I KNEW HOW TO SHOOT, HOW TO MAKE THE BULlet go from point A to point B. Sniper school taught me the science behind it all. One of the more interesting facts is that the barrel of a rifle cannot touch any part of the stock: they need to be freefloating to increase accuracy. (The barrel will "float" in the stock, due to the way the stock is cut out. It attaches only to the main body of the rifle.) When you shoot a round, a vibration comes through the barrel, known as barrel whip. Anything touching the barrel will affect that vibration, and, in turn, affect the accuracy. Then there are things like the Coriolis effect, which has to do with the rotation of the earth and the effect it has on a rifle bullet. (This comes into play only at extremely long distances.)

You live all of this technical data in sniper school. You learn about how far to lead someone when they're moving—if they're walking, if they're running, depending on the distance. You keep doing it until the understanding is embedded not just in your brain but in your arms and hands and fingers.

IN MOST SHOOTING SITUATIONS, I ADJUST FOR ELEVATION, BUT not for windage. (Simply put, adjusting for elevation means adjusting my aim to compensate for the drop of my bullet over the distance it travels; windage means compensating for the effect of the wind.) The wind is constantly changing. So about the time I adjust for wind, the wind changes. Elevation is a different story—though if you're in a combat situation, a lot of times you don't have the luxury of making a fine adjustment. You have to shoot or be shot.

TESTED

I WAS NOT THE BEST SNIPER IN MY CLASS. IN FACT, I FAILED THE practice test. That meant potentially washing out of the class.

Unlike the Marines, in the field we don't work with spotters. The SEAL philosophy is, basically, if you have a fellow warrior with you, he ought to be shooting, not watching. That said, we did use spotters in training.

After I failed the test, the instructor went through everything with me and my spotter, trying to figure out where I'd gone wrong. My scope was perfect, my dope was set, there was nothing mechanically wrong with the rifle . . .

Suddenly, he looked up at me.

"Dip?" he said, more a statement than a question.

"Oh . . ."

I hadn't put any chewing tobacco in my mouth during the test. It was the only thing I'd done differently . . . and it turned out to be the key. I passed the exam with flying colors—and a wad of tobacco in my cheek

SNIPERS AS A BREED TEND TO BE SUPERSTITIOUS. WE'RE LIKE baseball players with our little rituals and must-dos. Watch a baseball game, and you'll see a batter always does the same thing as he steps to the plate—he'll make the sign of the cross, kick the dirt, wave the bat. Snipers are the same way.

During training and even afterward, I kept my guns a certain way, wore the same clothes, had everything arranged precisely the same. It's all a matter of controlling everything on my end. I know the gun is going to do its job. I need to make sure I do mine.

THERE'S A LOT MORE TO BEING A SEAL SNIPER THAN SHOOTing. As training progressed, I was taught to study the terrain and the surroundings. I learned to see things with a sniper's eye.

If I were trying to kill me, where would I set up?
That roof. I could take the whole squad from there.

Once I identified those spots, I'd spend more time looking at them. I had excellent vision going into the course, but it wasn't so much seeing as learning to perceive—knowing what sort of movement should get your attention, discerning subtle shapes that can tip off a waiting ambush.

I had to practice to stay sharp. Observation is hard work. I'd go outside and just train myself to spot things in the distance. I always tried to hone my craft, even on leave. On a ranch in Texas, you see animals, birds—you learn to look in the distance and spot movement, shapes, little inconsistencies in the landscape.

For a while, it seemed like everything I did helped train me, even video games. I had a little handheld mahjongg game that a friend of mine had given us as a wedding present. I don't know if it was exactly appropriate as a wedding present—it's a handheld, one-person game—but as a training tool it was invaluable. In mahjongg, you scan different tiles, looking for matches. I would play timed sessions against the computer, working to sharpen my observation skills.

I said it before and I'll keep saying it: I'm not the best shot in the world. There were plenty of guys better than me, even in that class. I only graduated about middle of the pack.

As it happened, the guy who was the honor man or best in our class was part of our platoon. He never had as many kills as I did, though, at least partly because he was sent to the Philippines for a few months while I spent my time in Iraq. You need skill to be a sniper, but you also need opportunity. And luck.

BEATEN BY DOLPHINS, EATEN BY SHARKS

After spending the entire summer at sniper school, I returned to my platoon and got busy with the rest of our workup, going through the different training sessions as we prepared to deploy in a year. As usual, I had some of my hardest times in the water.

Everyone gets all warm and fuzzy about marine animals, but I've had close and personal encounters that were anything but.

While the Navy was testing a program using dolphins for harbor defense, they used us as targets, in a few cases without warning. The dolphins would come out and beat the shit out of us. They were trained to hit in the sides, and they could crack ribs. And if you hadn't been warned in advance of the exercise, you didn't know what was going on—your first reaction, or at least mine, was to think you were being attacked by sharks.

One time we were out and the dolphins were taking it to us. Getting beaten bad, I headed toward shore to dodge the bastards.

Spotting some piers, I ducked underneath—I knew they wouldn't follow me.

Safe.

All of a sudden, something clamped hard on my leg. Hard.

It was a sea lion. They were being trained to guard the piers.

I went back out into open water. I'd rather be beaten by a dolphin than eaten by a sea lion.

BUT SHARKS WERE, BY FAR, THE WORST.

One evening, we were supposed to swim across the bay off San Diego, in the dark, and plant a limpet mine on a particular ship. Simple, standard SEAL operation.

Not every SEAL hates the water like I do. In fact, a lot of them like it so much they'll swim around and play tricks on the others in the exercise. You might have a guy plant his mine, then sink to the bottom and wait for the next guy to come over with his. There's usually enough light from above that the second diver is silhouetted and easy to see. So when the victim—I mean, diver—comes to plant his mine, the first diver comes up, grabs his fin, and jerks it.

That scares the shit out of the second diver. Usually he thinks there's a shark in the water and screws up the rest of the exercise. And his gear may need a special cleaning.

On this particular day, I was beneath the ship and had just planted my mine when something grabbed my fin.

SHARK!!!

Then I put my heart back in my chest, remembering all the stories and warnings about my brethren SEALs.

Just one of the guys messing with my head, I told myself. I turned around to flip him off.

And found myself giving the finger to a shark who'd taken a particular liking to my flipper. He had it in his jaw.

He wasn't a huge shark, but what he lacked in size he made up for in pure orneriness. I grabbed my knife and cut off my fin—no sense keeping it now that it was all chewed up, right?

While he was munching on what remained of it, I swam up to the surface and flagged down the security boat. I grabbed onto the side and explained that they were taking me in RIGHT NOW!! because there was a SHARK!! out here, and he was one hungry mother.

During another training exercise—this one was before my first deployment—four of us were inserted on the California coast from a submarine. We came ashore in two Zodiacs, built a hide, and did some reconnaissance. When the time came, we all got in our Zodiacs and headed back out to meet the sub and go home.

Unfortunately, my officer had given the submarine the wrong grid coordinates for the rendezvous. In fact, they were so far off that there was an island between us and the sub.

Of course, we didn't know that at the time. We just circled around, trying to make radio coms with a vessel that was too far away to hear us. At some point, either our radio got wet or the battery drained, and all hope of connection was lost.

We spent just about the entire night out on the water in the Zodiacs. Finally, as dawn approached, our fuel was nearly gone. My raft was starting to go flat. We all decided we'd just go back ashore and wait. At least we would get some sleep.

As we were coming in, a sea lion swam up, all friendly-like. Being from Texas, I had never really had much of a chance to look at sea lions, so naturally I was curious and started watching this one. He was a pretty interesting, if ugly, critter.

All of a sudden—*splop*—he disappeared below the surface.

The next thing I knew, he—and we—were surrounded by large, pointy fins. Apparently, a number of sharks had decided to make breakfast of him.

Sea lions are big, but there were way too many sharks to be satisfied with just him. They started circling closer and closer to the sides of my raft, which looked increasingly thin and perilously close to the water.

I glanced toward shore. It was very far off.

Holy shit, I thought. *I'm going to get eaten.*

My companion in the raft was a rather round fellow, at least for a SEAL.

"If we go down," I warned him, "I'm shooting you. You'll be something for the sharks to munch on while I swim to shore."

He just cursed at me. I think he thought I was kidding.

I wasn't.

TATS

WE DID FINALLY MAKE SHORE WITHOUT GETTING EATEN. BUT meanwhile, the entire Navy was looking for us. The news media started carrying the story: FOUR SEALS LOST AT SEA.

Not exactly what we wanted to be famous for.

It took a while, but a patrol plane finally spotted us and an Mk-V was dispatched to pick us up. The commander of the assault boat took care of us and got us home.

THAT WAS ONE OF THE FEW TIMES WHEN I WAS REALLY GLAD to get aboard a boat or ship. Generally, when I've been out at sea I've been bored. Worrying about being assigned to sea duty was a big motivator during BUD/S.

Submarines are the worst. Even the largest feel cramped. The last time I was aboard one, we weren't even allowed to work out. The gym was located on the other side of the nuclear reactor from our quarters, and we weren't authorized to pass through the reactor area to get there.

Aircraft carriers are a hell of a lot larger, but they can be just as boring. At least they have lounges where you can play video games and there are no restrictions on getting to the gym to blow off steam.

In fact, on one occasion, we were specifically requested to go to the gym by the CO.

We were on the *Kitty Hawk* when they were having a problem with gangs. Apparently, some punk sailors who were gang members were causing quite a discipline problem aboard ship. The CO of the boat pulled us over and told us when the gang used the gym.

So we went down to work out, locked the door behind us, and fixed the gang problem.

DURING THIS WORKUP, I MISSED A DIVE SESSION BECAUSE I got sick. It was as if a light went off in my head. From that point on, just about every time diving turned up on our practice schedule, I came down with a very bad disease. Or I found a sniper-training trip that just *had* to be taken at that point.

The rest of the guys teased me that I had better ninja smoke than anybody.

And who am I to argue?

I ALSO GOT MY FIRST TATTOO AROUND THIS TIME. I WANTED to honor the SEALs, and yet I didn't feel as if I'd earned a Trident tattoo. (The official SEAL emblem had an eagle perched in an overwatch position on a trident that forms the crossbar of an anchor; a flintlock pistol sits in front of it. The insignia is known as the trident or, unofficially, a "Budweiser," the reference being to BUD/S . . . or the beer, depending on who you ask.)

So, instead, I got a "frog bone," a tattoo that looks like a frog skeleton. This, too, is a traditional SEAL and UDT symbol—in this case, honoring our dead comrades. I have the tattoo on my back, peeking over my shoulder—as if those who came before me were looking after me, offering some protection.

BIRTH

BESIDES BEING A SEAL, I WAS ALSO A HUSBAND. AND AFTER I came home, Taya and I decided to try and start a family.

Things went pretty well. She got pregnant about the first time we kissed without protection. And her pregnancy was near-perfect. It was the childbirth that got complicated.

For some reason, my wife had a problem with a low platelet count. Unfortunately, the problem wasn't discovered until too late, and because of that she couldn't get an epidural or other painkiller when it came time to give birth. So, she had to give birth naturally, without any training or preparation.

Our son was eight pounds, not a particularly small kid.

You learn a lot about a woman when she's under duress. I got bitched to high heaven. (She claims she didn't, but I know better. And who are you going to believe, a SEAL? Or a SEAL's wife?)

Taya was in labor for sixteen hours. Toward the end, they decided they could give her laughing gas to ease the pain. But before they did, they warned me of everything that could happen to my son, no matter how distant the possibility.

I didn't feel I had much of a choice. She was in tremendous pain. She needed relief. I told them to go ahead, though in the back of my mind I was worried that my boy would come out messed up.

Then the doctor told me my son was so big, he couldn't quite squeeze through the birth canal. They wanted to put a suction thing on his head to help him get out. Meanwhile, Taya was passing out cold between contractions.

"Okay," I said, not really understanding.

The doctor looked at me. "He may come out like a Conehead."

Oh great, I thought. *My child is not only going to be fucked up from the gas but he's going to be a Conehead.*

"Goddamnit, just get him out of there," I told him. "You're killing my wife. Do it!"

My boy came out just fine. But I have to say, I was a case the whole time. It was the most hopeless feeling in the world, seeing my wife in excruciating pain, without anything I could do.

I was a hell of a lot more nervous watching her give birth than I ever was in combat.

TAYA:

It was a very emotional time, with tremendous highs and lows. Both of our families were in town for the birth. We were all very happy, and yet, at the same time, we knew Chris would be leaving soon for Iraq.

That part sucked.

Chris had trouble handling the baby's crying at first, and that stressed me as well—you can handle war but you can't handle a few days of crying?

Most people don't deal too well with that. Chris certainly wasn't one of the exceptions.

I knew taking care of our son was all going to be on me for the next several months while he was away. More importantly, I knew that all the newness and magic was also going to be with me. I was nervous about how I would handle it, and sad that all the memories of our beautiful son would be mine alone as opposed to shared memories we could look back on together.

At the same time, I was angry he was leaving and terrified he wouldn't make it back. I also loved him like crazy.

NAV SCHOOL

BESIDES SNIPER SCHOOL, I HAD BEEN "VOLUNTEERED" FOR nav school by my chief. I went reluctantly.

Navigating is an important skill in combat—without a navigator, you don't know how to get to the battle, let alone how to get away when you're done. In a DA (direct action) scenario, the navigator figures out the best way to the target, comes up with alternatives, and guides the fire team to safety when you're done.

The problem is, SEAL navigators often don't get a chance to actually fight in the DA they navigate to. The way we set things up, the navigator is usually assigned to stay in the vehicle while the rest of the unit breaks into the house or whatever. That's so he can be ready in case we need to get out fast.

Sitting in the passenger seat plugging numbers into a computer was not exactly where I wanted to be. But my chief wanted someone he could count on planning the routes, and when your chief asks you to do something, you do it.

I spent the whole first week of nav school frowning at a desk in front of a Toughbook laptop computer, learning the computer's functions, how to hook up to a GPS and manipulate the satellite imagery and maps. I also learned how to take the images and paste them onto PowerPoint for briefings and the like.

Yes, even SEALs use PowerPoint.

The second week was a little more interesting. We drove around the city—we were in San Diego—plotting and following different routes. I'm not pretending it was cool, though—important, yes, but not very exciting.

As it happened, though, it was my skills as a navigator that got me to Iraq ahead of everyone else.

6

DEALING DEATH

BACK TO WAR

Toward the end of our workup, we found out that they were standing up a new unit in Baghdad to do direct action raids on suspected terrorists and resistance leaders. The unit was being run by the GROM, the Polish special operations unit. While the Poles would handle most of the heavy lifting, they needed some supplements—namely, snipers and navigators. And so, in September 2004, I was pulled from my platoon and sent to Iraq to help the GROM as a navigator. The rest of the platoon was due to come overseas the following month; I'd meet them there.

I felt bad about leaving Taya. She was still healing from the birth. But at the same time, I felt my duty as a SEAL was more important. I wanted to get back into action. I wanted to go to war.

At that point, while I loved my son, I hadn't yet bonded with him. I was never one of those dads who liked to feel my wife's belly when the baby was kicking. I tend to need to know someone well, even kin, before that part of me grows.

That changed over time, but at that point I still hadn't experienced the real depth of what being a father is all about.

Generally, when SEALs go out for a deployment or come back, we do so very quietly—that's the nature of special operations. There are usually few people around except for our immediate families; sometimes not even them. In this case, because of when I was heading out, it happened that I passed a small group of protesters demonstrating against the war. They had signs about baby killers and murderers and whatever, protesting the troops who were going over to fight.

They were protesting the wrong people. We didn't vote in Congress; we didn't vote to go to war.

I signed up to protect this country. I do not choose the wars. It happens that I love to fight. But I do not choose which battles I go to. Y'all send me to them.

I had to wonder why these people weren't protesting at their congressional offices or in Washington. Protesting the people who were ordered to protect them—let's just say it put a bad taste in my mouth.

I realize not everybody felt that way. I did see signs on some homes supporting the troops, saying "We love you" and that sort of thing. And there were plenty of tearful and respectful sendoffs and homecomings, some even on TV. But it was the ignorant protesters I remembered, years and years later.

And, for the record, it doesn't bother me that SEALs don't have big sendoffs or fancy homecomings. We are the silent professionals; we're covert operators and inviting the media to the airport is not in the program.

Still, it's nice to be thanked every so often for doing our job.

IRAQ

A LOT HAD HAPPENED IN IRAQ SINCE I LEFT IN THE SPRING OF 2003. The country had been liberated from Saddam Hussein and his army with the fall of Baghdad on April 9 of that year. But a variety of terrorist forces either continued or began fighting after Saddam was deposed. They fought both other Iraqis and the U.S. forces who were trying to help the country regain stability. Some were former members of Saddam's army and members of the Ba'athist Party that Saddam had headed. There were Fedayeen, members of a paramilitary resistance group the dictator had organized before the war. There were small, poorly organized groups of Iraqi guerrillas, who were also called Fedayeen, though, technically, they weren't connected with Saddam's organization. Though nearly all were Muslim, nationalism rather than religion tended to be their primary motive and organizing principle.

Then there were the groups organized primarily around religious beliefs. These identified themselves as mujahedeen, which basically means "people on jihad"—or murderers in the name of God. They were dedicated to killing Americans and Muslims who didn't believe in the brand of Islam that they believed in.

There was also al-Qaeda in Iraq, a mostly foreign group that saw the war as an opportunity to kill Americans. They were radical Sunni Muslims with an allegiance to Osama bin Laden, the terrorist leader who needs no introduction—and whom SEALs hunted down and gave a fitting sendoff in 2011.

There were also Iranians and their Republican Guard, who fought—sometimes directly, though usually through proxies—to both kill Americans and to gain power in Iraqi politics.

I'm sure there were a hell of a lot of others in what came to be known to the media as "the insurgency." They were all the enemy.

I never worried too much about who exactly it was who was pointing a gun at me or planting an IED. The fact that they wanted to kill me was all I needed to know.

Saddam was captured in December of 2003.

In 2004, the U.S. formally turned over authority to the interim government, giving control of the country back to the Iraqis, at least in theory. But the insurgency grew tremendously that same year. A number of battles in the spring were as fierce as those waged during the initial invasion.

In Baghdad, a hard-line Shiite cleric named Muqtada al-Sadr organized an army of fanatical followers and urged them to attack Americans. Sadr was especially strong in a part of Baghdad known as Sadr City, a slum named after his father, Mohammad Mohammad Sadeq al-Sadr, a grand ayatollah and an opponent of Saddam's regime during the 1990s. An extremely poor area even by Iraqi standards, Sadr City was packed with radical Shiites. Said to be about half the size of Manhattan in area, Sadr City was located northeast of Baghdad's Green Zone, on the far side of Army Canal and Imam Ali Street.

A lot of the places where regular Iraqis live, even if they are considered middle-class, look like slums to an American. Decades of Saddam's rule made what could have been a fairly rich country, due to its oil reserves, into a very poor one. Even in the better parts of the cities, a lot of the streets aren't paved and the buildings are pretty rundown.

Sadr City is truly a slum, even for Iraq. It began as a public housing area for the poor, and by the time of the war, it had become a refuge for Shiites, who were discriminated against by Saddam's Sunni-dominated government. After the war started, even more Shiites moved into the area. I've seen reports estimating that more than 2 million people lived within its roughly eight square miles.

Laid out in a grid pattern, the streets are fifty or one hundred yards long. Most areas have densely packed two- and three-story buildings. The workmanship on the buildings I saw was terrible; even on the fanciest buildings, the decorative lines didn't match up from one side to the other. Many of the streets are open sewers, with waste everywhere.

Muqtada al-Sadr launched an offensive against American forces in the spring of 2004. His force managed to kill a number of American troops and a far greater number of Iraqis before the fanatical cleric declared a cease-fire in June. In military terms, his offensive failed, but the insurgents remained strong in Sadr City.

Meanwhile, mostly Sunni insurgents took hold of al-Anbar province, a large sector of the country to the west of Baghdad. They were particularly strong in the cities there, including Ramadi and Fallujah.

That spring was the period when Americans were shocked by the images of four contractors, their bodies desecrated, hanging from a bridge in Fallujah. It was a sign of worse to come. The Marines moved into the city soon afterward, but their operations there were called off after heavy fighting. It's been estimated that at that point they controlled some 25 percent of the city.

As part of the pullout, an Iraqi force came into the city to take control. In theory, they were supposed to keep insurgents out. The reality was very different. By that fall, pretty much the only people who lived in Fallujah were insurgents. It was even more dangerous for Americans than it had been in the spring.

When I left for Iraq in September of 2004, my unit had begun training to join a new operation to secure Fallujah, once and for all. But I went to work with the Poles in Baghdad instead.

WITH THE GROM

"Kyle, you will come."

The Polish NCO doing the briefing stroked his bushy beard as he pointed at me. I didn't understand much Polish, and he didn't speak very good English, but what he was saying seemed pretty clear—they wanted me to go in the house with them during the operation.

"Fuck yeah," I said.

He smiled. Some expressions are universal.

After a week on the job, I had been promoted from navigator to a member of the assault team. I couldn't be happier.

I still had to navigate. My job was to figure out a safe route to and from the target house. While the insurgents were active in the Baghdad area, the fighting had slowed down and there wasn't yet the huge threat of IEDs and ambushes that you saw elsewhere. Still, that could change in an instant, and I was careful plotting my routes.

We got into our Hummers and set out. I had the front seat, next to the driver. I'd learned enough Polish to give directions—*Prawo kolei*: "right turn"—and guide him through the streets. The computer was on my lap; to my right was a swing arm for a machine gun. We'd taken the Hummer's doors off to make it easier to get in and out and fire. Besides the mounts on my side and in the back, we had a .50 in a turret at the back.

We reached the target and hauled ass out of the truck. I was psyched to finally get back into battle.

The Poles put me about sixth or seventh in the line to go in. That was a bit disappointing—that far back in the train you're unlikely to get any action. But I wasn't about to bitch.

The GROM hit houses essentially the way SEALs do. There are little variations here and there: the way they come around corners, for example, and the way they cover buddies during an operation. But for the most part, it's all violence of action. Surprise the target, hit them hard and fast, take control.

One difference I particularly like is their version of flash-crash grenades. American stun grenades explode with flash of light and an enormous bang. The Polish grenades, on the other hand, give a series of explosions. We called them seven-bangers. They sound like very loud gunfire. I tried to take as many of those from them as I could when it was time to move on.

We moved the instant the grenade started going off. I came in through the door, and caught sight of the NCO directing the team. He motioned me forward silently, and I ran to clear and secure my room.

The room was empty.

All clear.

I went back downstairs. Some of the others had found the guy we'd come for and were already loading him into one of the Hummers. The rest of the Iraqis who'd been in the house stood around, looking scared to death.

Back outside, I hopped into the Hummer and started directing the team back to base. The mission was uneventful, but as far as the GROM were concerned, my cherry had been burst—from that point on, I was a full-fledged member of the team.

BUFFALO-PISS VODKA

WE WENT ON DAs FOR ANOTHER TWO AND A HALF WEEKS, BUT there was only one where we had anything like real trouble. A guy wanted to fight as we were going in. Unfortunately for him, all he had were his bare fists. Here he's facing a squad of soldiers, each heavily armed and protected by body armor. He was either stupid or courageous, or maybe both.

The GROM took care of him quickly. One less asshole on the wanted list.

We picked up a pretty wide variety of suspects—financiers for al-Qaeda, bomb-makers, insurgents, foreign insurgents—one time we picked up a truckload of them.

The GROM were a lot like SEALs: extremely professional at work, and very hard-core partiers after hours. They all had Polish vodka, and they especially loved this one brand named Żubrówka.

Żubrówka has been around for hundreds of years, though I've never seen it in America. There's a blade of buffalo grass in each bottle; each blade comes from the same field in Poland. Buffalo grass is supposed to have medicinal properties, but the story related to me from my GROM friends was a lot more colorful—or maybe off-color. According to them, European bison known as wisent roam on this field and piss on the grass. The distillers put the blades in for an extra kick. (Actually, during the process, certain ingredients of the buffalo grass are safely neutralized, so just the flavor remains. But my friends didn't tell me that—maybe it was too hard to translate.)

I was a little dubious, but the vodka proved to be as smooth as it was potent. It definitely supported their argument that the Russians don't know anything about vodka and that Poles make it better.

BEING AN AMERICAN, OFFICIALLY I WASN'T SUPPOSED TO BE drinking. (And *officially,* I didn't.)

That asinine rule only applied to U.S. servicemen. We couldn't even buy a beer. Every other member of the coalition, be they Polish or whatever, could.

Fortunately, the GROM liked to share. They would also go to the duty-free shop at Baghdad airport and buy beer or whiskey or whatever the Americans working with them wanted.

I FORMED A FRIENDSHIP WITH ONE OF THEIR SNIPERS NAMED Matthew (they all took fake names, as part of their general security). We spent a lot of time talking about different rifles and scenarios. We compared notes on how they did things, the weapons they would use. Later on, I arranged to run some drills with them and gave them a bit of background on how SEALs operate. I taught them how we build our hides inside homes and showed them a few different drills to use to take home and train. We worked a lot with "snaps"—targets that pop up—and "movers"—targets that move left to right and vice versa.

What always seemed interesting to me was how well we communicated without using words, even on an op. They'd turn around and wave me up or back, whatever. If you're a professional, you don't need to be told what to do. You read off of each other and react.

GEARED UP

People are always asking me what sort of gear I carried in Iraq. The answer is: it depended. I adjusted my gear slightly from deployment to deployment. Here's how I usually went out:

Pistols

The standard SEAL-issued pistol was a SIG Sauer P226, chambered for 9-mm ammo. While that is an excellent weapon, I felt I needed more knockdown power than nine millimeters could provide, and later started carrying my own personal weapon in place of the P226. Let's face it—if you're using a pistol in combat, the shit has already hit the fan. You may not have the time for perfect shot placement. The bigger rounds may not kill your enemy, but they're more likely to put him down when you hit him.

In 2004, I brought over a Springfield TRP Operator, which used a .45-caliber round. It had a 1911 body style, with custom grips and a rail system that let me add a light and laser combo. Black, it had a bull barrel and was an excellent gun—until it took a frag for me in Fallujah.

I was actually able to get it repaired—those Springfields are tough. Still, not wanting to press my luck, I replaced it with a SIG P220. The P220 looked pretty much exactly like the P226, but was chambered for .45 caliber.

Carrying My Pistol

On my first two deployments, I had a drop-leg holster. (A drop-leg sits against the upper thigh, within easy reach of the pistol hand.)

The problem with that type of holster is that it tends to move around. During combat, or even if you're simply bouncing around, the rig slides over on your leg. So after the first two deployments, I went to a hip holster. That way, my gun was always where I expected it to be.

Med Gear

Everyone always carried their own "blowout kit," a small set of medical supplies. You always carried the bare necessities to treat a gunshot wound—bandages for different wounds, IV, clotting medicine. It had to be readily accessible—you didn't want the person helping you have to search for it. I put mine in my right-hand cargo pocket on my leg, under the holster. If I'd ever been shot, my buddies could have cut out the bottom of the cargo pocket and pulled out the kit. Most guys did it that way.

When you treat somebody in the field before the corpsman or a medic gets there, you always use the wounded man's kit. If you use your kit, who's to say you'll have it for the next guy—or yourself—if you need it?

Body Armor and Rig

During the first deployment, my SEAL body armor had the MOLLE system attached to it. (MOLLE stands for Modular Lightweight Load-carrying Equipment, a fancy acronym for a web system where different pouches and gear can be attached, allowing you to customize your webbing. The word *MOLLE* itself is a trademark for the system developed and manufactured by Natick Labs. However, a lot of people use the word to describe any similar system.)

On the deployments that followed, I had separate body armor with a separate Rhodesian rig. (Rhodesian describes a vest that allows you to set up a MOLLE or MOLLE-like rig. Again, the overall principle is that you can customize the way you carry your stuff.)

Having a separate vest allowed me to take my gear off and lay it down, while still wearing my body armor. This made it more comfortable to lie down and still be able to grab everything I needed. When I was going to be on the sniper rifle, lying behind it and peering through the scope, I would unclip the strap and lay out the vest. This made my ammo, which I had in the pouches, easier to access. Meanwhile, the vest was still attached to my shoulders; it would come with me and fall into place when I got up.

(One note about the body armor—Navy-issued body armor has been known to fall apart. In light of that fact, my wife's parents very generously bought me some Dragon Skin armor after my third deployment. It's super-heavy, but it's extremely good armor, the best you can get.)

I WORE A GPS ON MY WRIST, WITH A BACKUP IN MY VEST AND even a backup old-fashioned compass. I went through a couple of pairs of goggles per deployment; they had miniature fans inside to keep air circulating so they wouldn't fog up. And, of course, I had a pocketknife—I got a Microtech after graduating BUD/S—and Emerson and Benchmade fixed blades, depending on the deployment.

Among other equipment we'd carry would be a square of a VS-17 panel, used to alert pilots to a friendly position so they wouldn't fire on us. In theory, at least.

Initially, I tried to keep everything off my waist, even going so far as to carry my extra pistol mags in another drop-leg on my other side. (I cinched it up high so I could still access the pocket on my left leg.)

I NEVER WORE EAR PROTECTION IN IRAQ. THE EAR PROTECtion we had contained noise-canceling circuitry. While it was possible to hear gunshots fired by the enemy, the microphone that picked up those sounds was omnidirectional. That meant you couldn't tell what direction the shots were coming from.

And contrary to what my wife thinks, I wore my helmet from time to time. Admittedly, it was not often. It was a standard, U.S. military–issue helmet, uncomfortable and of minimal value against all but the weakest shots or shrapnel. To keep it from jostling on my head, I tightened it up using Pro-Tec pads, but it was still annoying to wear for long stretches. It added a lot of weight to my head while I was on the gun, making it harder to stay focused as the watch went on.

I'd seen that bullets, even from pistols, could easily go through a helmet, so I didn't have much incentive to deal with the discomfort. The general exception to this was at night. I'd wear the helmet so I had a place to attach my night vision to.

Otherwise, I usually wore a ball cap: a platoon cap with a Cadillac symbol adapted as our unit logo. (While officially we were Charlie Platoon, we usually took on alternate names with the same letter or sound at the beginning: Charlie becomes Cadillac, etc.)

Why a ball cap?

Ninety percent of *being* cool is looking cool. And you look so much cooler wearing a ball cap.

Besides my Cadillac cap, I had another favorite—a cap from a New York fire company that had lost some of its men during 9/11.

My dad had gotten it for me during a visit, after the attacks, to the "Lions Den," a historic city firehouse. There he met members of Engine 23; when the firemen heard that his son was going to war, they insisted he take the hat.

"Just tell him to get some payback," they said.

If they're reading this, I hope they know that I did.

ON MY WRIST, I'D WEAR A G-SHOCK WATCH. THE BLACK WATCH and its rubber wristband have replaced Rolex Submariners as standard SEAL equipment. (A friend of mine, who thought it was a shame the tradition died, recently got me one. I still feel a little strange wearing a Rolex, but it is a throwback to the frogmen who came before me.)

In cool weather, I brought a personal jacket to wear—a North Face—because, believe it or not, I had trouble convincing the supply mafia to issue me cold-weather gear. But that's a rant for a different day.

I WOULD STICK MY M-4 AND TEN MAGS (THREE HUNDRED rounds) in the front compartments of my web gear. I would also have my radio, some lights, and my strobe in those pockets. (The strobe can be used at night for rendezvousing with other units or aircraft, ships, boats, whatever. It also can be used to identify friendly troops.)

If I had one of my sniper rifles with me, I would have some two hundred rounds in my backpack. When I carried the Mk-11 instead of the Win Mag or .338, then I wouldn't bother carrying the M-4. In that case, the sniper rounds would be in my web gear, closer at hand. Rounding out my ammo were three mags for my pistol.

I wore Merrill high-top hiking boots. They were comfortable and held up to the deployment.

GET UP, KYLE

ABOUT A MONTH INTO MY TOUR WITH THE GROM, I WAS woken by a shake on my shoulder.

I jumped upright in bed, ready to deck whoever had snuck into my quarters.

"Hey, hey, it's cool," said the lieutenant commander who'd woken me. He was a SEAL, and my boss. "I need you to get dressed and come to my office."

"Yes, sir," I mumbled. I pulled on a pair of shorts and my flip-flops and went down the hall.

I thought I was in trouble, though I wasn't sure what for. I'd been on good behavior working with the Poles, no fights to speak of. I searched my mind as I walked toward his office, trying to prepare a defense. My mind was still fairly blank when I got there.

"Kyle, I'm going to need you to get your sniper rifle and pack up all your gear," the lieutenant commander told me. "You're going to Fallujah."

He started telling me about some of the arrangements and threw in some operational details. The Marines were planning a big push, and they needed snipers to help out.

Man, this is going to be good, I thought. *We are going to kill massive amounts of bad guys. And I'm going to be in the middle of it.*

AN ARMED CAMP

From a historical point of view, there were two battles for Fallujah. The first took place in the spring, as I've mentioned before. Political considerations, mostly driven by wildly distorted media reports and a lot of Arab propaganda, caused the Marines to back off their offensive soon after it was begun, and well before it achieved its aim of kicking the insurgents out of the city. In place of the Marines, Iraqis loyal to the interim government were supposed to take control and run the city.

That didn't work. Pretty much the moment the Marines pulled back, the insurgents completely took over Fallujah. Civilians who were not connected with the insurgency were killed, or fled the city. Anyone who wanted peace—anyone with any sense—left as soon as they could, or ended up dead.

Al-Anabar Province, the area that contained the city, was studded with insurgents of various forms. A lot were Iraqi mujahedeen, but there were also plenty of foreign nationals who were members of "al-Qaeda in Iraq" or other radical groups. The head of al-Qaeda in Iraq, Sheikh Abdullah al-Janabi—had his headquarters in the city. A Jordanian who had fought with Osama bin Laden in Afghanistan, he was committed to killing Americans. (Despite numerous reports to the contrary, as far as is known, Sheikh Abdullah al-Janabi escaped from Fallujah and is still at large.)

The insurgents were one-part terrorists, another-part criminal gangs. They would plant IEDs, kidnap officials and their families, attack American convoys, kill Iraqis who didn't share their faith or politics—anything and everything they could think of. Fallujah had become their safe haven, an anti-capital of Iraq dedicated to overthrowing the interim government and preventing free elections.

Al-Anabar Province and, more specifically, the general area around Fallujah became known through the media as the Sunni Triangle. That's a very, very rough approximation both of the area—contained between Baghdad, Ramadi, and Baqubah—and the ethnic composition.

(Some background on Islam in Iraq: There were two main groups of Muslims in Iraq, Sunnis and Shiites. Before the war, Shiites lived mostly in the south and east, say from Baghdad to the borders, and Sunnis dominated around Baghdad and to the northwest. The two groups coexisted but generally hated each other. While Shiites were the majority, during Saddam's time they were discriminated against and not allowed to hold important offices. Farther north, the areas are dominated by Kurds, who, though mostly Sunni, have separate traditions and often don't think of themselves as being part of Iraq. Saddam considered them to be an inferior people; during one political suppression, he ordered chemical weapons used and waged a despicable ethnic-cleansing campaign.)

WHILE USING FALLUJAH AS A BASE TO ATTACK THE SURROUNDING area and Baghdad, the insurgents spent considerable time fortifying the city so they could withstand another attack. They stockpiled ammo and weapons, prepared IEDs, and fortified houses. Mines were planted, and roads closed off so they could be used for ambushes. "Rat holes" were created in compound walls, allowing insurgents to move from one house to another, avoiding streets. Many if not all of the two hundred mosques in the city became fortified bunkers, since the insurgents knew that Americans respected houses of worship as sacred and therefore were reluctant to attack there. A hospital was turned into an insurgent headquarters and used as a base of operations for the insurgents' propaganda machine. In sum, the city was a terrorist fortress by the summer of 2004.

In fact, the insurgents were confident enough to regularly launch rocket attacks against U.S. bases in the area and ambush convoys moving on the main roads. Finally, the American command decided that enough was enough—Fallujah had to be retaken.

The plan they drew up was called Phantom Fury. The city would be cut off so that enemy supplies and reinforcements could no longer get in. The insurgents in Fallujah would be rooted out and destroyed.

While Marines from the First Marine Division made up the backbone of the attack force, all of the other services added key pieces. SEAL snipers were integrated with small Marine assault groups, providing overwatch and performing traditional sniper missions.

The Marines spent several weeks getting ready for the assault, launching a variety of operations to throw the insurgents off-balance. The bad guys knew something was coming; they just didn't know where and when. The eastern side of the city was heavily fortified, and the enemy probably thought that's where the attack would be launched.

Instead, the attack would come from the northwest and roll down into the heart of the city. That's where I was headed.

GETTING THERE

DISMISSED BY THE LIEUTENANT COMMANDER, I IMMEDIATELY gathered my gear, then headed outside to a pickup truck that was waiting to take me out to the helo. A 60—a Blackhawk H-60—

was waiting for me and another guy who'd been working with the GROM, a coms specialist named Adam. We looked at each other and smiled. We were thrilled to be getting into a real battle.

SEALs from all over Iraq were making a similar trip, heading toward the large Marine base south of the city at Camp Fallujah. They'd already established their own small base inside the camp by the time I arrived. I treaded my way through the narrow halls of the building, which had been dubbed the Alamo, trying not to knock into anything. The walls were lined with equipment and gear, gun boxes and metal suitcases, cartons and the odd box of soda. We could have been a traveling rock band, staging a stadium road show.

Except that our road show had very serious pyrotechnics.

Besides snipers from Team 3, men had been pulled from Team 5 and Team 8 to join the assault. I already knew most of the West Coast guys; the others I'd come to respect over the next few weeks.

The energy level was intense. Everyone was eager to get into the fight and help the Marines.

THE HOME FRONT

As the battle drew near, my thoughts wandered to my wife and son. My little baby boy was growing. Taya had started sending me photos and even videos showing his progress. She'd also sent images through e-mail for me to look at.

I can see some of those videos now in my mind—he'd be lying on his back, and shake his hands and feet, going as if he was running, a big ol' smile on his face.

He was a super-active kid. Just like his daddy.

Thanksgiving, Christmas—in Iraq, those dates didn't mean all that much to me. But missing my son's experience of them was a little different. The more I was gone, and the more I saw him grow, the more I wanted to help him grow—do the things a father does with and for a son.

I called Taya while I was waiting for the assault to begin.

It was a brief conversation.

"Look, babe, I can't tell you where I'm going, but I'm going to be gone for a while," I said. "Watch the news and you'll figure it out. I don't know when I'm going to be able to talk to you again."

That was going to have to do for a while.

IT BEGINS

ON THE EVENING OF NOVEMBER 7, I SQUEEZED INTO A Marine amtrac with a dozen Marines and a few SEALs, all keyed up for battle. The big armored vehicle rumbled to life, and slowly moved toward the head of a massive procession of armor heading out of camp and north of the city, into the open desert.

We sat knee to knee on benches facing each other in the barebones interior. A third row had been squeezed into the middle of the compartment. The AAV-7A1 wasn't exactly a stretch limo; you might try not to crowd out the guys on either side of you, but there was only so much you could do. Tight wasn't the word. Thankfully, just about everyone inside with me had showered recently.

At first, it was cold—this was November, and to a Texas boy it felt like deep winter—but within a few minutes the heater was choking us and we had to ask them to crank it down. I put my ruck down on the floor. With my Mk-11 propped between my legs and my helmet on the butt, I had a makeshift pillow. I tried to nap as we moved. Close your eyes, and time moves faster.

I didn't get all that much sleep. Every so often I glanced toward the slit windows in the rear door, but I couldn't see past the guys sitting there. That wasn't much of a loss—all they could see was the rest of the procession, a haze of dust, and a few patches of empty desert. We'd been practicing with the Marines for about a week, going over everything from getting in and out of their vehicles to figuring out exactly what sort of charges we would use to blow sniper holes through buildings. In between we'd worked on radio coms and general strategy, exchanged ideas about how to provide the best cover for the squads we'd be accompanying, and made a dozen tentative tactical decisions, such as deciding whether it would be generally better to shoot from the top floor or the one right below.

Now we were ready, but as often happens in the military, we were in hurry-up-and-wait mode. The tracked vehicles drove us up north of Fallujah, then stopped.

We sat there for what seemed like hours. Every muscle in my body cramped. Finally someone decided we could drop the ramp and stretch a bit. I unfolded myself from the bench and went out to shoot the shit with some of the other SEALs nearby.

Finally, just before daybreak, we loaded back up and began trundling toward the edge of the city. There was maximum adrenaline inside that tin can on treads. We were ready to get it on.

Our destination was an apartment complex overlooking the northwestern corner of the city. Roughly eight hundred yards from the start of the city proper, the buildings had a perfect view of the area where our Marines were going to launch their assault—an excellent location for snipers. All we had to do was take it.

"Five minutes!" yelled one of the NCOs.

I hooked one arm through my ruck and got a good grip on my gun.

The amtrac jerked to a halt. The rear ramp slammed down and I leapt out with the others, running toward a small grove with some trees and rocks for cover. I moved quickly—I wasn't afraid of getting shot as much as I was of being run over by one of the armada that had ferried us here. The mammoth amtracs didn't look like they'd stop for anybody.

I hit the dirt, got the ruck next to me, and began scanning the building, watching for anything suspicious. I worked my eyes around the windows and the surrounding area, expecting all the while to be shot at. The Marines, meanwhile, poured out their vehicles. Besides the tracked personnel carriers there were Hummers and tanks and dozens of support vehicles. The Marines just kept coming, swarming over the complex.

They started kicking in doors. I couldn't hear much, just the loud echoes of the shotguns they used to blow out the locks. The Marines detained a few women who had been outside, but otherwise the yard around the building was vacant.

My eyes never stopped moving. I scanned constantly, trying to find something.

Our radio guy came over and set up nearby. He was monitoring the Marine progress as they worked up through the apartment building, securing it. The few inhabitants they found inside had to be taken out and moved to safety. There was no resistance inside—if there were insurgents, they'd either gotten out when they saw us coming, or they pretended now that they were loyal Iraqis and friends of the U.S.

THE MARINES ENDED UP MOVING ABOUT 250 CIVILIANS FROM the complex, a fraction of what they had been told to expect. Each one was questioned first. Assuming they hadn't fired a weapon recently (the Marines did gunpowder checks), weren't on a wanted list, or were not otherwise suspicious, the head of each family was given $300 and told they had to leave. According to one of the Marine officers, they were allowed to go back to their apartments, take what they needed, and leave.

(A few known insurgents were captured and detained in the operation.)

WHILE WE WERE ON THE BERM WATCHING THE CITY, WE WERE also watching warily for an Iraqi sniper known as Mustafa. From the reports we heard, Mustafa was an Olympics marksman who was using his skills against Americans and Iraqi police and soldiers. Several videos had been made and posted, boasting of his ability.

I never saw him, but other snipers later killed an Iraqi sniper we think was him.

TO THE APARTMENTS

"ALL RIGHT," SAID OUR RADIO GUY FINALLY. "THEY WANT US inside."

I ran from the trees to the apartment complex, where a SEAL lieutenant was organizing the overwatches. He had a map of the city and showed us where the assault was going to take place the next day.

"We need to cover this area here, here, and here," he said. "Y'all go find a room to do it."

He gave us a building and off we went. I'd been paired with a sniper I'd met during BUD/S, Ray. (I've used the name to protect his identity.)

Ray is a big-time gun nut. Loves guns, and knows 'em real well. I'm not sure how good a shot he is, but he's probably forgotten more than I know about rifles.

We hadn't seen each other for years, but from what I remembered from BUD/S I figured we'd get along all right. You want to feel confident the guy you're working with is someone you can rely on—after all, you are literally trusting him with your life.

A Ranger we called Ranger Molloy had been shepherding our rifles and some gear with us in a Hummer. He came up and gave me my .300 Win Mag. The rifle's extra distance over the Mk-11 would be handy once I found a good hide to shoot from.

Running up the stairs, I sorted the situation out in my head. I knew what side of the building I wanted to be on, and roughly where I wanted to be. When I reached the top—I'd decided I wanted to shoot from a room rather than the roof—I started walking through the hall, scanning for an apartment that had the right view. Going inside, I looked for one with furniture I could use to set up.

To me, the home I was in was just another part of the battlefield. The apartments and everything in them were just things to be used to accomplish our goal—clearing the city.

Snipers need to either lie down or sit for a long period of time, so I needed to find furniture that would let me do that as comfortably as possible. You also need something to rest your rifle on. In this case, I was going to be shooting out of the windows, so I needed to be elevated. As I searched through the apartment, I found a room that had a baby crib in it. It was a rare find, and one I could put to good use.

Ray and I took it and flipped it over. That gave us a base. Then we pulled the door of the room off its hinges and put it on top. We now had a stable platform to work on.

Most Iraqis don't sleep on beds; they use bedrolls, thick mats, or blankets that are put directly on the floor. We found a few of them and laid them out on the door. That made a semi-comfortable, elevated bed to lie on while working the gun. A rolled mat gave us a place to rest the end of our guns on.

We opened the window and were ready to shoot.

We decided we'd work three hours on, three hours off, rotating back and forth. Ray took the first watch.

I started rummaging through the complex to see if I could find any cool shit—money, guns, explosives. The only thing I found worth acquisitioning was a handheld Tiger Woods golf game.

Not that I was authorized to take it, or even did take it, officially. If I *had* taken it, I would have played it the rest of the deployment. If I'd done that, it might explain why I am actually pretty good at the game now.

If I had taken it.

I GOT ON THE .300 WIN MAG IN LATE AFTERNOON. THE CITY I was looking out at was brownish-yellow and gray, almost as if everything was shaded the light sepia of an old photograph. Many, though not all, of the buildings were made of bricks or covered with stucco in this same color. The stones and roadways were gray. A fine mist of desert dust seemed to hover over the houses. There were trees and other vegetation, but the overall landscape looked like a collection of dully painted boxes in the desert.

Most of the buildings were squat houses, two stories high, occasionally three or four. Minarets or prayer towers poked out of the grayness at irregular intervals. There were mosque domes scattered around—here a green egg flanked by a dozen smaller eggs, there a white turnip glinting white in the sinking sun.

The buildings were packed in tight, the streets almost geometrical in their grid pattern. There were walls everywhere. The city had already been at war for some time, and there was plenty of rubble not only around the edges but in the main thoroughfares. Dead ahead of me but out of view was the infamous bridge where the insurgents had desecrated the bodies of the Blackwater contractors half a year earlier. The bridge spanned the Euphrates, which flowed in an inverted V just south of my position.

My immediate concern was a set of railroad tracks about eight hundred yards from the building. There was a berm and a train trestle over the highway south of me. To the east, on my left as I looked out the window, the train line ran to a switching yard and station outside the main part of the city.

The Marine assault would sweep across the tracks, driving down and into an area from the Euphrates to a highway at the eastern end of the city, marked by a cloverleaf. This was an area roughly three and one-third miles wide; the plan was to move about a mile and a half deep to Iraqi Route 10 by November 10, a little less than three days. That might not seem like a lot—most Marines can probably walk that far in a half hour—but the path lay through a rat's nest of booby-trapped streets and past heavily armed houses. Not only did the Marines expect to be fighting literally house to house and block to block, but they also realized that things would probably get worse as they went. You push the rats from one hole and they congregate in the next. Sooner or later, they run out of places to run.

Looking out the window, I was anxious for the battle to start. I wanted a target. I wanted to shoot someone.

I didn't have to wait all that long.

From the building, I had a prime view across to the railroad tracks and the berm, and then beyond that into the city.

I started getting kills soon after I got on the gun. Most were back in the area near the city. Insurgents would move into that area, trying to get into position to attack or maybe spy on the Marines. They were about eight hundred meters away, across the railroad tracks and below the berm, so probably, in their mind, they couldn't be seen and were safe.

They were badly mistaken.

I've already described what it felt like to take my first sniper shot; there may have been some hesitation in the back of my mind, an almost unconscious question: *Can I kill this person?*

But the rules of engagement were clear, and there was no doubt the man in my scope was an enemy. It wasn't just the fact he was armed and maneuvering toward the Marines' positions, though those were the important points for the ROEs. Civilians had been warned not to stay in the city, and while obviously not everyone had been able to escape, only small handfuls of innocents remained. The males of fighting age and sound minds within the city limits were almost all bad guys. They thought they were going to kick us out, just as they supposedly had kicked out the Marines in April.

After the first kill, the others come easy. I don't have to psych myself up, or do anything special mentally—I look through the scope, get my target in the crosshairs, and kill my enemy before he kills one of my people.

I got three that day; Ray got two.

I would keep both eyes open while I was on the scope. With right eye looking through the scope, my left eye could still see the rest of the city. It gave me better situational awareness.

WITH KILO

As the Marines moved into the city, they soon reached a position where we could no longer cover them from the apartment towers. We came down, ready for the next phase—working in the city itself.

I was assigned to Kilo Company, helping the Marine units on the western side of the city. They were the first wave of the assault, sweeping down block by block. Another company would come in behind them, securing the area and making sure that none of the insurgents snuck back in behind them. The idea was to clear Fallujah out, block by block.

The properties in this part of the city, as in many Iraqi cities, were walled off from their neighbors by thick brick and stucco walls. There were always nooks and crannies for insurgents to hide in. The backyards, usually flat with hard dirt or even cement, were rectangular mazes. It was a dry, dusty place, even with the river nearby. Most of the houses didn't have running water; the water supply would be on the roof.

I worked with Marine snipers for several days during the first week or so of that phase of the assault. For much of the time I was paired with two Marine snipers and a JTAC, a SEAL who could call in air strikes. There would also be a few support guys, Marines who would provide security and occasionally help out with different tasks. These were Marines who wanted to be snipers; after their deployment, they were hoping to ship out to the Marine sniper school.

Every morning would start with about twenty minutes of what we called "fires"—mortars, artillery, bombs, missiles, rockets—it amounted to a hell of a lot of ordnance being dumped on key enemy positions. The fire would take out ammo caches or dumps, or soften up spots where we thought we'd have a lot of resistance. Black funnels of smoke would rise in the distance, caches hit by the bombings; the ground and air would rumble with secondary explosions.

At first, we were behind the Marine advance. But it didn't take long before I realized we could do a better job by getting ahead of the squad on the ground. It gave us a better position, allowing us to surprise any insurgents who tried rallying to the ground unit.

It also gave us a hell of a lot more action. So we started taking houses to use as hides.

Once the bottom of the house was cleared, I'd run up the stairs from the top floor to the roof, emerging in the small shack that typically sheltered the entrance to the roof. Sure the roof was clear, I'd move over to the wall at the edge, get my bearings, and set up a position. Usually there would be something on the roof I could use—a chair or rugs—to make things more comfortable; if not, there was always something downstairs. I'd switched back to the Mk-11, realizing that most of my shots would be relatively close, because of the way the city was laid out. The weapon was more convenient than the Win Mag, and at these ranges just as deadly.

Meanwhile, the Marines on the ground would work down the street, usually side to side, clearing the houses. Once they reached a point where we could no longer cover them well, we'd move up and take a new spot, and the process would start over again.

GENERALLY, WE SHOT FROM ROOFS. THEY GAVE THE BEST VIEW and were often already equipped with chairs and the like. Most in the city were ringed by low-rise walls that provided protection when the enemy shot back. Plus, using the roofs allowed us to move quickly; the assault wouldn't wait for us to take our time getting in position.

If the roof was no good, we would shoot from the upper story, usually out of a window. Once in a while, we would have to blow a sniper hole in the side of a wall to set up a firing position. That was rare, though; we didn't want to draw more attention to our position by setting off an explosion, even if it was relatively small. (The holes were patched after we left.)

One day we set up inside a small office building that had been vacated some time before. We pulled the desks back from the windows and sat deep in the room; the natural shadows that played on the wall outside helped hide the position.

THE BAD GUYS

THE ENEMIES WE WERE FIGHTING WERE SAVAGE AND WELL-armed. In just one house, the Marines found roughly two dozen guns, including machine guns and sniper rifles, along with homemade rocket stands and a mortar base.

That was just one house on a long block. It was a nice house, in fact—it had air conditioning, elaborate chandeliers, and fancy Western furniture. It made a good place to rest while we took a break one afternoon.

The houses were all searched carefully, but the weapons were usually pretty easy to find. The Marines would go inside and see a grenade launcher propped against a china cabinet—with rockets stacked next to the teacups below. At one house, Marines found dive tanks—apparently the insurgent who had been staying at the house used them to sneak across the river and make an attack.

Russian equipment was also common. Most of it was very old—in one house there were rifle grenades that could have been made during World War II. We found binoculars with old Communist hammer-and-sickle emblems. And IEDs, including some cemented into walls, were everywhere.

A LOT OF PEOPLE WHO HAVE WRITTEN ABOUT THE BATTLES IN Fallujah mention how fanatical the insurgents were. They *were* fanatical, but it wasn't just religion that was driving them. A good many were pretty doped up.

Later on in the campaign, we took a hospital they'd been using at the outskirts of the city. There we found cooked spoons, drug works, and other evidence of how they prepared themselves. I'm not an expert, but it looked to me that they would cook up heroin and inject it before a battle. Other things I've heard said they would use prescription drugs and basically anything they could get to help get their courage up.

You could see that sometimes when you shot them. Some could take several bullets without seeming to feel it. They were driven by more than just religion and adrenaline, even more than blood lust. They were already halfway to Paradise, in their minds at least.

UNDER THE RUBBLE

ONE DAY I CAME DOWN FROM A ROOF TO TAKE A BREAK AND headed out into the backyard of the house with another SEAL sniper. I pulled open the bipod on my rifle and set it down.

All of a sudden there was an explosion right across from us, maybe ten feet away. I ducked, then turned and saw the cement block wall crumbling. Just beyond it were two insurgents, AKs slung over their shoulders. They looked as stunned as we must have; they, too, had been taking a break when a stray rocket hit or maybe some sort of IED went off.

It felt like an old western duel—whoever got to their pistol the quickest was going to live.

I grabbed mine and started shooting. My buddy did the same.

We hit them, but the slugs didn't drop them. They turned the corner and ran through the house where they'd been, then cut out into the street.

As soon as they cleared the house, the Marines pulling security on the road shot them down.

AT ONE POINT EARLY IN THE BATTLE AN RPG HIT THE BUILDING I was working from.

It was an afternoon when I'd set up back from a window on the top floor. The Marines on the ground had started to take fire on the street ahead. I began covering them, taking down targets one by one. The Iraqis started firing back at me, fortunately not too accurately, which was usually the way they shot.

Then an RPG hit the side of the house. The wall took the brunt of the explosion, which was good news and bad news. On the plus side, it saved me from getting blasted. But the explosion also took down a good chunk of the wall. It crashed onto my legs, slamming my knees into the concrete and temporarily pinning me there.

It hurt like hell. I kicked some of the rubble off and kept firing at the bastards down the block.

"Everybody okay?" yelled one of the other boys I was with.

"I'm good, I'm good," I yelled back. But my legs were screaming the opposite. They hurt like a son of a bitch.

The insurgents pulled back, then things stoked up again. That was the way it would go—a lull, followed by an intense exchange, then another lull.

When the firefight finally stopped, I got up and climbed out of the room. Downstairs, one of the boys pointed at my legs.

"You're limping," he said.

"Fuckin' wall came down on me."

He glanced upward. There was a good-sized hole in the house where the wall had been. Until that point, no one had realized that I'd been in the room where the RPG had hit.

I LIMPED FOR A WHILE AFTER THAT. A LONG WHILE—I eventually had to have surgery on both knees, though I kept putting it off for a couple of years.

I didn't go to a doctor. You go to a doctor and you get pulled out. I knew I could get by.

FRY ME NOT

YOU CANNOT BE AFRAID TO TAKE YOUR SHOT. WHEN YOU SEE someone with an IED or a rifle maneuvering toward your men, you have clear reason to fire. (The fact that an Iraqi had a gun would not necessarily mean he could be shot.) The ROEs were specific, and in most cases the danger was obvious.

But there were times when it wasn't *exactly* clear, when a person almost surely was an insurgent, probably was doing evil, but there was still some doubt because of the circumstances or the surroundings—the way he moved, for example, wasn't toward an area where troops were. A lot of times a guy seemed to be acting macho for friends, completely unaware that I was watching him, or that there were American troops nearby.

Those shots I didn't take.

You couldn't—you had to worry about your own ass. Make an unjustified shot and you could be charged with murder.

I often would sit there and think, "I know this motherfucker is bad; I saw him doing such and such down the street the other day, but here he's not doing anything, and if I shoot him, I won't be able to justify it for the lawyers. I'll fry." Like I said, there is paperwork for everything. Every confirmed kill had documentation, supporting evidence, and a witness.

So I wouldn't shoot.

There weren't a lot of those, especially in Fallujah, but I was always extremely aware of the fact that every killing might have to be justified to the lawyers.

My attitude was: if my justification is I *thought* my target would do something bad, then I wasn't justified. He had to be *doing* something bad.

Even with that standard, there were plenty of targets. I was averaging two and three a day, occasionally less, sometimes much more, with no end in sight.

A SQUAT WATER TOWER ROSE ABOVE THE ROOFTOPS A FEW blocks from one of the roofs where we were perched. It looked like a wide yellow tomato.

We'd already moved a few blocks past the tower when a Marine decided to climb up and retrieve the Iraqi flag flying from the grid work. As he climbed, the insurgents who had lain low during the earlier attack began firing on him. Within seconds, he was shot up and trapped.

We backtracked over, moving along the streets and across the rooftops until we found the men shooting at him. When we had the area cleared, we sent up one of our guys to retrieve the flag. After we got it down, we sent it to the Marine in the hospital.

RUNAWAY SHOWS HIS COLORS

NOT LONG AFTERWARD, A GUY I'LL CALL RUNAWAY AND I WERE on the street when we had contact with Iraqi insurgents. We ducked into a shallow setback in the wall next to the street, waiting for the hail of bullets to die down.

"We'll work our way back," I told Runaway. "You go first. I'll cover you."

"Good."

I leaned out and laid down cover fire, forcing the Iraqis back. I waited a few seconds, giving Runaway time to get into position so he could cover me. When I thought enough time had passed, I jumped out and started running.

Bullets began flying all around, but not from Runaway. They were all coming from the Iraqis, who were trying to write their names in my back with bullets.

I threw myself against the wall, sliding next to the gate. For a moment I was disoriented: where was Runaway?

He should have been nearby, waiting under cover for me so we could leapfrog back. But he was nowhere to be seen. Had I passed him on the street?

No. Motherfucker was busy earning his nickname.

I was trapped, hung up by the insurgents and without my mysteriously disappearing friend.

The Iraqi gunfire got so intense that I ended up having to call for backup. The Marines sent a pair of Hummers, and with their firepower backing up everything I could lay down, I was finally able to get out.

By then I'd figured out what had happened. When I met with Runaway a short time later, I practically strangled him—I probably would have, if it hadn't been for the officer there.

"Why the hell did you run away?" I demanded. "You ran all the way down the block without covering me."

"I thought you were following me."

"Bullshit."

It was the second time that week Runaway had taken off on me under fire. The first time I'd cut him slack, giving him the benefit of the doubt. But it was now clear he was a coward. Once he was under fire, he just pussied out.

Command separated us. It was a wise thing to do.

"WE'RE JUST GONNA SHOOT"

A LITTLE AFTER RUNAWAY'S EXCITING ADVENTURE, I CAME down from my position on one of the roofs when I heard a shit-ton of rounds go off nearby. I ran outside but couldn't see the firefight. Then I heard a radio call that there were men down.

A fellow I'll call Eagle and I ran up the block until we came across a group of Marines who'd retreated after taking fire about a block away. They told us that a group of insurgents had pinned down some other Marines not too far away, and we decided we'd try and help them.

We tried getting an angle from a nearby house, but it wasn't tall enough. Eagle and I moved closer, trying another house. Here we found four Marines on the roof, two of whom had been wounded. Their stories were confusing, and we couldn't get shots from there, either. We decided to take them out so the wounded could be helped; the kid I carried down had been gut-shot.

Down on the street, we got better directions from the two Marines who hadn't been shot, finally realizing that we had been targeting the wrong house. We started down an alley in the direction of the insurgents, but after a short distance we came to obstructions we couldn't get around, and we reversed course. Just as I came around the corner back out onto the main street, there was an explosion behind me—an insurgent had seen us coming and tossed a grenade.

One of the Marines following me went down. Eagle was a corpsman as well as a sniper, and after we pulled the injured kid away from the alley he went to work on him. Meanwhile, I took the rest of the Marines and continued down the road in the direction of the insurgents' stronghold.

We found a second group of Marines huddled at a nearby corner, pinned down by fire from the house. They'd set out to rescue the first group but stalled. I got everyone together and I told them that a small group of us would rush up the street while the others laid down fire. The trapped Marines were about fifty yards away, about one full block.

"It doesn't matter if you can see them or not," I told them. "We're all just gonna shoot."

I got up to start. A terrorist jumped out into the middle of the road and began unleashing hell on us, spitting bullets from a belt-fed weapon. Returning fire as best we could, we ducked back for cover. Everybody checked themselves for holes; miraculously, no one had been shot.

By now, somewhere between fifteen and twenty Marines were there with me.

"All right," I told them. "We're going to try this again. Let's do it this time."

I jumped out from around the corner, firing my weapon as I ran. The Iraqi machine gunner had been hit and killed by our earlier barrage, but there were still plenty of bad guys farther up the street.

I'd taken only a few steps when I realized that none of the Marines had followed me.

Shit. I kept running.

The insurgents began focusing their fire on me. I tucked my Mk-11 under my arm and fired back as I ran. The semiautomatic is a great, versatile weapon, but in this particular situation its twenty-round magazine seemed awful small. I blew through one mag, popped the release, slammed in a second, and kept firing.

I found four men huddled near a wall not far from the house. It turned out that two of them were reporters who'd been embedded with the Marines; they were getting a hell of a better view of the battle than they had bargained for.

"I'll cover you," I shouted. "Get the hell out of here."

I jumped up and laid down fire as they ran. The final Marine tapped me on the shoulder as he passed, signaling that he was the last man out. Ready to follow, I glanced to my right, checking my flank.

Out of the corner of my eye, I saw a body sprawled on the ground. He had Marine camis.

Where he came from, whether he'd been there when I arrived or crawled there from somewhere else, I have no idea. I ran over to him, saw that he'd been shot in both legs. I slapped a new mag into my gun, then grabbed the back of his body armor and pulled him with me as I retreated.

At some point as I ran, one of the insurgents threw a frag. The grenade exploded somewhere nearby. Pieces of wall peppered my side, from my butt cheek down to my knee. By some lucky chance, my pistol took the biggest fragment. It was pure luck—it might have put a nice hole in my leg.

My butt was sore for a while, but it still seems to work well enough.

WE MADE IT BACK TO THE REST OF THE MARINES WITHOUT either of us getting hit again.

I never found out who that wounded guy was. I've been told

he was a second lieutenant, but I never had a chance to track him down.

The other Marines said I saved his life. But it wasn't just me. Getting all those guys to safety was a joint effort; we all worked together.

The Corps was grateful that I had helped rescue their people, and one of the officers put me in for a Silver Star.

According to the story I heard, the generals sitting at their desks decided that, since no Marines had gotten Silver Stars during the assault, they weren't going to award one to a SEAL. I got a Bronze Star with a V (for valor in combat) instead.

Makes me smirk just to think about it.

Medals are all right, but they have a lot to do with politics, and I am not a fan of politics.

All told, I would end my career as a SEAL with two Silver Stars and five Bronze Medals, all for valor. I'm proud of my service, but I sure as hell didn't do it for any medal. They don't make me any better or less than any other guy who served. Medals never tell the whole story. And like I said, in the end they've become more political than accurate. I've seen men who deserved a lot more and men who deserved a lot less rewarded by higher-ups negotiating for whatever public cause they were working on at the time. For all these reasons, they are not on display at my house or in my office.

My wife is always encouraging me to organize or frame the paperwork on them and display the medals. Political or not, she still thinks they are part of the story of my service.

Maybe I'll get around to it someday.

More likely, I won't.

My uniform was covered with so much blood from the assault that the Marines got one of their own for me. From that point on, I looked like a Marine in digi cami.

It was a little weird to be wearing someone else's uniform. But it was also an honor to be considered a member of the team to the point where they'd outfit me. Even better, they gave me a fleece jacket and a fleece beanie—it was cold out there.

Taya:

After one deployment, we were driving in the car and Chris said, just out of the blue, "Did you know there is a certain kind of smell when someone dies in a particular way?"

And I said, "No. I didn't know that."

And gradually I got the story.

It was suitably gruesome.

Stories would just come out. A lot of times, he said things to see what I could handle. I told him I really, truly did not care what he did in wartime. He had my unconditional support. Still, he needed to go slow, to test the waters. I think he needed to know I wouldn't look at him differently, and perhaps more than that, he knew he would deploy again and he didn't want to scare me.

As far as I can see it, anyone who has a problem with what guys do over there is incapable of empathy. People want America to have a certain image when we fight. Yet I would guess if someone were shooting at them and they had to hold their family members while they bled out against an enemy who hid behind their children, played dead only to throw a grenade as they got closer, and who had no qualms about sending their toddler to die from a grenade from which they personally pulled the pin—they would be less concerned with playing nicely.

Chris followed the ROEs because he had to. Some of the more broad-spectrum ROEs are fine. The problem with the ROEs covering minutiae is that terrorists really don't give a shit about the Geneva Convention. So picking apart a soldier's every move against a dark, twisted, rule-free enemy is more than ridiculous; it's despicable.

I care about my husband and other Americans coming home alive. So other than being concerned for his safety, I truly wasn't afraid to hear anything he wanted to share. Even before I heard the stories, I don't think I was ever under illusions that war is pretty or nice.

When he told me the story about killing someone up close, all I thought was, Thank God he's okay.

Then I thought, You're kind of a bad-ass. Wow.

Mostly, we didn't talk about killing, or the war. But then it would intrude.

Not always in a bad way: one day, Chris was getting his oil changed at a local shop. Some men were in the lobby with him. The guy behind the counter called Chris's name. Chris paid his bill and sat back down.

One of the guys waiting for his own vehicle looked at him and said, "Are you Chris Kyle?"

And Chris said, "Yeah."

"Were you in Fallujah?"

"Yeah."

"Holy shit, you're the guy who saved our ass."

The guy's father was there and he came over to thank

Chris and shake his hand. They were all saying, "You were great. You got more kills than anyone."

Chris got embarrassed and very humbly said, "Y'all saved my ass, too."

And that was it.

7

DOWN IN THE SHIT

ON THE STREET

The kid looked at me with a mixture of excitement and disbelief. He was a young Marine, eager but tempered by the fight we'd been waging the past week.

"Do you want to be a sniper?" I asked him. "Right now?"

"Hell yeah!" he said finally.

"Good," I told him, handing over my Mk-11. "Give me your M-16. You take my sniper rifle. I'm going in the front door."

And with that, I headed over to the squad we'd been working with and told them I was helping them hit the houses.

Over the past few days, the insurgents had stopped coming out to fight us. Our kill rate from the overwatches had declined. The bad guys were all staying inside, because they knew if they came outside, we were going to shoot them.

They didn't give up. Instead, they would take their stands inside the houses, ambushing and battling the Marines in the small rooms and tiny hallways. I was seeing a lot of our guys being carried out and medevac'd.

I'd been turning the idea of going down on the street over in my head for a while, before finally deciding to go ahead with it. I picked out one of the privates who'd been helping the sniper team. He seemed like a good kid, with a lot of potential.

Part of the reason I went down on the streets was because I was bored. The bigger part was that I felt I could do a better job protecting the Marines if I was with them. They were going in the front door of these buildings and getting whacked. I'd watch as they went in, hear gunshots, and then the next thing I knew, they'd be hauling someone out in a stretcher because he just got shot up. It pissed me off.

I love the Marines, but the truth is these guys had never been taught to do room clearances like I had. It's not a Marine specialty. They were all tough fighters, but they had a lot to learn about urban warfare. Much was simple stuff: how to hold your rifle as you come into a room so it's hard for someone else to grab; where to move as you enter the room; how to fight 360 degrees in a city—things that SEALs learn so well we can do them in our sleep.

The squad didn't have an officer; the highest-ranking NCO was a staff sergeant, an E6 in the Marine Corps. I was an E5, junior to him, but he didn't have a problem letting me take control of the takedowns. We'd already been working together for a while, and I think I'd won a certain amount of respect. Plus, he didn't want his guys getting shot up, either.

"Look, I'm a SEAL, you're Marines," I told the boys. "I'm no better than you are. The only difference between you and me is I've spent more time specializing and training in this than you did. Let me help you."

We trained a little bit during the break. I gave some of my explosives to one of the squad members with experience in explosives. We did a little run-through on how to blow locks off. Until that point, they'd had such a small amount of explosives that they'd mostly been knocking the doors in, which, of course, took time and made them more vulnerable.

Break time over, we started going in.

INSIDE

I TOOK THE LEAD.

Waiting outside the first house, I thought about the guys I saw being pulled out.

I did not want to be one of them.

I could be, though.

It was hard to get that idea out of my mind. I also knew that I would be in a shitload of trouble if I did get hurt—going down on the streets was not what I was supposed to be doing, at least from an official point of view. It was definitely right—what I felt I *had* to do—but it would severely piss the top brass off.

But that would be the least of my problems if I got shot, wouldn't it?

"Let's do it," I said.

We blew the door open. I led the way, training and instincts taking over. I cleared the front room, stepped to the side, and started directing traffic. The pace was quick, automatic. Once things got started and I began to move into the house, something took over inside me. I didn't worry about casualties anymore. I didn't think about anything except the door, the house, the room—all of which was plenty enough.

GOING INTO A HOUSE, YOU NEVER KNEW WHAT YOU WERE going to find. Even if you cleared the rooms on the first floor without any trouble, you couldn't take the rest of the house for granted. Going up to the second floor, you might start to get a feeling that the rooms were empty or that you weren't going to have any problems up there, but that was a dangerous feeling. You never really know what's anywhere. Each room had to be cleared, and even then, you had to be on your guard. Plenty of times after we secured a house we took rounds and grenades from outside.

While many of the houses were small and cramped, we also made our way through a well-to-do area of the city as the battle progressed. Here the streets were paved, and the buildings looked like miniature palaces from the outside. But once you got past the façade and looked in the rooms, most were broken messes. Any Iraqi who had that much money had fled or been killed.

DURING OUR BREAKS, I WOULD TAKE THE MARINES OUT AND go through some drills with them. While other units were taking their lunch, I was teaching them everything I'd learned about room clearance.

"Look, I don't want to lose a guy!" I yelled at them. I wasn't about to get an argument there. I ran them around, busting their asses while they were supposed to be resting. But that's the thing with Marines—you beat them down and they come back for more.

WE BROKE INTO ONE HOUSE WITH A LARGE FRONT ROOM. WE'D caught the inhabitants completely by surprise.

But I was surprised as well—as I burst in, I saw a whole bunch of guys standing there in desert camouflage—the old brown chocolate-chip stuff from Desert Storm, the First Gulf War. They were all wearing gear. They were all Caucasian, including one or two with blond hair, obviously not Iraqis or Arabs.

What the fuck?

We looked at each other. Something flicked in my brain, and I flicked the trigger on the M-16, mowing them down.

A half-second's more hesitation, and I would have been the one bleeding out on the floor. They turned out to be Chechens, Muslims apparently recruited for a holy war against the West. (We found their passports after searching the house.)

OLD MAN

I HAVE NO IDEA HOW MANY BLOCKS, LET ALONE HOW MANY houses, we took down. The Marines were following a carefully laid out plan—we had to be at a certain spot each lunchtime, then reach another objective by nightfall. The entire invasion force moved across the city in choreographed order, making sure there were no holes or weak spots the insurgents could use to get behind us and attack.

Every once in a while, we'd come across a building still occupied by families, but for the most part, the only people we were seeing were insurgents.

We would do a full search of each house. In this one house,

we heard faint moans as we went down into the basement. There were two men hanging from chains on the wall. One was dead; the other barely there. Both had been severely tortured with electric shock and God knows what else. They were both Iraqi, apparently mentally retarded—the insurgents had wanted to make sure they wouldn't talk to us, but decided to have a little fun with them first.

The second man died while our corpsman worked on him.

There was a black banner on the floor, the kind the fanatics liked to show on their videos when beheading Westerners. There were amputated limbs, and more blood than you can imagine.

It was a nasty-smelling place.

AFTER A COUPLE OF DAYS, ONE OF THE MARINE SNIPERS DEcided to come down with me, and both of us started leading the DAs.

We would take a house on the right side of the street, then cross to the left and take the house across the way. Back and forth, back and forth. All of this took a lot of time. We'd have to go around the gates, get to the doors, blow up the doors, rush in. The scum inside had plenty of time to get prepared. Not to mention the fact that even with what I'd contributed, we were running out of explosives.

A Marine armored vehicle was working with us, moving down the center of the street as we went. It only had a .50-cal for a weapon, but its real asset was its size. No Iraqi wall could stand up to it once it got a head of steam.

I went over to the commander.

"Look, here's what I want you to do," I told him. "We're running out of explosives. Run through the wall in front of the house and put about five rounds of .50-cal through the front door. Then back up and we'll take it from there."

So we started doing it that way, saving explosives and moving much faster.

Pounding up and down the stairs, running to the roof, coming back down, hitting the next house—we got to where we were taking from fifty to one hundred houses a day.

The Marines were hardly winded, but I lost over twenty pounds in those six or so weeks I was in Fallujah. Most of it I sweated off on the ground. It was exhausting work.

The Marines were all a lot younger than me—practically teenagers, some of them. I guess I still had a bit of a baby face, because when we'd get to talking, and for some reason or another I'd tell them how old I was, they'd stare at me and say, "You're *that* old?"

I was thirty. An old man in Fallujah.

JUST ANOTHER DAY

As the Marine drive neared the southern edge of the city, the ground action in our section started to peter out. I went back up on the roofs and started doing overwatches again, thinking I would catch more targets from there. The tide of the battle had turned. The U.S. had mostly wrested control of the city from the bad guys, and it was now just a matter of time before resistance collapsed. But being in the middle of the action, I couldn't tell for sure.

Knowing that we considered cemeteries sacred, the insurgents typically used them to hide caches of weapons and explosives. At one point, we were in a hide overlooking the walled-in boundaries of a large cemetery that sat in the middle of the city. Roughly three football fields long by two football fields wide, it was a cement city of the dead, filled with tombstones and mausoleums. We set up on a roof near a prayer tower and mosque overlooking the cemetery.

The roof we were on was fairly elaborate. It was ringed with a brick wall punctuated with iron grates, giving us excellent firing positions; I sat down on my haunches and spotted in my rifle through a gap in the grid work, studying the paths between the stones a few hundred yards out. There was so much dust and grit in the air, I kept my goggles on. I'd also learned in Fallujah to keep my helmet cinched tight, wary of the chips and cement frags that flew from the battered masonry during a firefight.

I picked out some figures moving through the cemetery yard. I zeroed in on one and fired.

Within seconds, we were fully engaged in a firefight. Insurgents kept popping up from behind the stones—I don't know if there was a tunnel or where they came from. Brass flew from the 60 nearby.

I studied my shots as the Marines around me poured out fire. Everything they did faded into the background as I carefully put my scope on a target, steadied the aim on center mass, then squeezed ever so smoothly. When the bullet leapt from the barrel, it was almost a surprise.

My target fell. I looked for another. And another. And on it went.

Until, finally, there were no more. I got up and moved a few feet to a spot where the wall completely shielded me from the cemetery. There I took my helmet off and leaned back against the wall. The roof was littered with spent shells—hundreds if not thousands.

Someone shared a large plastic bottle of water. One of the Marines pulled his ruck over and used it as a pillow, catching some sleep. Another went downstairs, to the store on the first story of the building. It was a smoke shop; he returned with cartons of flavored cigarettes. He lit a few, and a cherry scent mingled with the heavy stench that always hung over Iraq, a smell of sewage and sweat and death.

Just another day in Fallujah.

The streets were covered with splinters and various debris. The city, never exactly a showcase, was a wreck. Squashed water bottles sat in the middle of the road next to piles of wood and twisted metal. We worked on one block of three-story buildings where the bottom level was filled with shops. Each of their awnings were covered with a thick layer of dust and grit, turning the bright colors of the fabric into a hazy blur. Metal shields blocked most of the storefronts; they were pockmarked with shrapnel chips. A few had handbills showing insurgents wanted by the legitimate government.

I have a few photos from that time. Even in the most ordinary and least dramatic scenes, the effects of war are obvious. Every so often, there's a sign of normal life before the war, something that has nothing to do with it: a kid's toy, for example.

War and peace don't seem to go together right.

THE BEST SNIPER SHOT EVER

The Air Force, Marines, and Navy were flying air support missions above us. We had enough confidence in them that we could call in strikes just down the block.

One of our com guys working a street over from us was with a unit that came under heavy fire from a building packed with insurgents. He got on the radio and called over to the Marines, asking permission to call in a strike. As soon as it was approved, he got on the line with a pilot and gave him the location and details.

"Danger close!" he warned over the radio. "Take cover."

We ducked inside the building. I have no idea how big the bomb he dropped was, but the explosion rattled the walls. My buddy later reported it had taken out over thirty insurgents—as much an indication of how many people were trying to kill us as how important the air support was.

I have to say that all of the pilots we had overhead were pretty accurate. In a lot of situations, we were asking for bombs and missiles to hit within a few hundred yards. That's pretty damn close when you're talking about a thousand or more pounds of destruction. But we didn't have any incidents, and I was also pretty confident that they could handle the job.

ONE DAY, A GROUP OF MARINES NEAR US STARTED GETTING fire from a minaret in a mosque a few blocks away. We could see where the gunman was shooting from but we couldn't get a shot on him. He had a perfect position, able to control a good part of the city below him.

While, ordinarily, anything connected to a mosque would have been out of bounds, the sniper's presence made it a legitimate target. We called an air strike on the tower, which had a high, windowed dome at the top, with two sets of walkways running around it that made it look a little like an air traffic control tower. The roof was made of panels of glass, topped by a spiked pole.

We hunkered down as the aircraft came in. The bomb flew through the sky, hit the top of the minaret, and went straight through one of the large panes at the top. It then continued down into a yard across the alley. There it went low-order—exploding without much visible impact.

"Shit," I said. "He missed. Come on—let's go get the son of a bitch ourselves."

We ran down a few blocks and entered the tower, climbing what seemed an endless flight of stairs. At any moment, we expected the sniper's security or the sniper himself to appear above and start firing at us.

No one did. When we made it to the top, we saw why. The sniper, alone in the building, had been decapitated by the bomb as it flew through the window.

But that wasn't all the bomb did. By chance, the alley where it landed had been filled with insurgents; we found their bodies and weapons a short time later.

I think it was the best sniper shot I ever saw.

REDISTRIBUTED

AFTER I'D BEEN WORKING WITH KILO COMPANY FOR ABOUT two weeks, the commanders called all the SEAL snipers back so they could redistribute us where we were needed.

"What the hell are you doing out there?" asked one of the first SEALs I met. "We're hearing shit that you're down there on the ground."

"Yeah, I am. No one's coming out on the street."

"What the hell are you doing?" he said, pulling me aside. "You know if our CO finds out you're doing this, you're out of here."

He was right, but I shrugged him off. I knew in my heart what I had to do. I also felt pretty confident in the officer who was my immediate commander. He was a straight shooter and all about doing the job that needed to get done.

Not to mention the fact that I was so far out of touch with my top command that it would have taken a long time for them to find out, let alone issue the orders to get me pulled out.

A bunch of other guys came over and started agreeing with me: down on the street was where we needed to be. I have no idea what they ended up doing; certainly, for the record, they all remained on the roofs, sniping.

"Well hell, instead of using that Marine M-16," said one of the East Coast boys, "I brought my M-4 with me. You can borrow it if you want."

"Really?"

I took it and wound up getting a bunch of kills on it. The M-16 and the M-4 are both good weapons; the Marines prefer the latest model of the M-16 for various reasons that have to do with the way they usually fight. Of course, my preference in close quarters combat was for the short-barreled M-4, and I was glad to borrow my friend's gun for the rest of my time in Fallujah.

I was assigned to work with Lima Company, which was operating a few blocks away from Kilo. Lima was helping fill in holes—taking down pockets of insurgents who had crept in or been bypassed. They were seeing a lot of action.

That night, I went over and talked to the company leadership in a house they'd taken over earlier in the day. The Marine commander had already heard what I'd been doing with Kilo, and after we talked a bit, he asked what I wanted to do.

"I'd like to be down on the street with y'all."

"Good enough."

Lima Company proved to be another great group of guys.

DON'T TELL MY MOM

A FEW DAYS LATER, WE WERE CLEARING A BLOCK WHEN I heard shooting on a nearby street. I told the Marines I was with to stay where they were, then ran over to see if I could help.

I found another group of Marines, who had started up an alley and run into heavy fire. They'd already pulled back and gotten under cover by the time I got there.

One kid hadn't quite made it. He was lying on his back some yards away, crying in pain.

I started laying down fire and ran up to grab him and pull him back. When I got to him, I saw he was in pretty bad shape, gut-shot. I dropped and got an arm under each of his, then started hauling him backward.

Somehow I managed to slip as I went. I fell backward, with him on top of me. By that point, I was so tired and winded I just lay there for a few minutes, still in the line of fire as bullets shot by.

The kid was about eighteen years old. He was really badly hurt. I could tell he was going to die.

"Please don't tell my momma I died in pain," he muttered.

Shit, kid, I don't even know who you are, I thought. *I'm not telling your momma anything.*

"Okay, okay," I said. "Don't worry. Don't worry. Everybody will make it sound great. Real great."

He died right then. He didn't even live long enough to hear my lies about how everything was going to be okay.

A bunch of Marines came. They lifted him off me and put him in the back of a Hummer. We called in a bomb strike and took out the shooting positions where the fire had come from, at the other end of the alley.

I went on back to my block and continued the fight.

THANKSGIVING

I THOUGHT ABOUT THE CASUALTIES I'D SEEN, AND THE FACT that I could be the next one carried out. But I wasn't going to quit.

I wasn't going to stop going into houses or stop supporting them from the roofs. I couldn't let down these young Marines I was with.

I told myself: *I'm a SEAL. I'm supposed to be tougher and better. I'm not going to give up on them.*

It wasn't that I thought I was tougher or better than they were. It was that I knew that was the way people looked at us. And I didn't want to let those people down. I didn't want to fail in their eyes—or in mine.

That's the line of thinking that's beaten into us: *We're the best of the best. We're invincible.*

I don't know if I'm the best of the best. But I did know that if I quit, I wouldn't be.

And I certainly did feel invincible. I had to be: I'd made it through all sorts of shit without getting killed . . . so far.

Thanksgiving shot past while we were in the middle of the battle.

I remember getting my Thanksgiving meal. They halted the assault for a little bit—maybe a half-hour—and brought up food to us on the rooftop where we'd set up.

Turkey, mashed potatoes, stuffing, green beans for ten—all in a large box.

Together. No separate boxes, no compartments. All in one pile.

Also no plates, no forks, no knives, no spoons.

We dipped our hands in and ate with our fingers. That was Thanksgiving.

Compared to the MREs we'd been eating, it was awesome.

ATTACKING THE MARSH

I STAYED WITH LIMA FOR ROUGHLY A WEEK, THEN WENT BACK to Kilo. It was terrible to hear who'd been hit and who they'd lost in the time I'd been gone.

WITH THE ASSAULT ABOUT FINISHED, WE WERE GIVEN A NEW task: set up a cordon to make sure no insurgents were able to get back in. Our sector was over by the Euphrates, on the western side of the town. From this point on, I was a sniper again. And figuring that my shots would now mostly be at longer range, I went back to the .300 Win Mag.

We set up in a two-story house overlooking the river a few hundred yards down from Blackwater Bridge. There was a marshy area immediately across the river, completely overgrown with weeds and everything. It was near a hospital the insurgents had converted into a headquarters before our assault, and even now the area seemed to be a magnet for savages.

Every night, we'd have someone trying to probe in from there. Every night I would get my shots off, taking out one or two or sometimes more.

The new Iraqi army had a camp nearby. Those idiots took it in their head to send a few shots our way as well. Every day. We hung a VF panel over our position—an indicator showing we were friendly—and the shots kept coming. We radioed their command. The shots kept coming. We called back and cussed out their command. The shots kept coming. We tried everything to get them to stop, short of calling in a bomb strike.

RUNAWAY'S RETURN

Runaway joined me again at Kilo. I had cooled off by now and more or less kept it civil, though my feelings toward him hadn't changed.

Nor, I guess, had Runaway. It was pathetic.

He was up on the roof with us one night when we started taking shots from insurgents somewhere.

I ducked behind the four-foot perimeter wall. Once the gunfire subsided, I glanced over the roof and looked to see where the shots had come from. It was too dark, though.

More shots were fired. Everybody ducked again. I went down just a little, hoping to see a muzzle flash in the dark when the next shot came over. I couldn't see anything.

"Come on," I said. "They're not accurate. Where are they firing from?"

No answer from Runaway.

"Runaway, look for the muzzle flash," I said.

I didn't hear a response. Two or three more shots followed, without me being able to figure out where they'd come from. Finally, I turned around to ask if he had seen anything.

Runaway was nowhere to be found. He'd gone downstairs—for all I know, the only thing that stopped him was the blocked door where the Marines were pulling security.

"I could get killed up there," he said when I caught up with him.

I left him downstairs, telling him to send up one of the Marines pulling security in his place. At least I knew that guy wouldn't run.

Runaway was eventually transferred somewhere where he wouldn't go into combat. He had lost his nerve. He should have pulled himself out of there. That would have been embarrassing, but how much worse could it have been? He had to spend his time convincing everyone else that he wasn't really a pussy, when the evidence was there for everyone to see.

Being the great warrior he was, Runaway declared to the Marines that SEALs and snipers were being wasted on sniper overwatch.

"SEALs shouldn't be here. This isn't a spec op mission," he told them. But the problem wasn't just the SEALs, as he soon made clear. "Those Iraqis are going to regroup and overrun us."

His prediction turned out to be just a little off. But hey, he has a bright future as a military planner.

THE MARSH

OUR REAL PROBLEM WAS WITH THE INSURGENTS USING THE marsh across the river as cover. The river coast was dotted with countless little islands with trees and brush. Here and there an old foundation or a pile of dredged dirt and rock poked up between the bushes.

Insurgents would pop up from the vegetation, take their shots, then squirrel back into the brush where you couldn't see them. The vegetation was so thick they could get pretty close not just to the river but to us—often within a hundred yards without being seen. Even the Iraqis could hit something from that distance.

Making things even more complicated, a herd of water buffalo lived in the swamp, and they'd tromp through every so often. You'd hear something or see the grass move and not know whether it was an insurgent or an animal.

We tried getting creative, requesting a napalm hit on the marsh to burn down the vegetation.

That idea was vetoed.

As the nights went on, I realized the number of insurgents was growing. It became obvious that I was being probed. Eventually, the insurgents might be able to get enough men together that I couldn't kill them all.

Not that I wouldn't have had fun trying.

THE MARINES BROUGHT IN A FAC (FORWARD AIR CONTROLler), to call in air support against the insurgents. The fellow they sent over was a Marine aviator, a pilot, working on a ground rotation. He tried a few times to vector in air attacks, but the requests were always denied higher up the chain of command.

At the time, I was told that there had been so much devastation in the city that they didn't want any more collateral damage. I don't see how blowing up a bunch of weeds and muck would make Fallujah look any worse than it already did, but then I'm just a SEAL and obviously don't understand those sorts of complicated issues.

Anyway, the pilot himself was a good guy. He didn't act stuck up or high and mighty; you'd never know he was an officer. We all liked him and respected him. And just to show there were no hard feelings, we let him get on the rifle every so often and look around. He never got off any shots.

Besides the FAC, the Marines sent a heavy-weapons squad, more snipers, and then mortarmen. The mortarmen brought some white phosphorous shells with them, and they tried launching those in an attempt to burn down the brush. Unfortunately, the shells would only set small pieces of the marsh on fire—they'd burn a bit, then fizzle and go out because it was so wet.

Our next try was throwing thermite grenades. A thermite grenade is an incendiary device that burns at four thousand degrees Fahrenheit and can go through a quarter-inch of steel in a few seconds. We went down to the river and hauled them across.

That didn't work, either, so we started making our own homegrown concoctions. Between the Marine sniper detail and the mortarmen, there was a great deal of creative brainpower focused on that marsh. Of all the plans, one of my personal favorites involved the creative use of the shaped "cheese" charges the mortarmen typically carried. (The cheese is used to propel mortar rounds. Distance can be adjusted by varying the amount of cheese used to fire the projectile.) We'd shove some cheese in a tube, add a bunch of det cord, some diesel, and add a time fuse. Then we'd heave the contraption across the river and see what happened.

We got some pretty flashes, but nothing we came up with worked real well.

If only we'd had a flamethrower . . .

THE MARSH REMAINED A "TARGET RICH ENVIRONMENT" filled with insurgents. I must have gotten eighteen or nineteen myself that week; the rest of the guys brought the total up to the area of thirty or more.

The river seemed to hold a special fascination for bad guys. While we were trying various ways to burn down the marsh, they were attempting all sorts of ways to get across.

The most bizarre involved beach balls.

BEACH BALLS AND LONG SHOTS

I WAS WATCHING FROM THE ROOF ONE AFTERNOON WHEN A group of roughly sixteen fully armed insurgents emerged from cover. They were wearing full body armor and were heavily geared.

(We found out later that they were Tunisians, apparently recruited by one of the militant groups to fight against Americans in Iraq.)

Not unusual at all, except for the fact that they were also carrying four very large and colorful beach balls.

I couldn't really believe what I was seeing—they split up into groups and got into the water, four men per beach ball. Then, using the beach balls to keep them afloat, they began paddling across.

It was my job not to let that happen, but that didn't necessarily mean I had to shoot each one of them. Hell, I had to conserve ammo for future engagements.

I shot the first beach ball. The four men began flailing for the other three balls.

Snap.

I shot beach ball number two.

It was kind of fun.

Hell—it was a *lot* of fun. The insurgents were fighting among themselves, their ingenious plan to kill Americans now turned against them.

"Y'all gotta see this," I told the Marines as I shot beach ball number three.

They came over to the side of the roof and watched as the insurgents fought among themselves for the last beach ball. The ones who couldn't grab on promptly sank and drowned.

I watched them fight for a while longer, then shot the last ball. The Marines put the rest of the insurgents out of their misery.

THOSE WERE MY STRANGEST SHOTS. MY LONGEST CAME around the same time.

One day, a group of three insurgents appeared on the shore upriver, out of range at around 1,600 yards. (That's just under a mile.) A few had tried that before, standing there, knowing that we wouldn't shoot them, because they were so far away. Our ROEs allowed us to take them, but the distance was so great that it really didn't make sense to take a shot. Apparently realizing they were safe, they began mocking us like a bunch of juvenile delinquents.

The FAC came over and started laughing at me as I eyed them through the scope.

"Chris, you ain't never gonna reach them."

Well, I didn't say I was going to try, but his words made it seem like almost a challenge. Some of the other Marines came over and told me more or less the same thing.

Anytime someone tells me I can't do something, it gets me thinking I can do it. But 1,600 yards was so far away that my scope wouldn't even dial up the shooting solution. So I did a little mental calculation and adjusted my aim with the help of a tree behind one of the grinning insurgent idiots making fun of us.

I took the shot.

The moon, Earth, and stars aligned. God blew on the bullet, and I gut-shot the jackass.

His two buddies hauled ass out of there.

"Get 'em, get 'em!" yelled the Marines. "Shoot 'em."

I guess at that point they thought I could hit anything under the sun. But the truth is, I'd been lucky as hell to hit the one I was aiming at; there was no way I was taking a shot at people who were running.

That would turn out to be one of my longest confirmed kills in Iraq.

MISPERCEPTIONS

People think that snipers take such incredibly long shots all the time. While we do take longer shots than most guys on the battlefield, they're probably a lot closer than most people think.

I never got all caught up in measuring how far I was shooting. The distance really depended on the situation. In the cities, where most of my kills came, you're only going to be shooting anywhere from two hundred to four hundred yards anyway. That's where your targets are, so that's where your shots are.

Out in the countryside, it's a different story. Typically, the shots out there would run from eight hundred to twelve hundred yards. That's where the longer-range guns like the .338 would come in handy.

Someone once asked me if I had a favorite distance. My answer was easy: the closer the better.

As I mentioned earlier, another misperception people have about snipers is that we always aim for the head. Personally, I almost never target the head, unless I'm absolutely sure I'm going to make the shot. And that's rare on the battlefield.

I'd much rather aim center mass—shoot for the middle of the body. I've got plenty of room to play with. No matter where I hit him, he's going down.

BACK TO BAGHDAD

After a week on the river, I was pulled out, swapping places with another SEAL sniper, who'd been injured briefly earlier in the operation and was ready to get back into action. I'd had more than my fair share of kills as a sniper; it was time to let someone else have a go.

Stick 'em up, Yankee . . .

Young hunters and their prey. My brother (*left*) is still one of my best friends.

I've been a cowboy pretty much from birth. Look at those fine boots I wore as a four-year-old.

Here I am in junior high, practicing with my Ithaca pump shotgun. Ironically, I've never been much of a shot with a scattergun.

You're not a real cowboy until you learn to lasso . . .

And I eventually got to where I was halfway decent at it.

It's a rough way to make a living, but I'll always be a cowboy at heart.

Fallujah in '04. Here I am with my .300 WinMag and some of the snipers I worked with. One was a SEAL, the others were Marines. (You can tell their service by the camis.)

All kitted up with my Mk-12 sniper rifle, the gun I was carrying when I rescued the trapped Marines and reporters in Fallujah.

The sniper hide we used when covering the Marines staging for the assault on Fallujah. Note the baby crib turned on its side.

Air Force Chief of Staff General Norton Schwartz hands me the Grateful Nation Award from JINSA, the Jewish Institute for National Security Affairs. JINSA gave me the award in 2005 in recognition of my service and achievements in Fallujah.

Charlie Platoon of SEAL Team 3 during the Ramadi deployment. The only faces that are shown are Marc Lee's (*left*), Ryan Job's (*middle*), and mine (*right*).

Marc Lee leading the platoon on patrol in Ramadi. With the help of the Marines, we were able to use the river to launch several ops against insurgents.

We made our own logo, reminiscent of the Punisher character. We spray-painted it on our vests and much of our gear. Like him, we were righting wrongs. *Photograph courtesy of 5.11*

Here I am with the boys in '06, just back from an op with my Mk-11 sniper rifle in my right hand.

Set up on a roof in Ramadi. The tent provided me a bit of relief from the sun.

Another sniping position I used in the same battle.

We chose roofs in Ramadi that provided us with good vantage points. Sometimes, though, the job called for more than a sniper rifle—that black smoke in the background is an enemy position obliterated by a tank.

Marc Lee.

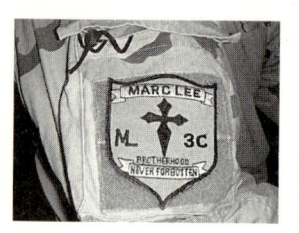

After Marc died, we created a patch to honor his memory. We will never forget.

Ryan Job.

A close-up of my Lapua .338, the gun I made my longest kill with. You can see my "dope" card—the placard on the side contains the come-ups (adjustments) needed for long-range targets. My 2,100-yard shot exceeded the card's range, and I had to eyeball it.

When not on the gun myself, I like to help others improve their skills. This was taken during my last deployment, while instructing a little class for some Army snipers.

Leading a training session for Craft International, the company I started after leaving the Navy. We make our sessions as realistic as possible for the operators and law enforcement officers we teach. *Photograph courtesy of 5.11*

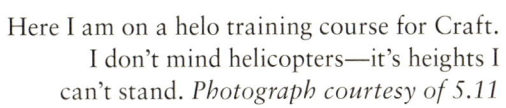

Here I am on a helo training course for Craft. I don't mind helicopters—it's heights I can't stand. *Photograph courtesy of 5.11*

Our company logo and slogan ("Despite what your momma told you . . . violence does solve problems") honor my SEAL brethren, especially my fallen comrades. I'll never forget them.

Me and Taya, the love of my life and better half. *Photograph courtesy of Heather Hurt/Calluna Photography*

My son and I check out a C-17.

Command sent me back to Camp Fallujah for a few days. It was one of the few breaks in the war that I actually welcomed. After the pace of the battle in the city, I was definitely ready for a brief vacation. The hot meals and showers felt pretty damn good.

After chilling out for a few days, I was ordered back to Baghdad to work with GROM again.

We were on the way to Baghdad when our Hummer was hit by a buried IED. The improvised explosive blew up just behind us; everybody in the vehicles freaked—except me and another guy who'd been at Fallujah since the start of the assault. We looked at each other, winked, then closed our eyes and went back to sleep. Compared to the month's worth of explosions and shit we'd just lived through, this was nothing.

WHILE I'D BEEN IN IRAQ, MY PLATOON WAS SENT TO THE Philippines on a mission to train up the local military to fight radical terrorists. It wasn't exactly the most exciting assignment. Finally, with that mission complete, they were sent to Baghdad.

I went out with some other SEALs to the airport to greet them.

I was expecting a big welcome—here my family was finally coming in.

They came off the plane cussin' me.

"Hey asshole."

And much worse than that. Like everything else they do, SEALs excel at foul language.

Jealousy, thy name is SEAL.

I'd wondered why I hadn't heard anything from them over the past few months. In fact, I was wondering why they were jealous—as far as I knew, they hadn't heard about anything I'd been doing.

Come to find out, my chief had been regaling them with the after-action reports of my sniping in Fallujah. They'd been sitting around hand-holding the Filipinos and hating life, while I'd been having all the fun.

They got over it. Eventually, they even asked me to do a little presentation on what I'd done, complete with pointers and stuff. One more chance to use PowerPoint.

FUN WITH THE BIG SHOTS

Now that they were here, I joined them and started doing some DAs. Intel would find an IED-maker or maybe a financer, give us the intel, and we'd go in and snag him. We'd hit them very early in the morning—blow his door down, rush inside, and take him before he even had a chance to get out of bed.

This went on for about a month. By now, DAs were pretty much an old routine; they were a hell of a lot less dangerous in Baghdad than in Fallujah.

We were living out near BIAP—Baghdad International Airport—and working from there. One day, my chief came over and gave me a chiefly grin.

"You've got to have some fun, Chris," he told me. "You need to do a little PSD."

He was using SEAL sarcasm. PSD stands for "personal security detail"—bodyguard duty. The platoon had been assigned to provide security for high-ranking Iraqi officials. The insurgents had started kidnapping them, trying to disrupt the government. It was a pretty thankless job. So far, I'd been able to avoid it, but it seemed my ninja smoke had run out. I left and went over to the other side of the city and the Green Zone. (The Green Zone was a section of central Baghdad that was created as a safe area for the allies and the new Iraqi government. It was physically cut off from the rest of the city by cement walls and barbed wire. There were only a few ways in and out, and these were under strict control. The U.S. and other allied embassies were located there, as were Iraqi government buildings.)

I lasted an entire week.

The Iraqi officials, so-called, were notorious for not telling their escorts what their schedules were or giving details on who was supposed to be traveling with them. Given the level of security in the Green Zone, that was a significant problem.

I acted as "advance." That meant I would go ahead of an official convoy, make sure the route was safe, and then stand at the security checkpoint and ID the convoy vehicles as they came through. This way the Iraqi vehicles could move through the checkpoints quickly without becoming targets.

One day, I was advance for a convoy that included the Iraqi vice president. I'd already checked the route and arrived at a Marine checkpoint outside the airport.

Baghdad International was on the other side of the city from the Green Zone. While the grounds themselves were secure, the area around it and the highway leading to the gate still came under occasional fire. It was a prime terror target, since the insurgents could pretty much figure that anyone going in or out was related to the Americans or the new Iraqi government in some way.

I was on radio coms with one of my boys in the convoy. He gave me the details on who was in the group, how many vehicles we had, and the like. He also told me that we had an Army Hummer in the front and an Army Hummer in the back—simple markers I could pass along to the guards.

The convoy came flying up, Hummer in the lead. We counted off the vehicles and lo, there was the last Hummer taking up the rear.

All good.

All of a sudden, two more vehicles appeared behind them in hot pursuit.

The Marines looked at me.

"Those two are not mine," I told them.

"What do you want us to do?"

"Pull your Hummer out and train that .50 on them," I yelled, pulling up my M-4.

I jumped out in the roadway, gun raised, hoping that would get their attention.

They didn't stop.

Behind me, the Hummer had pulled up, and the gunner was locked and loaded. Still unsure whether I was dealing with a kidnapping or just some stray vehicles, I fired a warning shot.

The cars veered off and hauled ass the other way.

Thwarted kidnapping? Suicide bombers who'd lost their nerve?

No. Come to find out, these were two friends of the vice president. He'd forgotten to tell us about them.

He wasn't too pleased. My command wasn't too pleased, either. I got fired from my PSD job, which wouldn't have been all that bad except that I then had to spend the next week sitting in the Green Zone doing nothing.

My platoon leadership tried to get me back for some DAs. But the head shed had decided to stick it to me a bit, and kept me twiddling my thumbs. That is the worst possible torture for a SEAL—missing out on the action.

Luckily, they didn't hang on to me for too long.

HAIFA STREET

In December 2005, Iraq geared up for national elections, its first since the fall of Saddam—and the first free and fair ones the country had ever held. The insurgency was doing everything it could to stop them. Election officials were being kidnapped left and right. Others were executed in the streets.

Talk about your negative campaigning.

Haifa Street in Baghdad was a particularly dangerous place. After three election officials were killed there, the Army put together a plan to protect officials in the area.

The strategy called for snipers to do overwatches.

I was a sniper. I was available. I didn't even have to raise my hand.

I joined an Army unit from the Arkansas National Guard, a great bunch of good ol' boys, warriors all.

People who are used to the traditional separation between the different military branches may think it's unusual for a SEAL to be working with the Army, or even the Marines for that matter. But the forces were often well-integrated during my time in Iraq.

Any unit could put in an RFF (Request for Forces). That request would then get filled by whatever service was available. So if a unit needed snipers, as they did in this case, whatever branch had available snipers would ship them over.

There's always back-and-forth between sailors, soldiers, and Marines. But I saw a lot of respect between the different branches, at least during the fighting. I certainly found most of the Marines and soldiers I worked with to be top-notch. You had your exceptions—but then you have your exceptions in the Navy, too.

THE FIRST DAY I REPORTED FOR MY NEW ASSIGNMENT, I thought I'd need an interpreter. Some people like to harass me about my Texas twang, but these hillbillies—holy shit. The important information came from the senior enlisted and the officers, who spoke regular English. But the privates and junior guys straight out of the backwoods could have been talking Chinese, for all I knew.

We started working on Haifa Street right near where the three election officials had been killed. The National Guard would secure an apartment building to use as a hide. Then I'd go in, pick out an apartment, and set up.

Haifa Street was not exactly Hollywood Boulevard, though it was the place to be if you were a bad guy. The street ran about two miles, from Assassin's Gate at the end of the Green Zone and up to the northwest. It was the scene of numerous firefights and gun battles, all sorts of IED attacks, kidnappings, assassinations—you name it and it happened on Haifa. American soldiers dubbed it Purple Heart Boulevard.

The buildings we used for overwatches were fifteen to sixteen stories tall, and had a commanding view of the road. We moved around to the extent that we could, shifting locations to keep the insurgents off-balance. There were an untold number of hideouts in the squat buildings beyond the immediate highway, all up and down the street. The bad guys didn't have much of a commute to get to work.

The insurgents here were a real mix; some were mujahedeen, former Baath or Iraqi Army guys. Others were loyal to al-Qaeda in Iraq or Sadr or some of the other whackadoos out there. At the start, they'd wear black or sometimes these green sashes, but once they realized that set them apart, they resorted to wearing regular civilian clothes just like everyone else. They wanted to mix with civilians to make it more difficult for us to figure out who they were. They were cowards, who not only would hide behind women and children, but probably hoped we'd kill the women and children, since in their minds it helped their cause by making us look bad.

One afternoon, I watched a young teenage kid waiting for the bus below me. When the bus pulled up, a group of older teenagers and young adults got off. All of a sudden, the kid I was watching turned and started walking very quickly in the opposite direction.

The group caught up quickly. One of them pulled out a pistol and put his arm around the kid's neck.

As soon as he did that, I started shooting. The kid I was protecting took off. I got two or three of his would-be kidnappers; the others got away.

The sons of the election officials were a favorite target. The insurgents would use the families to put pressure on the officials to drop out. Or else they'd just kill the family members as a warning to others not to help the government hold the elections or even vote.

THE SALACIOUS AND THE SURREAL

ONE EVENING, WE TOOK OVER WHAT WE THOUGHT WAS AN abandoned apartment, since it was empty when we arrived. I was rotating with another sniper, and while I was off, I went hunting around to see if there was something I might use to make the hide more comfortable.

In an open drawer of a bureau, I saw all this sexy lingerie. Crotchless panties, nightgowns—very suggestive stuff.

Not my size, though.

There was often an odd, almost surreal mix of things inside the buildings, items that would seem out of place under the best circumstances. Like the car tires we found on the roof in Fallujah, or the goat we found in the bathroom of a Haifa Street apartment.

I'd see something, then spend the rest of the day wondering what the story was. After a while, the bizarre came to seem natural.

Not quite surprising were the TVs and satellite dishes. They were everywhere. Even in the desert. Many times we'd come upon a little nomad settlement with tents for houses and nothing but a couple animals and open land around them. Still, they were bristling with satellite dishes.

CALLING HOME

ONE NIGHT, I WAS ON AN OVERWATCH AND THINGS WERE quiet. Nights were normally slow in Baghdad. Insurgents usually wouldn't attack then, because they knew we had the advantage with our technology, including our night-vision gear and infrared sensors. So I thought I'd take a minute and call my wife back home, just to tell I was thinking of her.

I took our sat phone and dialed home. Most times, when I talked to Taya, I'd tell her I was back at base, even though I was really on an overwatch or in the field somewhere. I didn't want to worry her.

This night, for some reason, I told her what I was doing.

"Is it all right to talk?" she asked.

"Oh yeah, it's all good," I said. "There's nothing going on."

Well, I got maybe another two or three sentences out of my mouth when someone started firing at the building from the street.

"What's that?" she asked.

"Oh, nothing," I said nonchalantly.

Of course, the gunfire stoked up real loud as the words came out of my mouth.

"Chris?"

"Well, I think I'm going to get going now," I told her.

"Are you okay?"

"Oh yeah. It's all good," I lied. "Nothing happening. Talk to you later."

Just then, an RPG hit the outside wall right near me. Some of the building smacked into my face, giving me a couple of beauty marks and temporary tattoos courtesy of the insurgency.

I dropped the phone and started returning fire. I spotted the guys down the street and popped one or two; the snipers who were with me downed a bunch more before the rest got the hell out of there.

Fight over, I grabbed up the phone. The batteries had run out, so I couldn't call back.

Things got busy for a few days, and it wasn't until two or three days later when I finally got a chance to call Taya and see how she was.

She started crying as soon as she answered the phone.

It turned out I hadn't actually ended the call before I put down the phone. She'd heard the whole gunfight, complete with shots and curses, before the batteries had finally run out. Which, of course, happened all of a sudden, adding to the anxiety.

I tried to calm her down, but I doubt what I said really eased her mind.

She was always a good sport, always insisting that I didn't have to hide things from her. She claimed her imagination was a lot worse than anything that really could happen to me.

I don't know about that.

I MADE A FEW OTHER CALLS HOME DURING LULLS IN BATTLES during my deployments. The overall pace of the action was so intense and continuous that there weren't many alternatives. Waiting until I got back to our camp might mean waiting for a week or more. And while I'd call then, too, if I could, it wasn't always possible.

And I got used to the battles. Getting shot at was just part of the job. RPG round? Just another day at the office.

My dad has a story about hearing from me at work one day when I hadn't had a chance to call in a while. He picked up the phone and was surprised to hear my voice.

He was even more surprised that I was whispering.

"Chris, why is your voice so hushed?" he asked.

"I'm on an op, Dad. I don't want them to know where I'm at."

"Oh," he answered, a little shaken.

I doubt I was actually close enough for the enemy to hear anything, but my father swears that a few seconds later, there were gunshots in the background.

"Gotta go," I said, before he had a chance to find out what the sound was. "I'll get back to you."

According to my father, I called back two days later to apologize for hanging up so abruptly. When he asked if he had overheard the start of a firefight, I changed the subject.

BUILDING MY REP

My knees were still hurting from being pinned under rubble back in Fallujah. I tried to get cortisone shots but couldn't. I didn't want to push too hard: I was afraid of getting pulled out because of my injury.

Every once in a while, I took some Motrin and iced them down; that was about it. In battle, of course, I was fine—when your adrenaline is pumped, you don't feel anything.

Even with the pain, I loved what I was doing. Maybe war isn't really fun, but I certainly was enjoying it. It suited me.

By this time, I had a bit of a reputation as a sniper. I'd had a lot of confirmed kills. It was now a very good number for such a short period—or any period, really.

Except for the Team guys, people didn't really know my name and face. But there were rumors around, and my stay here added to my reputation, such as it was.

It seemed like everywhere I set up, I'd get a target. This started to piss off some of the other snipers, who could spend whole shifts and even days without seeing *anybody,* let alone an insurgent.

One day, Smurf, a fellow SEAL, started following me around as we went into an apartment.

"Where are you setting up?" he asked.

I looked around and found a place I thought looked good.

"Right there," I told him.

"Good. Get the hell out of here. I'm taking this spot."

"Hey, you take it," I told him. I went off to find another spot—and promptly got a kill from there.

For a while, it didn't seem to matter what I did, things would happen in front of me. I wasn't inventing the incidents—I had witnesses for all my shots. Maybe I saw a little farther, maybe I anticipated trouble better than other people. Or, most likely, I was just lucky.

Assuming being a target for people who want to kill you can be considered luck.

One time, we were in a house on Haifa Street, where we had so many snipers that the only possible place to shoot from was a tiny window above a toilet. I had to actually stand up the whole time.

I still got two kills.

I was just one lucky motherfucker.

ONE DAY, WE GOT INTEL THAT THE INSURGENTS WERE USING A cemetery at the edge of town near Camp Independence at the airport to cache weapons and launch attacks. The only way I could get a view of the place was to climb up on this tall, tall crane. Once at the top, I then had to go out on a thin-mesh platform.

I don't know how high I went. I don't want to know. Heights are not my favorite thing—it makes my balls go in my throat just thinking about it.

The crane did give me a decent view of the cemetery, which was about eight hundred yards away.

I never took a shot from there. I never saw anything aside from mourners and funerals. But it was worth a try.

BESIDES LOOKING FOR PEOPLE WITH IEDs, WE HAD TO WATCH out for the bombs themselves. They were everywhere—occasionally, even in the apartment buildings. One team narrowly escaped one afternoon, the explosives going off just after they collapsed down and left the building.

The Guard was using Bradleys to get around. The Bradley looks a bit like a tank, since it has a turret and gun on top, but it's actually a personnel carrier and scout vehicle, depending on its configuration.

I believe it's made to fit six people inside. We would try and cram eight or ten in. It was hot, muggy, and claustrophobic. Unless you were sitting by the ramp, you couldn't see anything. You kind of sucked it up and waited to get wherever it was you were going.

One day, the Bradleys picked us up from a sniper op. We had just turned off Haifa onto one of the side streets, and all of a sudden—*buh-lam*. We'd been hit by a massive IED. The back of the vehicle lifted up and slammed back down. The inside filled with smoke.

I could see the guy across from me moving his mouth, but I couldn't hear a word: the blast had blown out my ears.

The next thing I knew, the Bradley started moving again. That was one tough vehicle. Back at the base, the commander kind of shrugged it off.

"Didn't even knock the tracks off," he said. He almost sounded disappointed.

IT'S A CLICHÉ, BUT IT'S TRUE: YOU FORM TIGHT FRIENDSHIPS in war. And then suddenly circumstances change. I became close friends with two guys in the Guard unit, real good friends; I trusted them with my life.

Today I couldn't tell you their names if my life depended on it. And I'm not even sure that I can describe them in a way that would show you why they were special.

Me and the boys from Arkansas seemed to get along real well together, maybe because we were all just country boys.

Well, they were hillbillies. You've got your regular redneck like me, then you got your hillbilly who's a whole sight different animal.

ONWARD

THE ELECTIONS CAME AND WENT.

The media back in the States made a big thing of the Iraqi government elections, but it was a nonevent for me. I wasn't even out that day; I caught it on TV.

I never really believed the Iraqis would turn the country into a truly functioning democracy, but I thought at one point that there was a chance. I don't know that I believe that now. It's a pretty corrupt place.

But I didn't risk my life to bring democracy to Iraq. I risked my life for my buddies, to protect my friends and fellow countrymen. I went to war for *my* country, not Iraq. My country sent me out there so that bullshit wouldn't make its way back to our shores.

I never once fought for the Iraqis. I could give a flying fuck about them.

A SHORT WHILE AFTER THE ELECTION, I WAS SENT BACK TO MY SEAL platoon. Our time in Iraq was growing short, and I was starting to look forward to going home.

Being at camp in Baghdad meant I had my own little room. My personal gear filled four or five cruise boxes, two big Stanley roller boxes, and assorted rucks. (Cruise boxes are the modern equivalent of footlockers; they're waterproof and roughly three feet long.) On deployment, we pack heavy.

I also had a TV set. All the latest movies were on pirated DVDs selling at Baghdad street stands for five bucks. I bought a box set of James Bond movies, some Clint Eastwood, John Wayne—I love John Wayne. I love his cowboy movies especially, which makes sense I guess. *Rio Bravo* may be my favorite.

Besides movies, I spent a bit of time playing computer games—Command and Conquer became a personal favorite. Smurf had a PlayStation, and we started getting into playing Tiger Woods.

I kicked his butt.

DAS, HELOS, AND HEIGHTS

WITH BAGHDAD SETTLING DOWN, AT LEAST FOR THE MOMENT, the head shed decided they wanted to open up a SEAL base in Habbaniyah.

Habbaniyah is twelve miles to the east of Fallujah, in Anabar Province. It wasn't quite the hotbed of the insurgency that Fallujah had been, but it wasn't San Diego, either. This is the area where before the First Gulf War, Saddam built chemical plants devoted to manufacturing weapons of mass destruction, such as nerve gas and other chemical agents. There weren't a lot of America supporters out there.

There was a U.S. Army base though, run by the famous 506th Regiment—the Band of Brothers. They'd just come over from Korea and, to be polite, had no fucking clue what Iraq was all about. I suppose everybody's gotta learn the hard way.

Habbaniyah turned out to be a real pain in the ass. We'd been given an abandoned building, but it was nowhere near adequate for what we needed. We had to build a TOC—a tactical operations command—to house all the computers and com gear that helped support us during our missions.

Our morale sunk. We weren't doing anything useful for the

war; we were working as carpenters. It's an honorable profession, but it's not ours.

Taya:

It was on this deployment that the medical doctors did a test and, for some reason, thought Chris had TB. The doctors told him he would eventually die of the disease.

I remember talking to him right after he got the news. He was fatalistic about it. He'd already accepted that he was going to die, and he wanted to do it there, not at home from a disease he couldn't fight with a gun or his fists.

"It doesn't matter," he told me. "I'll die and you'll find someone else. People die out here all the time. Their wives go on and find someone else."

I tried to explain to him that he was irreplaceable to me. When that didn't seem to faze him, I tried another equally valid point. "But you've got our son," I told him.

"So what? You'll find someone else and that guy will raise him."

I think he was seeing death so often that he started to believe people were replaceable.

It broke my heart. He truly believed that. I still hate to think that.

He thought dying on the battlefield was the greatest. I tried to tell him differently, but he didn't believe it.

They redid the tests, and Chris was cleared. But his attitude about death stayed.

Once the camp was settled, we started doing DAs. We'd be given the name and location of a suspected insurgent, hit his house at night, then come back and deposit him and whatever evidence we gathered at the DIF—Detention and Interrogation Facility, your basic jail.

We'd take pictures along the way. We weren't sightseeing; we were covering our butts, and, more important, those of our commanders. The pictures proved we hadn't beaten the crap out of him.

Most of these ops were routine, without much trouble and almost never any resistance. One night, though, one of our guys went into a house where a rather portly Iraqi decided he didn't want to come along nicely. He started to tussle.

Now, from our perspective, our brother SEAL was getting the shit kicked out of him. According to the SEAL in question, he had actually slipped and was in no need of assistance.

I guess you can interpret it any way you want. We all rushed in and grabbed the fatso before he could do much harm. Our friend got ribbed about his "fall" for a while.

ON MOST OF THESE MISSIONS, WE HAD PHOTOS OF THE PERSON we were supposed to get. In that case, the rest of the intelligence tended to be pretty accurate. The guy was almost always where he was supposed to be, and things pretty much followed the outline we had drawn up.

But some cases didn't go so smoothly. We began realizing that if we didn't have a photo, the intelligence was suspect. Knowing that the Americans would bring a suspect in, people were using tips to settle grievances or feuds. They'd talk to the Army or some other authority, making claims about a person helping the insurgency or committing some other crime.

It sucked for the person we arrested, but I didn't get all that worked up about it. It was just one more example of how screwed up the country was.

SECOND-GUESSED

ONE DAY, THE ARMY ASKED FOR A SNIPER OVERWATCH FOR A 506th convoy that was coming into base.

I went out with a small team and we took down a three- or four-story building. I set up in the top floor and started watching the area. Pretty soon the convoy headed down the road. As I was watching the area, a man came out of a building near the road and began maneuvering in the direction the convoy was going to take. He had an AK.

I shot him. He went down.

The convoy continued through. A bunch of other Iraqis came out and gathered around the guy I'd shot, but nobody that I could see made any threatening motions toward the convoy or looked to be in a position to attack it, so I didn't fire.

A few minutes later, I heard on the radio that the Army is sending a unit out to investigate why I shot him.

Huh?

I had already told the Army command on the radio what had happened, but I got back on the radio and repeated it. I was surprised—they didn't believe me.

A tank commander came out and interviewed the dead man's wife. She told them her husband was on his way to the mosque carrying a Koran.

Uh-huh. The story was ridiculous, but the officer—whom, I'm guessing, hadn't been in Iraq very long—didn't believe me. The soldiers began to look around for the rifle, but by that time so many people had been in the area that it was long gone.

The tank commander pointed out my position. "Did it come from there?"

"Yes, yes," said the woman, who, of course, had no idea where the shot had come from, since she hadn't been anywhere nearby. "I know he's Army, because he's wearing an Army uniform."

Now, I was two rooms deep, with a screen in front of me, wearing a gray jacket over my SEAL camis. Maybe she hallucinated in her grief, or maybe she just said whatever she thought would give me grief.

We were recalled to base and the entire platoon put on standdown. I was told I was not "operationally available"—I was confined to base while the 506th investigated the incident further.

The colonel wanted to interview me. My officer came with me.

We were all pissed. The ROEs had been followed; I had plenty of witnesses. It was the Army "investigators" who had screwed up.

I had trouble holding my tongue. At one point, I told the Army colonel, "I don't shoot people with Korans—I'd like to, but I don't." I guess I was a little hot.

Well, after three days and God only knows how much other "investigation," he finally realized that it had been a good kill and dropped the matter. But when the regiment asked for more overwatches, we told them to fuck off.

"Any time I shoot someone, you're just going to try and have me executed," I said. "No way."

We were heading home in two weeks anyway. Aside from a few more DAs, I spent most of that time playing video games, watching porn, and working out.

I FINISHED THAT DEPLOYMENT WITH A SUBSTANTIAL NUMBER of confirmed sniper kills. Most happened in Fallujah.

Carlos Norman Hathcock II, the most famous member of the sniping profession, a true legend and a man whom I look up to, tallied ninety-three confirmed kills during his three years of tours in the Vietnam War.

I'm not saying I was in his class—in my mind, he was and always will be the *greatest* sniper ever—but in sheer numbers, at least, I was close enough for people to start thinking I'd done a hell of a job.

8

FAMILY CONFLICTS

TAYA:
We went out to the tarmac to wait for the plane when it came in. There were a few wives and children. I came out with our baby and I felt so excited. I was over the moon.

I remember turning to one of the women I was with and saying, "Isn't this great? Isn't this exciting? I can't stand it."

She said, "Ehhh."

I thought to myself, well, maybe I'm still new to it.

Later on, she and her husband, a SEAL in Chris's platoon, got divorced.

BONDING

I'D LEFT THE STATES SOME SEVEN MONTHS BEFORE, ONLY TEN days after my son was born. I loved him, but as I mentioned earlier, we hadn't really had a chance to bond. Newborns are just a bundle of needs—feed them, clean them, get them to rest. Now he had a personality. He was crawling. He was more of a person. I'd seen him growing up in the photos Taya had sent me, but this was more intense.

He was my son.

We'd lie on the floor in our pajamas and play together. He'd crawl all over me and I'd boost him up and carry him all around. Even the simplest things—like him touching my face—were a joy.

But the transition from war to home was still a shock. One day, we'd been fighting. The next, we'd crossed the river to al-Taqaddum Airbase (known to us as TQ) and started back for the States.

War one day; peace the next.

Every time you come home, it's weird. Especially in California. The simplest things can upset you. Take traffic. You're driving on the road, everything's crowded, it's craziness. You're still thinking IEDs—you see a piece of trash and you swerve. You drive aggressively toward other drivers, because that's the way you do it in Iraq.

I would shut myself in for about a week. I think that's where Taya and I started having problems.

BEING PARENTS FOR THE FIRST TIME, WE HAD THE DISAGREEments everyone has about children. Co-sleeping, for instance—Taya had my son sleep with her in a co-sleeper in the bed while I was gone. When I came home, I wanted to change that. We disagreed quite a bit on that. I thought he should be in his own crib in his own room. Taya saw it as depriving her of her closeness with him. She thought we should transition him gradually.

That wasn't how I saw it at all. I felt children should sleep in their own beds and rooms.

FAMILY CONFLICTS

I know now that issues like that are common, but there was added stress. She'd been raising him completely on her own for months now, and I was intruding on her routines and ways of doing things. They were incredibly close, which I thought was great. But I wanted to be with them, too. I wasn't trying to come between them, just add myself back into the family.

As it happened, none of that was a big deal for my son; he slept just fine. And he still has a very special relationship with his mom.

LIFE AT HOME HAD ITS INTERESTING MOMENTS, THOUGH THE drama was very different. Our neighbors and close friends were completely respectful of my need for time to decompress. Once that was over, they put together a little welcome-home barbecue.

They'd all been great while I was gone. The people across the street arranged to have someone cut our grass, which was huge to us financially and helped Taya with the heavy load she carried while I was gone. It seemed like a little thing, but it was big to me.

Now that I was home, of course, it was my job to take care of things like that. We had a small, itty-bitty backyard; it took all of five minutes to cut the grass back there. But on one side of the yard were climbing roses that climbed up these potato bush trees we had. The bushes had little purple flowers on them year-round.

The combination looked really pretty. But the roses had thorns in them that could pierce an armored vest. Every time I'd mow the yard and come around the corner, I'd get snagged by them.

One day, those roses just went too far, tearing at my side. I decided to take care of them once and for all: I picked up my lawnmower, held it up about chest-high, and trimmed the mothers (the roses and the trees) down.

203

"What! Are you kidding me?" yelled Taya. "Are you trimming the bushes with a lawnmower?"

Hey, it worked. They never snagged me again.

I did do some genuinely goofy stuff. Having fun and making other people smile and laugh has always been something I like to do. One day, I saw our backyard neighbor through our kitchen window, so I stood on a chair and knocked on the window to get her attention. I proceeded to moon her. (Her husband happened to be a Navy pilot, so I'm sure she was familiar with such things.)

Taya rolled her eyes. She was amused, I think, though she wouldn't admit it.

"Who does that?" she said to me.

"She laughed, didn't she?" I said.

"You are thirty years old," she said. "Who does that?"

There's a side of me that loves to pull pranks on people, to get them to laugh. You can't just do regular stuff—I want them to have a good time. Belly laughs. The more extreme the better. April Fools' Day is a particularly tough time for my family and friends, though more because of Taya's pranks than my own. I guess we both like to have a good laugh.

ON THE DARKER SIDE, I WAS EXTREMELY HOT-HEADED. I HAVE always had a temper, even before becoming a SEAL. But it was more explosive now. If someone cut me off—not a very rare occurrence in California—I could get crazy. I might try and run them off the road, or even stop and whup their ass.

I had to work at calming down.

OF COURSE, HAVING A REPUTATION AS A SEAL DOES HAVE ITS advantages.

At my sister-in-law's wedding, the preacher and I got to talking. At some point, she—the preacher was a lady—noticed a bulge in my jacket.

"You have a gun?" she asked.

"Yes, I do," I said, explaining that I was in the military.

She may or may not have known that I was a SEAL—I didn't tell her, but word tends to get around—but when she was ready to start the ceremony and couldn't get anyone in the crowd to be quiet and get into place, she came over to me, patted me on the back, and said, "Can you get everyone to sit down?"

"Yes, I can," I told her.

I barely had to raise my voice to get that little ceremony going.

TAYA:

People talk about physical love and need when someone comes home from a long absence: "I want to rip your clothes off." That sort of thing.

I felt that way in theory, but the reality was always a little different.

I needed to get to know him again. It was strange. There's so much anticipation. You miss them so much when they deploy, and you want them to be home, but then when they are, things aren't perfect. And you feel as if they should be. Depending on the deployment and what I'd been through, I also had emotions ranging from sadness to anxiety to anger.

When he came back after this deployment, I felt almost shy. I was a new mother and had been doing things on my own for months. We were both changing and growing in totally separate worlds. He had no firsthand knowledge of mine and I had no firsthand knowledge of his.

I also felt bad for Chris. He was wondering what was wrong. There was distance between us that neither one of us could really fix, or even talk about.

BREAKING AND ENTERING

WE HAD A LONG BREAK FROM WAR, BUT WE WERE BUSY THE whole time, retraining and, in some cases, learning new skills. I went to a school run by FBI agents and CIA and NSA officers. They taught me how to do things like pick locks and steal cars. I loved it. The fact that it was in New Orleans didn't hurt, either.

Learning how to blend in and go undercover, I cultivated my inner jazz musician and grew a goatee. Lock-picking was a revelation. We worked on a variety of locks, and by the end of the class I don't think there was a lock that could have kept me or anyone else in our class at bay. Stealing cars was a little harder, but I got pretty good at that, too.

We were trained to wear cameras and eavesdropping devices without getting caught. To prove that we could, we had to get the devices into a strip club and return with (video) evidence that we'd been there.

The sacrifices you make for your country . . .

I stole a car off Bourbon Street as part of my final. (I had to put it back when we were done; as far as I know, the owner was none the wiser.) Unfortunately, these are all perishable skills—I can still pick a lock, but it'll take me longer now. I'll have to brush up if I ever decide to go crooked.

FAMILY CONFLICTS

AMONG OUR MORE NORMAL ROTATIONS WAS A RECERTIFICAtion class for parachuting.

Jumping out of planes—or, I should say, *landing safely* after jumping out of planes—is an important skill, but it's a dangerous one. Hell, I've heard it said the Army figures in combat, if they get 70 percent of the guys in a unit to land safely enough to rally and fight, they're doing well.

Think about that. A thousand guys—three hundred don't make it. Not a big deal to the Army.

Oh-*kay*.

I went to Fort Benning to train with the Army right after I first became a SEAL. I guess I should have realized what I was in for on the first day of school, when a soldier just ahead of me refused to jump. We all stood there waiting—and thinking—while the instructors tended to him.

I'm afraid of heights as it is, and this didn't build my confidence. *Holy shit*, I wondered, *what's he seeing that I'm not?*

Being a SEAL, I had to make a good showing—or at least not look like a wimp. Once he was taken out of the way, I closed my eyes and plunged ahead.

It was on one of those early static jumps (jumps where the cord is automatically pulled for you, a procedure usually used for beginners) that I made the mistake of looking up to check my canopy as I left the plane.

They tell you not to do that. I was wondering why when the chute deployed. My tremendous sense of relief that I had a canopy and wasn't going to die was mitigated by the rope burns on both sides of my face.

The reason they tell you not to look up is so that you don't get hit by the risers as they fly by your head when the chute opens. Some things you learn the hard way.

And then there are night jumps. You can't see the land coming.

You know you have to roll into PLFs—parachute landing falls—but when?

I tell myself, the first time I feel something I'm going to roll. The first . . . time . . . *the f-i-r-s-t* . . . !!

I think I banged my head every time I jumped at night.

I WILL SAY I PREFERRED FREEFALL TO STATIC JUMPING. I'M not saying I *enjoyed* it, just that I liked it a lot better. Kind of like picking the firing squad over being hanged.

In freefall, you came down a lot slower and had much more control. I know there are all these videos of people doing stunts and tricks and having a grand ol' time doing HALO (high altitude, low opening) jumps. There are none of me. I watch my wrist altimeter the whole time. That chord is pulled the split-second I hit the right altitude.

ON MY LAST JUMP WITH THE ARMY, ANOTHER JUMPER CAME right under me as we descended. When that happens, the lower canopy can "steal" the air beneath you. The result is . . . you fall faster than you were falling.

The consequences can be pretty dramatic, depending on the circumstances. In this case, I was seventy feet from the ground. I ended up falling from there, and having a couple of tree branches and the ground beat the crap out of me. I walked away with some bumps and bruises and a few broken ribs.

Fortunately, it was the last jump of the school. My ribs and I soldiered on, glad to be done.

FAMILY CONFLICTS

OF COURSE, AS BAD AS PARACHUTING IS, IT BEATS SPY-RIGGING. Spy-rigging may look cool, but one wrong move and you can spin off in Mexico. Or Canada. Or maybe even China.

Strangely, though, I like helos. During this workup, my platoon worked with MH-6 Little Birds. Those are very small, very fast scout-and-attack helicopters adapted for Special Operations work. Our versions had benches fitted to each side; three SEALs can sit on each bench.

I loved them.

True, I was scared to death getting on the damn thing. But once the pilot took off and we were in the air, I was hooked. It was a tremendous adrenaline rush—you're low and fast. It's awesome. The momentum of the aircraft keeps you in place; you don't even feel any wind buffeting.

And hell—if you fall, you'll never feel a thing.

THE PILOTS WHO COMMANDED THOSE AIRCRAFT ARE AMONG the best in the world. They were all members of the 160th SOAR—the Special Operations air wing, handpicked to work with spec warfare personnel. There's a difference, and it's noticeable.

When you're fast-roping from a chopper with a "regular" pilot, you may find yourself at the wrong altitude, too high for the rope to reach the ground. At that point, it's too late to do anything about it except grunt or groan as you hit the ground. A lot of pilots also have trouble holding station—staying put long enough for you to get in the right spot on the ground.

Not so with the guys from SOAR. Right place, first time, every time. That rope drops, it's where it belongs.

AMERICAN SNIPER: MEMORIAL EDITION

MARCUS

The Fourth of July 2005 was a beautiful California day: perfect weather, not a cloud in the sky. My wife and I took our son and drove out to a friend's house in the foothills outside of town. There we spread a blanket and gathered in the tailgate of my Yukon to watch the fireworks display put on at an Indian reservation in the valley. It was a perfect spot—we could see down as the fireworks came up to us, and the effect was spectacular.

I've always loved celebrating the Fourth of July. I love the symbolism, meaning of the day, and of course the fireworks and the barbecues. It's just a wonderful time.

But that day, as I sat back and watched the red, white, and blue sparkles, sadness suddenly spread over me. I fell into a deep black hole.

"This sucks," I muttered as the fireworks exploded.

I wasn't critiquing the show. I had just realized that I might never see my friend Marcus Luttrell again. I hated to be unable to do anything to help my friend, who was facing God only knew what kind of trouble.

We'd gotten word a few days before that he was missing. I'd also heard through the SEAL grapevine that the three guys he was with were dead. They'd been ambushed by the Taliban in Afghanistan; surrounded by hundreds of Taliban fighters, they fought ferociously. Another sixteen men in a rescue party were killed when the Chinook they were flying in was shot down. (You can and should read the details in Marcus's book, *Lone Survivor*.)

To that point, losing a friend in combat seemed if not impossible, at least distant and unlikely. It may seem strange to say, given everything I'd been through, but at that point we were feeling pretty sure of ourselves. Cocky, maybe. You just get to a point where you think you're such a superior fighter that you can't be hurt.

Our platoon had come through the war without any serious injuries. In some respects, training seemed more dangerous.

There had been accidents in training. Not long before, we were doing ship takedowns when one of our platoon members fell while going up the side. He landed on two other guys in the boat. All three had to go to the hospital; one of the men he landed on broke his neck.

We don't focus on the dangers. The families, though, are a different story. They're always very aware of the dangers. The wives and girlfriends often take turns sitting in the hospital with the families of people who are injured. Inevitably, they realize they could be sitting there for their own husband or boyfriend.

I REMAINED TORN UP ABOUT MARCUS FOR THE REST OF THE night, in my own private black hole. I stayed there for a few days.

Work, of course, continued. One day, my chief popped his head into the room and signaled me to join him outside.

"Hey, they found Marcus," he said as soon as we were alone.

"Great."

"He's fucked up."

"So what? He's going to make it." Anyone who knew Marcus knew that was true. The man cannot be kept down.

"Yeah, you're right," said my chief. "But he's pretty tore up, beat up. It'll be hard."

It was hard, but Marcus was up to it. In fact, despite health issues that continue to dog him, he would deploy again not long after leaving the hospital.

EXPERT, SO-CALLED

BECAUSE OF WHAT I'D DONE IN FALLUJAH, I WAS PULLED OUT a few times to talk to head shed types about how I thought snipers should be deployed. I was now a Subject Matter Expert—an SME in militarese.

I hated it.

Some people might find it flattering to be talking to a bunch of high-ranking officers, but I just wanted to do my job. It was torture sitting in the room, trying to explain what the war was like.

They'd ask me questions like, "What kind of gear should we have?" Not unreasonable, I guess, but all I could think of was: *God, you guys are really all pretty stupid. This is basic stuff you should have figured out long ago.*

I would tell them what I thought, how we should train up snipers, how we should use them. I suggested more training about urban overwatches and creating hides in buildings, things I'd learned more or less as I went. I gave them ideas about sending snipers into an area before the assault, so they could provide intel to the assault teams before they arrived. I made suggestions on how to make snipers more active and aggressive. I suggested that snipers take shots over the heads of an assault team during training, so the teams could get used to working with them.

I told the brass about gear issues—the dust cover of the M-11, for example, and suppressors that jiggled at the end of the barrel, hurting the accuracy of the rifle.

It was all extremely obvious to me, but not to them.

Asked for my opinion, I'd give it. But most times they didn't *really* want it. They wanted me to validate some decision they'd already made or some thought they'd already had. I'd tell them about a given piece of gear I thought we should have; they'd answer that they'd already bought a thousand of something else. I'd offer them a strategy I'd used successfully in Fallujah; they'd quote me chapter and verse on why it wouldn't work.

Taya:

We had a lot of confrontations while he was home. His enlistment was coming up, and I didn't want him to re-up.

I felt he had done his duty to the country, even more than anyone could ask. And I felt that we needed him.

I've always believed that your responsibility is to God, family, and country—in that order. He disagreed—he put country ahead of family.

And yet he wasn't completely obstinate. He always said, "If you tell me not to reenlist, I won't."

But I couldn't do that. I told him, "I can't tell you what to do. You'll just hate me and resent me all your life.

"But I will tell you this," I said. "If you do reenlist, then I will know exactly where we stand. It will change things. I won't want it to, but I know in my heart it will."

When he reenlisted anyway, I thought, Okay. Now I know. Being a SEAL is more important to him than being a father or a husband.

NEW GUYS

WHILE WE WERE TRAINING UP FOR OUR NEXT DEPLOYMENT, the platoon got a group of new guys. A few of them stood out—Dauber and Tommy, for example, who were both snipers and corpsmen. But I think the new guy who made the biggest impression was

Ryan Job. And the reason was that he did not look like a SEAL; on the contrary, Ryan looked like a big lump.

I was floored that they let this guy come to the Team. Here we all were, buff, in great shape. And here was a round, soft-looking guy.

I went up to Ryan and got in his face. "What's your problem, fat fuck? You think you're a *SEAL*?"

We all gave him shit. One of my officers—we'll call him LT—knew him from BUD/S and stuck up for him, but LT was a new guy himself, so that didn't carry too much weight. Being a new guy, we would have beat Ryan's ass anyway, but his weight made things a lot worse for him. We actively tried to make him quit.

But Ryan (whose last name was pronounced "jobe," rhyming with "ear lobe") wasn't a quitter. You couldn't compare his determination with anyone else's. That kid started working out like a maniac. He lost weight and got into better shape.

More importantly, anything we told him to do, he did. He was such a hard worker, so sincere, and so damn funny, that at some point we just went, *I love you. You are the man*. Because no matter how he looked, he truly *was* a SEAL. And a damn good one.

We tested him, believe me. We'd find the biggest man in the platoon and make him carry him. He did it. We'd have him take the hardest jobs in training; he did them without complaint. And he'd crack us up in the process. He had these great facial expressions. He could point his upper lip, screw his eyes around and then twist in a certain way, and you'd lose it.

Naturally, this ability led to a certain amount of fun. For us, at least.

One time we told him to go do the face to our chief.

"B-but . . ." he stammered.

"Do it," I told him. "Go get in his face. You're the new guy. Do it."

He did. Thinking Ryan was trying to be a jerk, the chief grabbed him by the throat and tossed him to the ground.

That only encouraged us. Ryan had to show the face a lot. Every time, he'd go and get his ass beat. Finally, we had him do it to one of our officers—a huge guy, definitely not someone to be messed with, even by another SEAL.

"Go do it to him," one of us said.

"Oh God, no," he protested.

"If you don't do it right now, we're going to choke you out," I warned.

"Can you please just choke me out right now?"

"Go do it," we all said.

He went and did it to the officer. He reacted about how you would expect. After a little while, Ryan tried to tap out.

"There's no tapping out," he snarled, continuing his pounding.

Ryan survived, but that was the last time we made him do the face.

EVERYBODY GOT HAZED WHEN THEY JOINED THE PLATOON. We were equal-opportunity ballbusters—officers got it just as bad as enlisted men.

At the time, new guys didn't receive their Tridents—and thus weren't really SEALs—until after they had passed a series of tests with the team. We had our own little ritual that involved a mock boxing match against their whole platoon. Each new guy had to get through three rounds—once you're knocked down, that's a round—before being formally pinned and welcomed to the brotherhood.

I was Ryan's safety officer, making sure he didn't get too busted up. He had a head guard and everyone wore boxing gloves, but the hazing can get kind of enthusiastic, and the safety officer is there to make sure it doesn't get out of hand.

Ryan wasn't satisfied with three rounds. He wanted more. I think he thought if he fought long enough, he'd beat them all.

Not that he lasted too much longer. I had warned him that I was his safety and whatever he did, he was not to hit me. In the confusion of his head being bounced off the platoon's gloves, he swung and hit me.

I did what I had to do.

MARC LEE

With our deployment rapidly approaching, our platoon was beefed up. Command brought a young SEAL named Marc Lee over from another unit to help round us out. He immediately fit in.

Marc was an athletic guy, in some ways exactly the sort of tough physical specimen you expect to be a SEAL. Before joining the Navy, he had played soccer well enough to be given a tryout with a professional team, and may very well have been a pro if a leg injury hadn't cut short his career.

But there was a lot more to Marc than just physical prowess. He'd studied for the ministry, and while he left because of what he saw as hypocrisy among the seminary students, he was still very religious. Later on during our deployment, he led a small group in prayer before every op. As you'd expect, he was very knowledgeable about the Bible and religion in general. He didn't push it on you, but if you needed or wanted to talk about faith or God, he was always willing.

Not that he was a saint, or even above the horseplay that is part of being a SEAL.

Soon after he joined us, we went on a training mission in Nevada. At the end of the day, a group of us piled into a four-door truck and headed back to the base to get to bed. Marc was in the back with me and a SEAL we'll call Bob. For some reason, Bob and I started talking about being choked out.

With new-guy enthusiasm—and maybe naiveté—Marc said, "I've never been choked out."

"'Scuse me?" I said, leaning over to get a good look at this virgin. Being choked out is a mandatory SEAL occupation.

Marc looked at me. I looked at him.

"Bring it on," he said.

As Bob leaned over, I dove and choked Marc out. My work completed, I leaned back.

"You mother," said Bob, straightening. "I wanted to do it."

"I thought you were leaning over to let me get him," I told him.

"Hell no. I was just handing my watch up front so it wouldn't get broken."

"Well, okay," I said. "He'll wake up, then you get him."

He did. I think half the platoon had a shot at him before the night was out. Marc took it well. Of course, as a new guy, he had no choice.

COMMAND

I LOVED OUR NEW CO. HE WAS OUTSTANDING, AGGRESSIVE, and stayed out of our hair. He not only knew each one of us by name and face, he knew our wives and girlfriends. He took it personally when he lost people, and yet was able to stay aggressive at the same time. He never held us back in training, and, in fact, approved extra training for snipers.

My command master chief, whom I'll call Primo, was another top-notch commander. He didn't give a flying fuck about promotions, about looking good, or covering his butt: he was all about successful missions and getting the job done. And he was a Texan—as you can tell, I'm a little partial—which meant he was a bad-ass.

His briefs always started the same way: "What are you sons of bitches doing?" he'd snarl. "Are you gonna get out there and kick some ass?"

Primo was all about getting into battle. He knew what SEALs are supposed to do, and he wanted us to do it.

He was also a good ol' boy off the battlefield.

You always have team guys getting in trouble during off-time and training. Bar fights are a big problem. I remember him pulling us aside when he came on.

"Listen, I know you're going to get into fights," he told us. "So here's what you do. You hit fast, you hit hard, and you run. If you don't get caught, I don't care. Because when you get caught is when I have to get involved."

I took that advice to heart, though it wasn't always possible to follow.

Maybe because he was from Texas, or maybe because he had the soul of a brawler himself, he took a liking to me and another Texan, whom we called Pepper. We became his golden boys; he'd cover our asses when we got in trouble. There were times when I may have told off an officer or two; Chief Primo took care of it. He might chew me out himself, but he always smoothed the way with head shed. On the other side of things, he knew he could count on Pepper and me to get a job done if it needed doing.

TATS

W HILE I WAS HOME, I HAD A PAIR OF NEW TATTOOS ADDED TO my arm. One was a Trident. Now that I felt like a real SEAL, I felt I had earned it. I had it put on the inside of my arm where not everyone would see, but I knew it was there. I didn't want it to be out there bragging.

On the front of my arm, I had a crusader cross inked in. I wanted everyone to know I was a Christian. I had it put in in red, for blood. I hated the damn savages I'd been fighting. I always will. They've taken so much from me.

E VEN THE TATTOOS BECAME A CAUSE FOR STRESS BETWEEN MY wife and myself. She didn't like tattoos in general, and the way I got these—staying out late one evening when she was expecting me home, surprising her with them—added to our friction.

Taya saw it as one more sign that I was changing, becoming somebody she didn't know.

I didn't think of it that way at all, though I admit I knew she wouldn't like it. But it's better to ask for forgiveness than permission.

Actually, I had wanted full sleeves, so, in my mind, it was a compromise.

GETTING READY TO GO

W HILE I WAS HOME, T AYA BECAME PREGNANT WITH OUR SEC- ond child. Again, that was a lot of strain for my wife.

My father told Taya that he was sure once I saw my son and

spent time with him, I wouldn't want to reenlist or go back to war.

But while we talked a lot about it, in the end I didn't feel there was much of a question about what to do. I was a SEAL. I was trained for war. I was made for it. My country was at war and it needed me.

And I missed it. I missed the excitement and the thrill. I loved killing bad guys.

"If you die, it will wreck all our lives," Taya told me. "It pisses me off that you would not only willingly risk your life, but risk ours, too."

For the moment, we agreed to disagree.

As it came up to the time to deploy, our relationship became more distant. Taya would push me away emotionally, as if she were putting on armor for the coming months. I may have done the same thing.

"It's not intentional," she told me, in one of the rare moments when we both could realize what was happening and actually talk about it.

We still loved each other. It may sound strange—we were close and not close, needing each other and yet needing distance between us. Needing to do other things. At least in my case.

I was anticipating leaving. I was excited about doing my job again.

GIVING BIRTH

A few days before we were scheduled to deploy, I went to the doctor to see about getting a cyst in my neck removed. Inside his examining room, he numbed the area around it with a local anesthesia, then they stuck a needle in my neck to suction the material out.

I think. I don't actually know, because as soon as the needle went in, I passed out with a seizure. When I came to, I was out flat on the examining table, my feet where my head should have been.

I had no other ill effects, not from the seizure or the procedure. No one really could figure out why I'd reacted the way I did. As far as anyone could tell, I was fine.

But there was a problem—a seizure is grounds for being medically discharged from the Navy. Luckily, there was a corpsman whom I'd served with in the room. He persuaded the doctor not to include the seizure in his report, or to write what happened in a way that wouldn't affect my deployment or my career. (I'm not sure which.) I never heard anything about it again.

BUT WHAT THE SEIZURE *did* DO WAS KEEP ME FROM GETTING to Taya. While I'd been passing out, she had been having a routine pregnancy checkup. It was about three weeks before our daughter was due and days before I was supposed to deploy. The checkup included an ultrasound, and when the technician looked away from the screen, my wife realized something was wrong.

"I have a feeling you're having this baby right away," was the most the technician would say before getting up and fetching the doctor.

The baby had her umbilical cord around her neck. She was also breached and the amount of amniotic fluid—liquid that nourishes and protects the developing infant—was low.

"We'll do a C-section," said the doc. "Don't worry. We'll get this baby out tomorrow. You'll be fine."

Taya had called me several times. By the time I came to, she was already at the hospital.

We spent a nervous night together. The next morning, the doctors performed a C-section. As they were working, they hit some kind of artery and splashed blood all over the place. I was deathly afraid for my wife. I felt real fear. Worse.

Maybe it was a touch of what she'd gone through every moment of my deployment. It was a terrible hopelessness and despair.

A hard thing to admit, let alone stomach.

Our daughter was fine. I took her and held her. I'd been as distant toward her as I had been toward our son before he was born; now, holding her, I started to feel real warmth and love.

Taya looked at me strangely when I tried to hand her the baby.

"Don't you want to hold her?" I asked.

"No," she said.

God, I thought, *she's rejecting our daughter. I have to leave and she's not even bonding.*

A few moments later, Taya reached out and took her.

Thank God.

Two days later, I deployed.

9

THE PUNISHERS

"I'M HERE TO GET THOSE MORTARS"

You would think an army planning a major offensive would have a way to get its warriors right to the battle area.

You would think wrong.

Because of the medical situation with the cyst and then my daughter's birth, I ended up leaving the States about a week behind the rest of my platoon. By the time I landed in Baghdad in April 2006, my platoon had been sent west to the area of Ramadi. No one in Baghdad seemed to know how to get me out there. It was up to me to get over to my boys.

A direct flight to Ramadi was impossible—things were too hot there. So I had to cobble together my own solution. I came across an Army Ranger who was also heading for Ramadi. We hooked up, pooling our creative resources as we looked for a ride at Baghdad International Airport.

At some point, I overheard an officer talking about problems the Army was having with some insurgent mortarmen at a base to the west. By coincidence, we heard about a flight heading to that same base; the Ranger and I headed over to try to get onto the helicopter.

A colonel stopped as we were about to board.

"Helicopter's full," he barked at the Ranger. "Why do you need to be on it?"

"Well, sir, we're the snipers coming to take care of your mortar problem," I told him, holding up my gun case.

"Oh yes!" the colonel yelled to the crew. "These boys need to be on the very next flight. Get them right on."

We hopped aboard, bumping two of his guys in the process.

BY THE TIME WE GOT TO THE BASE, THE MORTARS HAD BEEN taken care of. We still had a problem, though—there were no flights heading for Ramadi, and the prospects of a convoy were slimmer than the chance of seeing snow in Dallas in July.

But I had an idea. I led the Ranger to the base hospital, and found a corpsman. I've worked with a number as a SEAL, and in my experience, the Navy medics always know their way around problems.

I took a SEAL challenge coin out of my pocket and slipped it into my hand, exchanging it when we shook. (Challenge coins are special tokens that are created to honor members of a unit for bravery or other special achievements. A SEAL challenge coin is especially valued, both for its rarity and symbolism. Slipping it to someone in the Navy is like giving him a secret handshake.)

"Listen," I told the corpsman. "I need a serious favor. I'm a SEAL, a sniper. My unit is in Ramadi. I got to get there, and he's coming with me." I gestured to the Ranger.

"Okay," said the corpsman, his voice almost a whisper. "Come into my office."

We went into his office. He took out a rubber stamp, inked our hands, then wrote something next to the mark.

It was a triage code.

The corpsman medevac'd us *into* Ramadi. We were the first, and probably only, people to be medevac'd into a battle rather than out of it.

And I thought only SEALs could be *that* creative.

I have no idea why that worked, but it did. No one on the chopper we were hustled into questioned the direction of our flight, let alone the nature of our "wounds."

SHARK BASE

RAMADI WAS IN AL-ANBAR, THE SAME PROVINCE AS FALLUJAH, about thirty miles farther west. Many of the insurgents who'd been run out of Fallujah were said to have holed up there. There was plenty of evidence: attacks had ratcheted up ever since Fallujah had been pacified. By 2006, Ramadi was considered the most dangerous city in Iraq—a hell of a distinction.

My platoon had been sent to Camp Ramadi, a U.S. base along the Euphrates River outside the city. Our compound, named Shark Base, had been set up by an earlier task unit and was just outside the wire of Camp Ramadi.

When I finally arrived, my boys had been sent to work east of Ramadi. Arranging transportation through the city was impossible. I was pissed—I thought I'd gotten there too late to join in the action.

Looking for something to do until I could figure out how to get with the rest of the platoon, I asked my command if I could sit out on the guard towers. Insurgents had been testing the perimeters, sneaking as close as they dared and spraying the base with their AKs.

"Sure, go ahead," they told me.

I went out and took my sniper rifle. Almost as soon as I got into position, I saw two guys skirting around in the distance, looking for a spot to shoot from.

I waited until they popped up behind cover.

Bang.

I got the first one. His friend turned around and started to run.

Bang.

Got him, too.

SEVEN STORY

I WAS STILL WAITING FOR A CHANCE TO JOIN THE REST OF MY platoon when the Marine unit at the northern end of the city put in a request for snipers to help with an overwatch from a seven-story building near their outpost.

The head shed asked me to come up with a team. There were only two other snipers at the base. One was recovering from wounds and looped out on morphine; the other was a chief who appeared reluctant to go.

I asked for the guy who was on morphine; I got the chief.

We found two 60 gunners, including Ryan Job, to provide a little muscle, and with an officer headed out to help the Marines.

Seven Story was a tall, battered building about two hundred yards outside the Marine outpost. Made of tan-colored cement and located near what had been a major road before the war, it looked almost like a modern office building, or would have if it weren't for the missing windows and huge holes where it had been hit by rockets and shells. It was the tallest thing around and had a perfect vantage into the city.

We went out in early evening with several Marines and local *jundi*s for security. The *jundi*s were loyal Iraqi militia or soldiers who were being trained; there were a number of different groups, each with its own level of expertise and efficiency—or, most often, the opposite of both.

While there was still light, we got a few shots here and there, all on isolated insurgents. The area around the building was pretty rundown, a whitewashed wall with a fancy iron gate separating one sand-strewn empty lot from another.

Night fell, and suddenly we were in the middle of a flood of bad guys. They were on their way to assault the Marine outpost and we just happened to be along the route. There were a ton of them.

At first, they didn't realize we were there, and it was open season. Then, I saw three guys with RPGs taking aim at us from about a block away. I shot each of them in succession, saving us the hassle of ducking from their grenades.

The firefight quickly shifted our way. The Marines called us over the radio and told us to collapse back to them.

Their outpost was a few hundred treacherous yards away. While one of the 60 gunners, my officer, and I provided cover fire, the rest of our group went downstairs and moved over to the Marine base. Things got hot so fast that by the time they were clear we were surrounded. We stayed where we were.

RYAN REALIZED OUR PREDICAMENT AS SOON AS HE ARRIVED at the Marine outpost. He and the chief got into an argument over whether to provide cover for us. The chief claimed that their job was to stay with the Iraqi *jundi*s, who were already hunkered down inside the Marine camp. The chief ordered him to stay; Ryan told him what he could do with that order.

Ryan ran upstairs on the roof of the Marine building, where he joined the Marines trying to lay down support fire for us as we fought off the insurgents.

THE MARINES SENT A PATROL OVER TO PULL US OUT. AS I watched them coming from the post, I spotted an insurgent moving in behind them.

I fired once. The Marine patrol hit the dirt. So did the Iraqi, though he didn't get up.

"There's [an insurgent] sniper out there and he's good," their radio man called. "He nearly got us."

I got on my radio.

"That's me, dumbass. Look behind you."

They turned around and saw a savage with a rocket launcher lying dead on the ground.

"God, thank you," answered the Marine.

"Don't mention it."

The Iraqis did have snipers working that night. I got two of them—one who was up on the minaret of a mosque, and another on a nearby building. This was a fairly well-coordinated fight, one of the better-organized ones we would encounter in the area. It was unusual, because it took place at night; the bad guys generally didn't try and press their luck in the dark.

Finally, the sun came up and the gunfire slacked down. The Marines pulled out a bunch of armored vehicles to cover for us, and we ran back to their camp.

I went up to see their commander and brief him on what had happened. I had barely gotten a sentence out of my mouth when a burly Marine officer burst into the office.

"Who the hell was the sniper up there on Seven Story?" he barked.

I turned around and told him it was me, bracing myself to be chewed out for some unknown offense.

"I want to shake your hand, son," he said, pulling off his glove. "You saved my life."

He was the guy I'd called a dumbass on the radio earlier. I've never seen a more grateful Marine.

"THE LEGEND"

My boys returned from their adventures out east soon afterward. They greeted me with their usual warmth.

"Oh, we know the Legend's here," they said as soon as they saw me. "All of a sudden we hear there's two kills at Camp Ramadi. People are dying up north. We knew the Legend was here. You're the only motherfucker who's ever killed anyone out there."

I laughed.

The nickname "the Legend" had started back in Fallujah, around the time of the beach ball incident, or maybe when I got that really long shot. Before that, my nickname had been Tex.

Of course, it wasn't just "Legend." There was more than a little mocking that went with it—THE LEGEND. One of my guys—Dauber, I think it was, even turned it all around and called me THE MYTH, cutting me down to size.

It was all good-natured, in a way more of an honor than a full-uniform medal ceremony.

I really liked Dauber. Even though he was a new guy, he was a sniper, and a pretty good one. He could hold his own in a firefight—and trading insults. I had a real soft spot for him, and when it came time to haze him, I didn't hit him . . . much.

Even if the guys joked about it, Legend was one of the better nicknames you could get. Take Dauber. That's not his real name (at the moment, he's doing what we'll call "government work"). The nickname came from a character in the television series *Coach*. There, Dauber was the typical dumb-jock type. In real life, he's actually an intelligent guy, but that fact was of no consideration in his getting named.

But one of the best nicknames was Ryan Job's: Biggles.

It was a big, goofy name for a big, goofy guy. Dauber takes credit for it—the word, he claims, was a combination of "big" and "giggles" that had been invented for one of his relatives.

He mentioned it one day, applying it to Ryan. Someone else on the team used it, and within seconds, it had stuck.

Biggles.

Ryan hated it, naturally, which certainly helped it stick.

Along the way, someone later found a little purple hippo. Of course, it had to go to the guy who had the hippo face. And Ryan became Biggles the Desert Hippo.

Ryan being Ryan, he turned it all around. It wasn't a joke *on* him; it was *his* joke. Biggles the Desert Hippo, best 60 gunner on the planet.

He carried that hippo everywhere, even into battle. You just had to love the guy.

THE PUNISHERS

Our platoon had its own nickname, one that went beyond Cadillac.

We called ourselves the Punishers.

For those of you who are not familiar with the character, the Punisher debuted in a Marvel comic book series in the 1970s. He's a real bad-ass who rights wrongs, delivering vigilante justice. A movie by the same name had just come out; the Punisher wore a shirt with a stylized white skull.

Our comms guy suggested it before the deployment. We all thought what the Punisher did was cool: He righted wrongs. He killed bad guys. He made wrongdoers fear him.

That's what we were all about. So we adapted his symbol—a skull—and made it our own, with some modifications. We spray-painted it on our Hummers and body armor, and our helmets and all our guns. And we spray-painted it on every building or wall we could. We wanted people to know, *We're here and we want to fuck with you.*

It was our version of psyops.

You see us? We're the people kicking your ass. Fear us. Because we will kill you, motherfucker.

You are bad. We are badder. We are bad-ass.

Our sister platoon wanted to use the template we used to mark our gear, but we wouldn't let them. We told them *we* were the Punishers. They had to get their own symbol.

We went a bit light with our Hummers. They were named, mostly, for *G.I. Joe* characters, like Duke and Snake

Eyes. Just because war is hell doesn't mean you can't have a little fun.

WE HAD A GOOD TEAM THAT DEPLOYMENT, STARTING AT THE top. Decent officers, and a really excellent chief named Tony.

Tony had trained as a sniper. He was not only a bad-ass, he was an *old* bad-ass, at least for a SEAL—rumor has it he was forty that deployment.

SEALs usually do not make it to forty and stay out in the field. We're too beat-up. But Tony somehow managed it. He was a hardcore son of a bitch, and we would have followed him to hell and back.

I was the point man—snipers usually are—when we went on patrols. Tony was almost always right behind me. Generally, the chief will be toward the rear of the formation, covering everybody else's ass, but in this case our LT reasoned that having two snipers at the head of the platoon was more effective.

ONE NIGHT SOON AFTER THE ENTIRE PLATOON HAD GOTTEN back together, we traveled about seventeen kilometers east of Ramadi. The area was green and fertile—so much so that it looked to us like the Vietnamese jungle, compared to the desert we'd been operating in. We called it Viet Ram.

One night not long after the unit reunited, we were deposited at a patrol area and began walking toward a suspected insurgent stronghold on foot. Eventually, we came to a huge ditch with a bridge going across it. Most of the time, these bridges were booby-trapped, and in this case we had intel indicating this one definitely was. So I went up and stood there, shining my laser to look for a trip wire.

I played the light across the top of the bridge but saw nothing. I ducked a little lower and tried again. Still nothing. I looked everywhere I could think of, but found no contact wires, no IEDs, no booby-traps, nothing.

But since I'd been told the bridge was booby-trapped, I was sure there *had* to be something there.

I looked again. My EOD—the bomb disposal expert—was waiting behind me. All I had to do was find a trip wire or the bomb itself, and he'd have it disarmed in seconds.

But I couldn't find shit. Finally, I told Tony, "Let's go across."

Don't get the wrong image: I wasn't charging across that bridge. I had my rifle in one hand and the other parked protectively over my family jewels.

That wouldn't have saved my life if an IED exploded, but at least I'd be intact for the funeral.

The bridge was all of ten feet long, but it must have taken me an hour to get across that thing. When I finally reached the other side, I was soaking wet from sweat. I turned around to give the other guys the thumbs-up. But there was no one there. They'd all ducked behind some rocks and brush, waiting for me to blow up.

Even Tony, who, as point man, should have been right behind me.

"Motherfucker!" I yelled. "Where the hell did you go?"

"There's no reason for more than one of us to get blown up," he told me matter-of-factly as he came across.

TERPS

FALLUJAH HAD BEEN TAKEN IN AN ALL-OUT ASSAULT, MOVING through the city in a very organized fashion. While it had been successful, the attack had also caused a lot of damage, which had supposedly hurt support for the new Iraqi government.

You can argue whether that's true or not—I sure would—but the top American command didn't want the same thing to happen in Ramadi. So, while the Army worked on a plan for taking Ramadi with minimal destruction, we went to war in the area nearby.

We started with DAs. We had four interpreters—terps, as we called them—who helped us deal with the locals. At least one and usually two would go out with us.

One terp we all really liked was Moose. He was a bad-ass. He'd been working since the invasion in 2003. He was Jordanian, and he was the only one of the terps we gave a gun. We knew he would fight—he wanted to be an American so bad he would have died for it. Every time we got contacted, he would be out there shooting.

He wasn't a great shot, but he could keep the enemy's heads down. Most importantly, he knew when he could and couldn't shoot—not as easy a call as it might seem.

THERE WAS THIS LITTLE VILLAGE OUTSIDE SHARK BASE WE called Gay Tway. It was infested with insurgents. We would open the gates, walk out, and hit our target. There was one house we went to three or four times. After the first time, they didn't even bother putting the door back.

Why they kept going back to that house, I don't know. But we kept going back, too; we got to know the place pretty well.

It didn't take too long before we started getting a lot of contact in Gay Tway and the village of Viet Ram. An Army National Guard unit covered that area, and we started working with them.

TARGETS

AMONG OUR FIRST JOBS WAS TO HELP THE ARMY RECLAIM THE area around a hospital along the river in Viet Ram. The four-story concrete building had been started and then abandoned a few years before. The Army wanted to finish it for the Iraqis; decent medical care was a big need out there. But they couldn't get close to it to do any work, because as soon as they did, they came under fire. So we went to work.

Our platoon, sixteen guys, teamed up with about twenty soldiers to clear the nearby village of insurgents. Entering town early one morning, we split up and started taking houses.

I was at point, carrying my Mk-12, the first guy in each building. Once the house was secure, I'd go up to the roof, cover the guys on the ground, and look for insurgents, who we expected to attack once they knew we were there. The group leapfrogged forward, clearing the area as we went.

Unlike in the city, these houses weren't right next to each other, so the process took longer and was more spread-out. But soon enough, the terrorists realized where we were and what we were up to, and they put together a little attack from a mosque. Holed up behind its walls, they started raining AK fire at a squad of soldiers on the ground.

I was up on one of the roofs when the fight started. Within moments, we started firing everything we had at the bad guys: M-4s, M-60s, sniper rifles, 40-mm grenades, LAW rockets—everything we had. We lit that mosque up.

The momentum of the battle quickly shifted in our favor. The soldiers on the ground began maneuvering to assault the mosque, hoping to catch the insurgents before they could slide back into whatever sewer they'd emerged from. We shifted our fire higher, moving our aim above their heads to allow them to get in.

Somewhere in the middle of the fight, a piece of hot brass from another gun—probably an M-60 machine gun next to me—shot against my leg and landed in my boots next to my ankle. It burned like hell, but I couldn't do anything about it—there were too many bad guys popping up from behind the walls, trying to get my people.

I was wearing simple hiking boots rather than combat boots. That was my normal style—they were lighter and more comfortable, and ordinarily more than enough to protect my feet. Unfortunately, I hadn't bothered to lace them up very well before the battle, and there was a space between my pants and the boot where the brass happened to fall after it ejected.

What had the instructors told me in BUD/S about not being able to call "time out" in battle?

When things quieted down, I stood up and pulled out the casing. A good wedge of skin came out with it.

We secured the mosque, worked through the rest of the village, then called it a day.

DIFFERENT WAYS OF KILLING

WE WENT ON PATROLS WITH THE ARMY UNIT SEVERAL MORE times, trying to reduce resistance in the area. The idea was simple, if potentially risky: we'd make ourselves visible, trying to draw fire from the insurgents. Once they showed themselves, we could fire back and kill them. And usually we did.

Pushed from the village and the mosque, the insurgents retreated to the hospital. They loved hospital buildings, not only because they were big and usually well-made (and therefore protective), but because they knew we were reluctant to attack hospitals, even after they were taken over by terrorists.

It took a while, but the Army command finally decided to attack the building.

Good, we all told them when we heard the plan. Let's go do it.

We set up an overwatch in a house some two or three hundred yards from the hospital building, across a clear field. As soon as the insurgents saw us, they started letting us have it.

One of my guys shot off a Carl Gustav rocket at the top of the building where they were shooting from. The Gustav put a big ol' hole there. Bodies flew everywhere.

The rocket helped take some of the fight out of them, and as resistance weakened, the Army punched in and took the building. By the time they reached the grounds, there was almost no resistance. The few people we hadn't killed had run away.

It was always hard to tell how many insurgents were opposing us in a battle like that. A small handful could put up a pretty good fight. A dozen men fighting behind cover could hold up a unit advance for quite a while, depending on the circumstances. Once the insurgents were met with a lot of force, however, you could count on about half squirting out the back or wherever to get away.

We'd had the Carl Gustav with us earlier, but as far as I know, this was the first time we'd actually killed anyone with it, and it may have been the first time any SEAL unit did so. It was certainly the first time we used it against a building. Once word spread, of course, everyone wanted to use them.

Technically, the Carl Gustav was developed to combat armor, but as we found out, it was pretty potent against buildings. In fact, it was perfect in Ramadi—it just blew right through reinforced concrete and took out whoever was inside. The overpressure from the explosion wiped out the interior.

We had different rounds for the gun. (Remember, it's actually considered a recoilless rifle rather than a rocket launcher.) A lot of times, the insurgents would hide behind embankments and other barriers, well protected. In that case, you could set an air-burst round to explode over them. The air burst was a lot worse than anything that detonated on the ground.

The Gustav is relatively easy to use. You have to wear double ear-protection and be careful where you stood when it's fired, but the results are awesome. Everyone in the platoon wanted to use it after a while—I swear there were fights over who was going to launch it.

WHEN YOU'RE IN A PROFESSION WHERE YOUR JOB IS TO KILL people, you start getting creative about doing it.

You think about getting the most firepower you possibly can into the battle. And you start trying to think of new and inventive ways to eliminate your enemy.

We had so many targets out in Viet Ram we started asking ourselves, what weapons have we *not* used to kill them?

No pistol kill yet? You have to get at least one.

We'd use different weapons for the experience, to learn the weapon's capabilities in combat. But at times it was a game—when you're in a firefight every day, you start looking for a little variety. No matter what, there were plenty of insurgents, and plenty of firefights.

THE GUSTAV TURNED OUT TO BE ONE OF OUR MOST EFFECTIVE weapons when we came up against insurgents shooting from buildings. We had LAW rockets, which were lighter and easier to carry. But too many of them turned out to be duds. And once you fired a LAW, you were done; it wasn't a reloadable weapon. The Carl Gustav was always a big hit—pun intended.

Another weapon we used quite a bit was the 40-mm grenade launcher. The launcher comes in two varieties, one that attaches under your rifle and another that is a stand-alone weapon. We had both.

Our standard grenade was a "frag"—a grenade that exploded and sprayed an area with shrapnel or fragments. This is a traditional antipersonnel weapon, tried and true.

While we were on this deployment, we received a new type of projectile using a thermobaric explosive. Those had a lot more "boom"—a single grenade launched at an enemy sniper in a small structure could bring the whole building down because of the over-pressure created by the explosion. Most times, of course, we were firing at a larger building, but the destructive power was still intense. You'd have a violent explosion, a fire, and then no more enemy. Gotta love it.

You shoot grenades with what we call Kentucky windage—estimating the distance, adjusting the elevation of the launcher, and firing. We liked the M-79—the standalone version that was first used during the Vietnam War—because it had sights, making it a bit easier to aim and hit what you wanted. But one way or another, you quickly got the hang of things, because you were using the weapon so much.

We had contact every time we went out.

We loved it.

Taya:

I had a hard time with the kids after Chris deployed. My mom came and helped me, but it was just a difficult time.

I guess I wasn't ready to have another baby. I was mad at Chris, scared for him, and nervous about raising a baby and a toddler all by myself. My son was only a year and a half old; he was getting into everything, and the newborn happened to be really clingy.

I remember just sitting on the couch and crying in my bathrobe for days. I would be nursing her and trying to feed him. I'd sit there and cry.

The C-section didn't heal well. I had women tell me, "After my C-section, I was scrubbing the floors a week later and I was all good." Well, six weeks after mine I was still in pain, still hurting and not healing really well at all. I hated that I wasn't healing like those women. (I found out later it's usually the second C-section that women bounce back from. No one told me that part.)

I felt weak. I was mad at myself that I wasn't tougher. It just sucked.

THE DISTANCES EAST OF RAMADI MADE THE .300 WIN MAG my rifle of choice, and I started taking it regularly on patrols. After

THE PUNISHERS

the Army took the hospital, they continued taking fire and getting attacked. It didn't take too long before they started getting mortar fire as well. So we bumped out, fighting the insurgents who were shooting at them, and looking for the mortar crews.

One day, we set up in a two-story building a short distance from the hospital. The Army tried using special gear to figure out where the mortars were being fired from, and we chose the house because it was near the area they identified. But, for some reason, that day the insurgents decided to lie low.

Maybe they were getting tired of dying.

I decided to see if we could flush them out. I always carried an American flag inside my body armor. I took it out and strung some 550 cord (general-purpose nylon rope sometimes called *parachute cord*) through the grommets. I tied the line to the lip on the roof, then threw it over the side so it draped down the side of the building.

Within minutes, half a dozen insurgents stepped out with automatic machine guns and started shooting at my flag.

We returned fire. Half of the enemy fell; the other half turned and ran.

I still have the flag. They shot out two stars. Fair trade for their lives, by my accounting.

AS WE BUMPED OUT, THE INSURGENTS WOULD MOVE FARTHER away and try and put more cover between us and them. Occasionally, we'd have to call in air support to get them from behind walls or berms in the distance.

Because of the fear of collateral damage, command and the pilots were reluctant to use bombs. Instead, the jets would make strafing runs. We'd also get attack helicopters, Marine Cobras and Hueys, which would use machine guns and rockets.

One day, while we were on an overwatch, my chief and I spotted a man putting a mortar in the trunk of a car about eight hundred yards from us. I shot him; another man came out of the building where he'd been and my chief shot him. We called in an airstrike; an F/A-18 put a missile on the car. There were massive secondaries—they'd loaded the car with explosives before we saw them.

AMONG THE SLEEPERS

A NIGHT OR TWO LATER, I FOUND MYSELF WALKING IN THE dark through a nearby village, stepping over bodies—not of dead people, but sleeping Iraqis. In the warm desert, Iraqi families would often sleep outside.

I was on my way to take up a position so we could overwatch a raid on the marketplace where one of the insurgents had a shop. Our intelligence indicated this was where the weapons in the car we'd blown up had come from.

Four other guys and I had been dropped off about six kilometers away by the rest of the team, which was planning to mount a raid in the morning. Our assignment was to get into place ahead of them, scout and watch the area, then protect them as they arrived.

It wasn't as dangerous as you might think to walk through insurgent-held areas at night. They were almost always asleep. The Iraqis would see our convoys arrive during the day, and then leave before it got dark. So the bad guys would figure we were all back at the base. There'd be no guards posted, no lookouts, no pickets watching the area.

Of course, you had to watch where you stepped—one of my platoon members nearly stepped on a sleeping Iraqi as we walked to our target area in the dark. Fortunately, he caught himself at the last second, and we were able to walk on without waking anyone. The tooth fairy had nothing on us.

We found the marketplace and set up to watch it. It was a small row of tiny, one-story shacks used as stores. There were no windows—you open a door and sell your wares right out of the hut.

Not too long after we got to our hide, we received a radio call telling us that another unit was out somewhere in the area.

A few minutes later, I spotted a suspicious group of people.

"Hey," I said over the radio. "I see four guys carrying AKs and web gear, all mujed out. Are these our boys?"

Web gear is webbing or vest and strap gears used to hold combat equipment. The men I saw looked like mujahedeen—by "all mujed out" I meant they were dressed the way insurgents often did in the countryside, wearing the long man-jammies and scarves. (In the city, they often wore Western-style clothes—tracksuits and warm-ups were big.)

The four men were coming from the river, which would be where I expected the guys to be coming from.

"Hold on, we'll find out," said the com guy on the other end of the radio.

I watched them. I wasn't going to shoot them—no way I was going to take a chance and kill an American.

The unit took its time responding to our TOC, which, in turn, had to get a hold of my platoon guys. I watched as the men walked on.

"Not ours," came the call back finally. "They cancelled."

"Great. Well I just let four guys go in your direction."

(I'm sure if they had been out there, I never would have seen them. *Ninjas.*)

Everybody was pissed. My guys back at the Hummers sat ready, scanning the desert, waiting for the muj to appear. I went back to my own scan, watching the area they were supposed to hit.

A few minutes later, what did I see but the four insurgents who'd passed me earlier.

I got one; one of the other snipers got another before they could take cover.

Then another six or seven insurgents appeared behind them.

Now we were in the middle of a firefight. We started launching grenades. The rest of the platoon heard the gunfire and came hard. But fighters who'd stumbled past us melted away.

The element of surprise lost, the platoon went ahead with the raid on the marketplace in the dark. They found some ammo and AKs, but nothing important in terms of a real weapons cache.

We never found out what the insurgents who slipped past were up to. It was just another mystery of war.

THE ELITE ELITE

I think all SEALs highly respect our brothers in the elite anti-terror unit you've read so much about at home. They are an elite group within an elite group.

We didn't interact with them in Iraq much. The only other time I had much to do with them came a few weeks later, after we got into Ramadi proper. They had heard we were out there slaying a huge number of savages, and so they sent one of their snipers over to see what we were doing. I guess they wanted to find out what we were doing that worked.

Looking back, I regret not having tried to join. At the time, they weren't using snipers as heavily as the other teams were. The assaulters were doing the majority of the work, and I didn't want to be an assaulter. I was loving what I was doing. I wanted to be a sniper. I was getting to use my rifle, and killing enemies. Why give it up, move to the East Coast, and become a new guy all over again? And that's not even considering the BUD/S-like school you have to get through to prove you belong.

I would have had to spend a number of years as an assaulter before working my way up to be a sniper again. Why do that when I was already sniping, and loving it?

But now that I've heard about their ops and what they accomplished, I think I should have gone for it.

The guys have a reputation for being arrogant and more than a little full of themselves. That's plain wrong. I had the opportunity to meet a few after the war when they came out to a training facility I run. They were extremely down-to-earth, very humble about their achievements. I absolutely wished I was going back out with them.

CIVILIANS AND SAVAGES

THE OFFENSIVE IN RAMADI HAD YET TO START, OFFICIALLY, but we were getting plenty of action.

One day, intel came in concerning insurgents planting IEDs along a certain highway. We went out there and put it under surveillance. We'd also hit the houses and watch for ambushes on convoys and American bases.

It's true that it can be difficult to sort out civilians from insurgents in certain situations, but here the bad guys made it easy for us. UAVs would watch a road, for example, and when they saw someone planting a bomb, they could not only pinpoint the booby-trap but follow the insurgent back to his house. That gave us excellent intel on where the bad guys were.

Terrorists going to attack Americans would give themselves away by moving tactically against approaching convoys or when coming close to a base. They'd sneak around with their AKs ready—it was very easy to spot them.

They also learned to spot us. If we took over a house in a small hamlet, we would keep the family inside for safety. The people who lived nearby would know that if the family wasn't outside by nine o'clock in the morning, there were Americans inside. That was an open invitation for any insurgent in the area to come and try to kill us.

It became so predictable, it seemed to happen according to a time schedule. Around about nine in the morning you'd have a firefight; things would slack off around midday. Then, around three or four in the afternoon, you'd have another. If the stakes weren't life and death, it would have been funny.

And at the time, it *was* funny, in a perverse kind of way.

You didn't know which direction they'd attack from, but the tactics were almost always the same. The insurgents would start out with automatic fire, pop off a bit here, pop off there. Then you'd get the RPGs, a flurry of fire; finally, they'd scatter and try to get away.

ONE DAY, WE TOOK OUT A GROUP OF INSURGENTS A SHORT DIStance from the hospital. We didn't realize it at the time, but Army intel passed the word later on that the insurgent command had made a cell phone call to someone, asking for more mortarmen, because the team that had been hitting the hospital had just been killed.

Their replacements never showed up.

Shame. We would have killed them, too.

THE PUNISHERS

❦

EVERYONE KNOWS BY NOW ABOUT PREDATORS, THE UAVs that supplied a lot of intelligence to American forces during the war. But what many don't know is that we had our own backpack UAVs—small, man-launched aircraft about the size of an RC aircraft kids of all ages play with in the States.

They fit in a backpack. I never got to operate one, but they did seem kind of cool. The trickiest part—at least from what I could see—was the launch. You had to throw it pretty hard to get it airborne. The operator would rev the engine, then fling it into the air; it took a certain amount of skill.

Because they flew low and had relatively loud little engines, the backpack UAVs could be heard on the ground. They had a distinctive whine, and the Iraqis soon learned that the noise meant we were watching. They became cautious as soon as they heard it—which defeated the purpose.

THINGS GOT SO HEAVY AT SOME POINTS THAT WE HAD TO TAKE up two different radio bands, one to communicate with our TOC and one to use among the platoon. There was so much radio traffic back and forth that comms from the TOC would overrun us during contact.

When we first started going out, our CO told our top watch to wake him every time we got into a TIC—a military acronym that stands for "troops in contact," or combat. Then we were getting in so much combat that he revised the order—we were only to notify him if we'd been in a TIC for an hour.

Then it was, only notify me if someone gets injured.

Shark Base was a haven during this time, a little oasis of rest and recreation. Not that it was very fancy. It had a stone floor, and the windows were blocked by sandbags. At first, our cots were practically touching, and the only homey touch was the banged-up footlockers. But we didn't need much. We'd go out for three days, come back for a day. I'd sleep, then maybe play video games for the rest of the day, talk on the phone to back home, use the computer. Then it was time to gear up and go back out.

You had to be careful when you were talking on the phone. Operational security—OpSec, to use yet another military term—was critical. You couldn't say anything to anyone that might give away what we were doing, or what we planned to do, or even specifically what we had done.

All of our conversations from the base were recorded. There was software that listened for key words; if enough came up, they'd pull the conversation, and you could very well get in trouble. At one point, somebody ran their mouth about an operation, and we all got cut off for a week. He was pretty humiliated, and of course we reamed him out. He felt appropriately remorseful.

Sometimes, the bad guys made it easy for us.

One day we went out and set up in a village near the main road. It was a good spot; we were able to get a few insurgents as they tried passing through the area on their way to attack the hospital.

All of a sudden, a bongo truck—a small work vehicle with a cab and a bed in the back where a business might carry equipment—careened from the road toward our house. Rather than equipment, the truck was carrying four gunmen in the back, who started shooting at us as the truck drove across the fortunately wide yard.

I shot the driver. The vehicle drifted to a halt. The passenger in the front hopped out and ran to the driver's side. One of my buddies shot him before they could get going. We lit up the rest of the insurgents, killing them all.

A short while later, I spotted a dump truck heading down the main road. I didn't think all that much about it, until it turned into the driveway of the house and started coming straight at us.

We'd already interviewed the owners of the house, and knew no one there drove a dump truck. And it was pretty obvious from his speed that he wasn't there to pick up some dirt.

Tony shot the driver in the head. The vehicle veered off and crashed into another building nearby. A helo came in a short while later and blew up the truck. A Hellfire missile whooshed in, and the dump truck erupted: it had been filled with explosives.

FINALLY, A PLAN

BY EARLY JUNE, THE ARMY HAD COME UP WITH A PLAN TO take Ramadi back from the insurgents. In Fallujah, the Marines had worked systematically through the city, chasing and then pushing the insurgents out. Here, the insurgents were going to come to us.

The city itself was wedged between waterways and swampland. There was limited access by road. The Euphrates and the Habbaniyah canal bounded the city on the north and west; there was one bridge on either side near the northwestern tip. To the south and east, a lake, swamps, and a seasonal drainage canal helped form a natural barrier to the countryside.

The U.S. forces would come in from the perimeters of the city, the Marines from up north, and the Army on the other three sides. We would establish strongholds in various parts of the city, demonstrating that we were in control—and essentially daring the enemy to attack. When they did attack, we would fight back with everything we had. We'd set up more and more footholds, gradually extending control over the entire city.

The place was a mess. There was no functioning government, and it was beyond lawless. Foreigners entering the city were instant targets for killing or kidnapping, even if they were in armored convoys. But the place was a worse hell for ordinary Iraqis. Reports have estimated that there were more than twenty insurgent attacks against Iraqis every day. The easiest way to be killed in the city was to join the police force. Meanwhile, corruption was rife.

The Army analyzed the terrorist groups in the city and decided there were three different categories: hard-core Islamist fanatics, associated with al-Qaeda and similar groups; locals who were a little less fanatic though they still wanted to kill Americans; and opportunistic criminal gangs who were basically trying to make a living off the chaos.

The first group had to be eliminated because they would never give up; they would be our main focus in the coming campaign. The other two groups, though, might be persuaded to either leave, quit killing people, or work with the local tribal leadership. So, part of the Army plan would be to work with the tribal leadership to bring peace to the area. By all accounts, they had grown tired of the insurgents and the chaos they had brought, and wanted them gone.

The situation and plan were a lot more complicated than I can sum up. But to us on the ground, all of this was irrelevant. We didn't give a damn about the nuances. What we saw, what we knew, was that many people wanted to kill us. And we fought back.

THE JUNDIS

THERE WAS ONE WAY THE OVERALL PLAN DID AFFECT US, AND not for the better.

The Ramadi offensive wasn't supposed to be just about American troops. On the contrary, the new Iraqi army was supposed to be front and center in the effort to retake the city and make it safe.

The Iraqis were there. Front, no. Center—as a matter of fact, yes. But not quite in the way you're thinking.

BEFORE THE ASSAULT BEGAN, WE WERE ORDERED TO HELP PUT an "Iraqi face on the war"—the term command and the media used for pretending that the Iraqis were actually taking the lead in making their country safe. We trained Iraqi units, and when feasible (though not necessarily desirable) took them with us on operations. We worked with three different groups; we called them all *jundi*s, Arabic for soldiers, although, technically, some were police. No matter which force they were with, they were pathetic.

We had used a small group of scouts during our operations east of the city. When we went into Ramadi, we used SMPs—they were a type of special police. And then we had a third group of Iraqi soldiers that we used in villages outside of the city. During most operations, we would put them in the middle of our columns—Americans at the front, the Iraqis in the center, Americans at the rear. If we were inside a house, they would sit on the first floor, doing security and talking with the family, if there was one there.

As fighters went, they sucked. The brightest Iraqis, it seemed, were usually insurgents, fighting against us. I guess most of our *jundi*s had their hearts in the right place. But as far as proficient military fighting went . . .

Let's just say they were incompetent, if not outright dangerous.

One time a fellow SEAL named Brad and I were fixing to go into a house. We were standing outside the front door, with one of our *jundi*s directly behind us. Somehow the *jundi*'s gun got jammed. Idiotically, he flicked off the safety and hit the trigger, causing a burst of rounds to blow right next to me.

I thought they'd come from the house. So did Brad. We started returning fire, dumping bullets through the door.

Then I heard all this shouting behind me. Someone was dragging an Iraqi whose gun had gone off—yes, the gunfire had come from us, not anyone inside the house. I'm sure the *jundi* was apologizing, but I wasn't in the mood to listen, then or later.

Brad stopped firing and the SEAL who'd come up to get the door leaned back. I was still sorting out what the hell had happened when the door to the house popped open.

An elderly man appeared, hands trembling.

"Come in, come in," he said. "There's nothing here, nothing here."

I doubt he realized how close it came to that being true.

BESIDES BEING PARTICULARLY INEPT, A LOT OF *jundi*s WERE just lazy. You'd tell them to do something and they'd reply, *"Inshallah."*

Some people translate that as "God willing." What it really means is "ain't gonna happen."

Most of the *jundi*s wanted to be in the army to get a steady paycheck, but they didn't want to fight, let alone die, for their country. For their tribe, maybe. The tribe, their extended family—that was where their true loyalty lay. And for most of them, what was going on in Ramadi had nothing to do with that.

I realize that a lot of the problem has to do with the screwed-up culture in Iraq. These people had been under a dictatorship for all their lives. Iraq as a country meant nothing to them, or at least nothing good. Most were happy to be rid of Saddam Hussein, very happy to be free people, but they didn't understand what that really meant—the other things that come with being free.

The government wasn't going to be running their lives anymore, but it also wasn't going to be giving them food or anything else. It was a shock. And they were so backward in terms of education and technology that for Americans it often felt like being in the Stone Age.

You can feel sorry for them, but at the same time you don't want these guys trying to run your war for you.

And giving them the tools they needed to progress is *not* what my job was all about. My job was killing, not teaching.

We went to great lengths to make them look good.

At one point during the campaign, a local official's son was kidnapped. We got intel that he was being held at a house next to a local college. We went in at night, crashing through the gates and taking down a large building to use for the overwatch. While I watched from the roof of the building, some of my boys took down the house, freeing the hostage without any resistance.

Well, this was a big deal locally. So when it was photo op time, we called in our *jundi*s. They got credit for the rescue, and we drifted into the background.

Silent professionals.

That sort of thing happened all across the theater. I'm sure there were plenty of stories back in the States about how much good the

Iraqis were doing, and how we were training them. Those stories will probably fill the history books.

They're bullshit. The reality was quite a bit different.

I think the whole idea of putting an Iraqi face on the war was garbage. If you want to win a war, you go in and win it. *Then* you can train people. Doing it in the middle of a battle is stupid. It was a miracle it didn't fuck things up any worse than it did.

COP IRON

THE THIN DUST FROM THE DIRT ROADS MIXED WITH THE stench of the river and city as we came up into the village. It was pitch-black, somewhere between night and morning. Our target was a two-story building in the center of a small village at the south side of Ramadi, separated from the main part of the city by a set of railroad tracks.

We moved into the house quickly. The people who lived there were shocked, obviously, and clearly wary. Yet they didn't seem overly antagonistic, despite the hour. While our terps and *jundi*s dealt with them, I went up to the roof and set up.

It was June 17, the start of the action in Ramadi. We had just taken the core of what would become COP Iron, the first stepping stone of our move into Ramadi. (COP stands for Command Observation Post.)

I eyed the village carefully. We'd been briefed to expect a hell of a fight, and everything we'd been through over the past few weeks in the east reinforced that. I knew Ramadi was going to be a hell of a lot worse than the countryside. I was tense, but ready.

With the house and nearby area secured, we called the Army in. Hearing the tanks coming in the distance, I scanned even more carefully through the scope. The bad guys could hear it, too. They'd be here any second.

The Army arrived with what looked like a million tanks. They took over the nearby houses, and then began building walls to form a compound around them.

No insurgents came. Taking the house, taking the village—it was a nonevent.

Looking around, I realized the area we had taken was both literally and figuratively on the other side of the tracks from the main city. Our area was where the poorer people lived, quite a statement for Iraq, which wasn't exactly the Gold Coast. The owners and inhabitants of the hovels around us barely scratched out a living. They couldn't care less about the insurgency. They couldn't care even less about us.

Once the Army got settled, we bumped out about two hundred yards to protect the crews as they worked. We were still expecting a hell of a fight. But there wasn't much action at all. The only interesting moment came in the morning, when a mentally handicapped kid was caught wandering around writing in a notebook. He looked like a spy, but we quickly realized he wasn't right in the head and let him and his gibberish notes go.

We were all surprised by the calm. By noon, we were sitting there twiddling our thumbs. I won't say we were disappointed but . . . it felt like a letdown after what we had been told.

This was the most dangerous city in Iraq?

10

THE DEVIL OF RAMADI

GOING IN

A FEW NIGHTS LATER, I CLIMBED INTO A SHALLOW MARINE Corps riverboat known as a SURC ("small unit riverine craft"), ducking down onto the deck behind the armored gunwale. The Marines manning 60s near the bow kept watch as the boat and a second one with the rest of our group slipped upriver, heading quietly toward our insertion point.

Insurgent spies hid near the bridges and in various spots in the city. Had we been on land, they would have tracked our progress. But on the water, we weren't an immediate threat, and they didn't pay much attention.

We were traveling heavy. Our next stop was near the center of the city, deep in enemy territory.

Our boats eased into shore, running right up onto the bank of the canal. I rose and walked across the little bow doors, nearly losing my balance as I stepped off onto land. I trotted up the dry land, then stopped and waited for the rest of the platoon to rally around me. We'd taken eight Iraqis with us in the boats; counting our terps, we were just over two dozen strong.

The Marines slid back into the water and were gone.

Taking point, I started moving up the street toward our target. Small houses loomed ahead; there were alleys and wider roads, a maze of buildings, and the shadows of larger structures.

I hadn't gotten very far when the laser on my rifle crapped out. The battery had died. I halted our advance.

"What the hell's going on?" asked my lieutenant, coming up quickly.

"I need to change out my battery real quick," I explained. Without the laser, I would be aiming blind—little better than not aiming at all.

"No, get us out of here."

"All right."

So I started walking again, taking us up to a nearby intersection. A figure appeared in the darkness ahead, along the edge of a shallow drainage canal. I caught the shadow of his weapon, stared for a moment as I made out the details—AK-47, extra mag taped to one in the rifle.

Muj.

The enemy. His back was turned and he was watching the street rather than the water, but he was well-armed and ready for a fight.

Without the laser, I would have been shooting blind. I motioned to my lieutenant. He came up quick, right behind me, and—*boom*.

He took down the insurgent. He also damn near put a hole in my eardrum, blasting a few inches from my head.

There was no time to bitch. I ran forward as the Iraqi fell, unsure whether he was dead or if there were others nearby. The entire platoon followed, spreading out and "busting" the corners.

The guy was dead. I grabbed his AK. We ran up the street to the house we were going to take, passing some smaller houses on the way. We were a few hundred yards from the river, just off two main roads that would control that corner of the city.

Like many Iraqi houses, our target had a wall around it approximately six feet tall. The gate was locked, so I slung my M-4 on my shoulder, took out my pistol, and hauled up onto the wall, climbing up with one hand free.

When I got to the top, I saw there were people sleeping in the courtyard. I dropped down inside their compound, holding my gun on them, expecting one of my platoon mates to come over after me to open the gate.

I waited.

And waited. And waited.

"Come on," I hissed. "Get over here."

Nothing.

"*Come on!*"

Some of the Iraqis started to stir.

I eased toward the gate, knowing I was all alone. Here I was, holding a pistol on a dozen insurgents for all I knew, and separated from the rest of my boys by a thick wall and locked gate.

I found the gate and managed to jimmy it open. The platoon and our Iraqi *jundi*s ran in, surrounding the people who'd been sleeping in the courtyard. (There'd been a mix-up outside, and for some reason they hadn't realized I was in there alone.)

The people sleeping in the courtyard turned out to be just a regular extended family. Some of my guys got them situated without firing any shots, rounding them up and moving them to a safe area. Meanwhile, the rest of us ran in to the buildings, clearing each room as quickly as we could. There was a main building, and then a smaller cottage nearby. While my boys checked for weapons and bombs, anything suspicious, I raced to the rooftop.

One of the reasons we'd selected the building was its height—the main structure was three stories tall, and so I had a decent view of the surrounding area.

Nothing stirred. So far, so good.

"Building secure," the com guy radioed to the Army. "Come on in."

We had just taken the house that would become COP Falcon, and, once more, done so without a fight.

PETTY OFFICER/PLANNER

OUR HEAD SHED HAD HELPED PLAN THE COP FALCON OPERAtion, working directly with the Army commanders. Once they were done, they came to the platoon leadership and asked for our input. I got involved in the tactical planning process more deeply than I ever had before.

I had mixed feelings. On the one hand, I had experience and knowledge to add something useful. On the other hand, it got me doing the kind of work I don't like to do. It seemed a little "admin" or bureaucratic—coat-and-tie stuff, to use a civilian workplace metaphor.

AS AN E6, I WAS ONE OF THE MORE SENIOR GUYS IN THE PLAtoon. Usually you have a chief petty officer (E7), who's the senior enlisted guy, and an LPO, the lead petty officer. Generally the LPO is an E6, and the only one in the platoon. In our platoon, we had two. I was the junior E6, which was great—Jay, the other E6, was LPO, and so I missed a lot of the admin duties that go with that post. On the other hand, I had the benefits of the rank. For me, it was kind of like the story of Goldilocks and the Three Bears—I was too senior to do the bullshit jobs and too junior to do the political jobs. I was just right.

I hated sitting down at a computer and mapping everything out, let alone making a slideshow presentation out of it. I would have much rather just said, "Hey, follow me; I'll show what we're going to do on the fly." But writing it all down was important: if I went down, someone else would have to be able to step in and know what was going on.

I did get stuck with one admin job that had nothing to do with mission planning: evaluating the E5s. I truly hated it. (Jay arranged some sort of trip and left me with that—I'm sure because he didn't want to do it, either.) The bright side was that I realized how good our people were. There were absolutely no turds in that platoon—it was a real outstanding group.

Aside from my rank and experience, the head shed wanted me involved in planning, because snipers were taking a more aggressive role in battle. We had become, in military terms, a force multiplier, able to do a lot more than you might think based on our sheer numbers alone.

Most planning decisions involved details like the best houses to take for overwatch, the route to take in, how we'd be dropped off, what we would do after the initial houses were taken, etc. Some of the decisions could be very subtle. How you get to a sniper hide, for example. The preference would be to get there as stealthily as possible. That might suggest walking in, as we had in some of the villages. But you don't want to walk through narrow alleys where there's a lot of trash—too much noise, too many chances for an IED or an ambush.

There's a misperception among the general public that SpecOp troops always parachute or fast-rope into a trouble zone. While we certainly do both where appropriate, we didn't fly into any of the areas in Ramadi. Helicopters do have certain advantages, speed and the ability to travel relatively long distances being one of them. But they're also loud and attract attention in an urban environment. And they're relatively easy targets to shoot down.

In this case, coming in by water made a great deal of sense, because of the way Ramadi is laid out and where the target was located. It allowed us to get to a spot near the target area stealthily, comparatively quickly, and with less chance of contact than the overland routes. But that decision led to an unexpected problem—we had no boats.

ORDINARILY, SEALs WORK WITH SPECIAL BOAT TEAMS, known at the time and in the past as Special Boat Units, or SBUs. Same mission, different name. They drive the fast boats that insert SEALs and then retrieve them; we were rescued by one when we were "lost" on the California coast during training.

There was a bit of friction between SEALs and SBUs back home in the bars, where you'd occasionally hear some SBU members claiming to be SEALs. Team guys would think, and sometimes say, that's like a taxi driver claiming to be a movie star because he drove someone to the studio.

Whatever. There are some damn good guys out there. The last thing we need is to be picking fights with the people who are supporting us.

But that's a point that works both ways. Our problem in Ramadi came from the fact the unit that was supposed to be working with us refused to help.

They told us they were too important to be working with us. In fact, they claimed to be standing by for a unit with a higher priority, just in case they were needed. Which they weren't.

Hey, sorry. I'm pretty sure their job was to help whoever needed it, but whatever. We hunted around and found a Marine unit that was equipped with SURC boats—small, shallow-draft vessels that could get right up to the shore. They were armored and equipped with machine guns fore and aft.

The guys driving them were bad-ass. They did everything an SBU was supposed to do. Except that they did it for us.

They knew their mission. They didn't pretend to be someone else. They just wanted to get us there, the safest way possible. And when our mission was done, they came for us—even if it was a hot extract. These Marines would come in a heartbeat.

COP FALCON

THE ARMY ROLLED IN WITH TANKS, ARMORED VEHICLES, AND trucks. Soldiers humped sandbags and reinforced weak spots in the house. The house we were on was at the corner of a T-intersection of two major roads, one of which we called Sunset. The Army wanted the spot because of its strategic location; it was a choke point and a pretty clear presence inside the city.

Those factors also made it a prime target.

The tanks drew attention right away. A couple of insurgents began moving toward the house as they arrived. The bad guys were armed with AKs, maybe foolishly thinking they could scare the armor off. I waited until they were two hundred yards from the tanks before picking them off. They were easy shots, nailed before they could coordinate an organized attack.

A FEW HOURS PASSED. I KEPT FINDING SHOTS—THE INSURgents were probing the area, one or two at a time, trying to sneak in behind us.

It was never hot and heavy, but there was a steady stream of opportunity. Pop shots, I called them later.

The Army commander estimated we got two dozen insurgents in the first twelve hours of the fight. I don't know how accurate that is, but I did take down a few myself that first day, each with one shot. It wasn't particularly great shooting—they were all around four hundred yards and less. The .300 Win Mag is a hard-hitter at that range.

While it was still dark, the Army now had enough defenses at Falcon to hold their own if they were attacked. I went down off the roof and with my boys moved out again, running toward a rundown apartment building a few hundred yards away. The building, one of the tallest around, had a good vantage not only on Falcon but on the rest of the area. We called it Four Story; it would end up being a home away from home for much of the battle that followed.

We got in without trouble. It was empty.

WE DIDN'T SEE MUCH FOR THE REST OF THE NIGHT. BUT WHEN the sun came up, so did the bad guys.

They targeted COP Falcon, but ineptly. They'd walk, drive, ride mopeds, trying to get close enough to launch an attack. It was always obvious what they were doing: you'd see a couple of guys on a moped. The first would have an AK and the second would have a grenade launcher.

I mean, come on.

We started getting a lot of shots. Four Story was a great sniper hide. It was the tallest building around, and you couldn't get close enough to shoot at it without exposing yourself. It was easy to pick an attacker off. Dauber says we took twenty-three guys in the first twenty-four hours we were there; in the days that followed, we'd get plenty more targets.

Of course, after the first shot, it was a fighting position, not a sniper hide. But in a way, I didn't mind being attacked—the insurgents were just making it easier for me to kill them.

NUMBERS 100 AND 101

IF THE ACTION AROUND COP IRON HAD BEEN DULL TO NONE, the action around COP Falcon was the exact opposite: intense and thick. The Army camp was a clear threat to the insurgents, and they wanted it gone.

A flood of bad guys came at us. That only made it easier for us to defeat them.

Very shortly after Ramadi started, I reached a huge milestone for a sniper: I got my 100th and my 101st confirmed kills for that deployment. One of the guys took a photo of me for posterity, holding up the brass.

There was a little bit of a competition between myself and some of the other snipers during this deployment, to see who got the most kills. Not that we had all that much to do with the numbers—they were more a product of how many targets we had to shoot at. It's just the luck of the draw—you want to have the highest numbers, but there's not much you can do about it.

I did want to be the top sniper. At first, there were three of us who had the most kills; then two of us started pulling away. My "competition" was in my sister platoon, working on the east side of the city. His totals shot up at one point, pulling ahead.

Our big boss man happened to be on our side of the city, and he was keeping track of how the platoons were doing. As part of that, he had the sniper totals. He tweaked me a little as the other sniper pulled in front.

"He's gonna break your record," he'd tease. "You better get on that gun more."

Well, things evened out real fast—all of a sudden I seemed to have every stinkin' bad guy in the city running across my scope. My totals shot up, and there was no catchin' me.

Luck of the draw.

If you're interested, the confirmed kills were only kills that someone else witnessed, and cases where the enemy could be confirmed dead. So if I shot someone in the stomach and he managed to crawl around where we couldn't see him before he bled out, he didn't count.

WORKING WITH THE ARMY

With the initial attacks dying down after a couple of days, we foot-patrolled back to COP Falcon from Four Story. There we met with the captain of the force, and told him that we wanted to be based out of Falcon rather than having to go all the way back to Camp Ramadi every few days.

He gave us the in-law suite. We were the Army's in-laws.

We also told him that we would help him clear whatever area he wanted. His job was to clear the city around COP Falcon, and ours was to help him.

"What's the worst spot you got?" we asked.

He pointed it out.

"That's where we're going," we said.

He shook his head and rolled his eyes.

"You guys are crazy," he said. "You can have that house, you can outfit it however you want, you can go wherever you want. But I want you to know—I'm not coming to get you if you go out there. There are too many IEDs, I'm going to lose a tank. I can't do it."

LIKE A LOT OF THE ARMY, I'M SURE THE CAPTAIN INITIALLY looked at us skeptically. They all assumed we thought we were better than they were, that we had out-sized egos and shot off our mouths without being able to back it up. Once we proved to them that we didn't think we were better than them—more experienced, yes, but not stuck up, if you know what I mean—then they usually came around. We formed strong working relationships with the units, and even friendships that lasted after the war.

The captain's unit was doing cordon and search operations, where they would take an entire block and search it. We started working with them. We'd do daylight presence patrols—the idea was to make civilians see troops on a regular basis, gaining more confidence that they were going to be protected, or that at least we were there to stay. We would put half the platoon on an overwatch while the rest patrolled.

A lot of these overwatches would be near Four Story. The guys downstairs would patrol and almost always be contacted. I'd be upstairs with other snipers and nail whoever was trying to attack them.

Or we would bump out five hundred yards, six or eight hundred yards, going deep into Injun territory to look and wait for the bad guys. We'd set up on overwatch ahead of one of his patrols. As soon as his people showed up, they'd draw all sorts of insurgents toward them. We'd take them down. The bad guys would turn and try and fire on us; we'd pick them off. We were protectors, bait, and slayers.

After a few days, the captain came up to us and said, "Y'all are bad-ass. I don't care where you go, if you need me, I'm comin' to get you. I'll drive the tank to the front door."

And from that moment on, he had our faith and our back.

I WAS ON OVERWATCH AT FOUR STORY ONE MORNING WHEN some of our guys started doing a patrol nearby. As they moved to cross the street, I spotted some insurgents coming down J Street, which was one of the main roads in that area.

I took down a couple. My guys scattered. Not knowing what was going on, someone asked over the radio why the hell I was shooting at them.

"I'm shooting over your head," I told him. "Look down the street."

Insurgents started feeding into the area and a huge firefight erupted. I saw one guy with an RPG; I got him in my crosshairs, squeezed easy on the trigger.

He fell.

A few minutes later, one of his friends came out to grab the rocket launcher.

He fell.

This went on for quite a while. Down the block, another insurgent with an AK tried to get a shot on my boys. I took him down—then took down the guy who came to get his gun, and the next one.

Target-rich environment?! Hell, there were piles of insurgents littering the road. They finally gave up and disappeared. Our guys continued to patrol. The *jundi*s saw action that day; two of them died in a firefight.

It was tough to keep track of how many kills I got that day, but I believe the total was the highest I'd ever had in a single day.

WE KNEW WE WERE IN GOOD WITH THE ARMY CAPTAIN WHEN he came over to us one day and said, "Listen, y'all gotta do one thing for me. Before I get shipped out of here, I want to shoot my main tank gun one time. All right? So call me."

It wasn't too long after that we got in a firefight and we got his unit on the radio. We called him over, and he got his tank in and he got his shot.

There were a lot more in the days that followed. By the time he left Ramadi, he'd shot it thirty-seven times.

PRAYERS AND BANDOLIERS

BEFORE EVERY OP, A BUNCH OF THE PLATOON WOULD GATHER and say a prayer. Marc Lee would lead it, usually speaking from the heart rather than reciting a memorized prayer.

I didn't pray every time going out, but I did thank God every night when I got back.

There was one other ritual when we returned: cigars.

A few of us would get together and smoke them at the end of an op. In Iraq, you can get Cubans; we smoked Romeo y Julieta No. 3s. We'd light up to top off the day.

IN A WAY, WE ALL THOUGHT WE WERE INVINCIBLE. IN ANOTHER way, we also accepted the fact that we could die.

I didn't focus on death, or spend much time thinking about it. It was more like an idea, lurking in the distance.

IT WAS DURING THIS DEPLOYMENT THAT I INVENTED A LITTLE wrist bandolier, a small bullet-holder that allowed me to easily reload without disturbing my gun setup.

I took a holder that had been designed to be strapped on a gun stock and cut it up. Then I arranged some cord through it and tied it to my left wrist.

Generally, when I fired, I would have my fist balled up under the gun to help me aim. That brought the bandolier close. I could fire, take my right hand, and grab more bullets, and keep my eye sighted through the scope at all times.

AS LEAD SNIPER, I TRIED TO HELP THE NEW GUYS, TELLING them what details to look for. You could tell someone was an insurgent not just by the fact that he was armed but by the way he moved. I started giving advice I'd been given back at the beginning of Fallujah, a battle that by now seemed like a million years ago.

"Dauber, don't be afraid to pull the trigger," I'd tell the younger sniper. "If it's within the ROEs, you take him."

A little bit of hesitation was common for the new guys. Maybe all Americans are a little hesitant to be the first to shoot, even when it's clear that we're under attack, or will be shortly.

Our enemy seemed to have no such problem. With a little experience, our guys didn't, either.

But you could never tell how a guy was going to perform under the stress of combat. Dauber did real well—real well. But I noticed that, for some snipers, the extra strain made them miss shots that they would have no trouble with in training. One guy in particular—an excellent guy and a good SEAL—went through a spell where he was missing quite a lot.

You just couldn't tell how someone was going to react.

RAMADI WAS INFESTED WITH INSURGENTS, BUT THERE WAS A large civilian population. Sometimes they'd wander into firefights. You'd wonder what the hell they were thinking.

One day, we were in a house in another part of the city. We'd engaged a bunch of insurgents, killing quite a few, and were waiting through a lull in the action. The bad guys were probably nearby, waiting for another chance to attack.

Insurgents normally put small rocks in the middle of the road to warn others where we were. Civilians usually saw the rocks and quickly realized what was going on. They always stayed far away. Hours might pass before we saw any people again—and, of course, by that point, the people we would be seeing would have guns and be trying to kill us.

For some reason, this car came flying over the rocks and floored it, speeding toward us and passing all sorts of dead men on the way.

I threw a flash-crash but the grenade didn't get the driver to stop. So, I fired into the front of the car. The bullet went through the engine compartment. He stopped and bailed out of the car, yelling as he hopped around.

Two women were with him in the car. They must have been the stupidest people in the city, because even with all that had happened, they were oblivious to us or the danger around them. They started coming toward our house. I threw another flash grenade and finally they started moving back in the direction they'd come. Finally, they seemed to notice some of the bodies that were littered around and started screaming.

They seem to have gotten away okay, except for the foot wound. But it was a miracle they hadn't been killed.

THE PACE WAS HOT AND HEAVY. IT MADE US WANT MORE. WE ached for it. When the bad guys were hiding, we tried to dare them into showing themselves so we could take them down.

One of the guys had a bandanna, which we took and fashioned into a kind of mummy head. Equipped with goggles and a helmet, it looked almost like a soldier—certainly at a few hundred yards. So we attached it to a pole and held it up over the roof, trying to draw fire one day when the action slowed. It brought a couple of insurgents out and we bagged them.

WE WERE JUST SLAUGHTERING THEM.

There were times when we were so successful on overwatch that I thought our guys on the street were starting to get a little careless. I once spotted them going down the middle of the street, rather than using the side and ducking into the little cover area provided by the walls and openings.

I called down on the radio.

"Hey, y'all need to be going cover to cover," I told them, scolding them gently.

"Why?" answered one of my platoon mates. "You've got us covered."

He may have been joking, but I took it seriously.

"I can't protect you from something I don't see," I said. "If I don't see a glint or movement, the first time I know he's there is when he shoots. I can get him after he's shot you, but that's not going to help you."

HEADING BACK TO SHARK BASE ONE NIGHT, WE GOT INVOLVED in another firefight, a quick hit-and-run affair. At some point, a frag came over and exploded near some of the guys.

The insurgents ran off, and we picked ourselves back up and got going.

"Brad, what's with your leg?" someone in the platoon asked.

He looked down. It was covered with blood.

"Nothin'," he said.

It turned out he'd caught a piece of metal in his knee. It may not have hurt then—I don't know how true that is, since no SEAL has ever actually admitted feeling pain since the beginning of Creation—but when he got back to Shark Base, it was clear the wound wasn't something he could just blow off. Shrapnel had wedged itself behind his patella. He needed to be operated on.

He was airlifted out, our first casualty in Ramadi.

THE CONSTANT GARDENER

OUR SISTER PLATOON WAS ON THE EAST SIDE OF THE CITY, helping the Army put in COPs there. And to the north, the Marines were doing their thing, taking areas, holding and clearing them of insurgents.

We went back for a few days to work with the Marines when they took down a hospital north of the city on the river.

The insurgents were using the hospital as a gathering point. As the Marines came in, a teenager, I'd guess about fifteen, sixteen, appeared on the street and squared up with an AK-47 to fire at them.

I dropped him.

A minute or two later, an Iraqi woman came running up, saw him on the ground, and tore off her clothes. She was obviously his mother.

I'd see the families of the insurgents display their grief, tear off clothes, even rub the blood on themselves. *If you loved them,* I thought, *you should have kept them away from the war. You should have kept them from joining the insurgency. You let them try and kill us—what did you think would happen to them?*

It's cruel, maybe, but it's hard to sympathize with grief when it's over someone who just tried to kill you.

Maybe they'd have felt the same way about us.

People back home, people who haven't been in war, or at least not that war, sometimes don't seem to understand how the troops in Iraq acted. They're surprised—shocked—to discover we often joked about death, about things we saw.

Maybe it seems cruel or inappropriate. Maybe it would be, under different circumstances. But in the context of where we were, it made a lot of sense. We saw terrible things, and lived through terrible things.

Part of it was letting off pressure or steam, I'm sure. A way to cope. If you can't make sense of things, you start to look for some other way to deal with them. You laugh because you have to have some emotion, you have to express yourself somehow.

Every op could mix life and death in surreal ways.

On that same operation to take the hospital, we secured a house to scout the area before the Marines moved in. We'd been in the hide for a while when a guy came out with a wheelbarrow to plant an IED in the backyard where we were. One of our new guys shot him. But he didn't die; he fell and rolled around on the ground, still alive.

It happened that the man who shot him was a corpsman.

"You shot him, you save him," we told him. And so he ran down and tried to resuscitate him.

Unfortunately, the Iraqi died. And in the process, his bowels let loose. The corpsman and another new guy had to carry the body out with us when we left.

Well, they eventually reached a fence at the Marine compound, they didn't know what to do. Finally they just threw him up and over, then clambered after him. It was like *Weekend at Bernie's*.

In the space of less than an hour, we'd shot a guy who wanted to blow us up, tried to save his life, and desecrated his body.

The battlefield is a bizarre place.

Soon after the hospital was secured, we went back to

the river where the Marine boats had dropped us off. As we got down the bank, an enemy machine gun started tearing up the night. We hit the dirt, lying there for several long minutes, pinned down by a single Iraqi gunner.

Thank God he sucked at shooting.

It was always a delicate balance, life and death, comedy and tragedy.

TAYA:

I never played the video Chris had recorded of himself reading the book for our son. Part of it was the fact that I didn't want to see Chris getting all choked up. I was emotional enough as it was; seeing him choked up reading to our son would have torn me up more than I already was.

And part of it was just a feeling on my part—anger toward Chris, maybe—you left, you're gone, go.

It was harsh, but maybe it was a survival instinct.

I was the same way when it came to his death letters.

While he was deployed, he wrote letters to be delivered to the kids and me if he died. After the first deployment, I asked to read whatever he had written, and he said he didn't have it anymore. After that he never offered them up and I never asked to see them.

Maybe it was just because I was mad at him, but I thought to myself, We are not glorifying this after you're dead. If you feel loving and adoring, you better let me know while you're alive.

Maybe it wasn't fair, but a lot of life then wasn't fair and that's the way I felt.

Show me now. Make it real. Don't just say some sappy shit when you're gone. Otherwise, it's a load of crap.

GUARDIANS AND DEVILS

NINETY-SIX AMERICANS WERE KILLED DURING THE BATTLE OF Ramadi; countless more were wounded and had to be taken from the battlefield. I was lucky not to be one of them, though there were so many close calls I began to think I had a guardian angel.

One time we were in a building and we were hosed down by the insurgents outside. I was out in the hallway, and as the shooting died down, I went into one of the rooms to check on some of my guys. As I came in, I jerked straight back, falling backward as a shot came in through the window at my head.

The bullet flew just over me as I fell.

Why I went down like that, how I saw that bullet coming at me—I have no idea. It was almost as if someone had slowed time down and pushed me straight back.

Did I have a guardian angel?

No idea.

"Fuck, Chris is dead," said one of my boys as I lay on my back.

"Damn," said the other.

"No, no," I yelled, still flat on the floor. "I'm good, I'm good. I'm okay."

I checked for holes a few dozen times, but there were none.

All good.

IEDS WERE MUCH MORE COMMON IN RAMADI THAN THEY had been in Fallujah. The insurgents had learned a lot about setting them since the beginning of the war, and they tended to be pretty powerful—strong enough to lift a Bradley off the ground, as I'd found out earlier in Baghdad.

The EOD guys who worked with us were not SEALs, but we came to trust them as much as if they were. We'd stick them on the back of the train when we went into a building, then call them forward if we saw something suspicious. At that point, their job was to identify the booby-trap; if it was a bomb, and we were in a house, we would have gotten the hell out of there fast.

That never happened to us, but there was one time when we were in a house and some insurgents managed to plant an IED right outside the front door. They had stacked two 105-mm shells, waiting for us to come out. Fortunately, our EOD guy spotted it before we moved out. We were able to sledgehammer our way out through a second-story wall and escape across a low roof.

A WANTED MAN

ALL AMERICANS WERE WANTED MEN IN RAMADI, SNIPERS most of all. Reportedly, the insurgents put out a bounty on my head.

They also gave me a name: al-Shaitan Ramadi—"the Devil of Ramadi."

It made me feel proud.

The fact is, I was just one guy, and they had singled me out for causing them a lot of damage. They wanted me gone. I had to feel good about that.

They definitely knew who I was, and had clearly gotten intelligence from some fellow Iraqis who were supposedly loyal to us— they described the red cross I had on my arm.

The other sniper from my sister platoon got a bounty on his head as well. His ended up being more—well, that did make me a little jealous.

But it was all good, because when they put their posters together and made one of me, they used his photo instead of mine. I was more than happy to let them make that mistake.

The bounty went up as the battle went on.

Hell, I think it got so high, my wife may have been tempted to turn me in.

PROGRESS

We helped set up several more COPs, and meanwhile our sister platoon did the same on the eastern side of the city. As the weeks turned into months, Ramadi started to change.

The place was still a hellhole, extremely dangerous. But there were signs of progress. The tribal leaders were more vocal about wanting peace, and more began working together as a unified council. The official government still wasn't functioning here, and the Iraqi police and army were nowhere near capable of keeping order, naturally. But there were large sections of the city under relative control.

The "inkblot strategy" was working. Could those blots spread over the entire city?

Progress was never guaranteed, and even when we succeeded for a while there was no guarantee things wouldn't go backward. We had to return to the area near the river around COP Falcon several times, providing overwatch while the area was searched for caches and insurgents. We'd clear a block, it would be peaceful for a while, then we'd have to start all over again.

We worked a bit more with the Marines as well, stopping and inspecting small craft, going after a suspected weapons cache, and even running a few DAs for them. A few times we were tasked to check and then blow up abandoned boats to make sure they couldn't be used for smuggling.

Funny thing: the SBU unit that had blown us off earlier heard about how much action we were getting and contacted us, asking now if they could come up and work with us. We told them thanks but no thanks; we were doing just fine with the Marines.

WE GOT INTO A CERTAIN RHYTHM WORKING WITH THE ARMY as they continued cordoning off areas and searching them for weapons and bad guys. We'd drive in with them, take over a building, and go up on the roof for overwatch. Most times there would be three of us—myself and another sniper, along with Ryan on the 60.

Meanwhile, the Army would move out to the next building. That taken, they'd work their way down the street. Once they reached a certain spot where we couldn't see to provide them security, we'd come down and move to a new spot. The process would start all over again.

It was on one of these ops that Ryan got shot.

11

MAN DOWN

"WHAT THE HELL?"

ONE VERY HOT SUMMER DAY WE TOOK A SMALL APARTMENT building with a good view of one of the major east-west roads through the center of Ramadi. It was four stories high, the staircase lined with windows, the roof open and with a good view of the area. It was a clear day.

Ryan was joking with me as we went in. He was cracking me up—he always made me laugh, made me relax. Smiling, I posted him to watch the road. Our troops were working on a side street on the other side of the roof, and I figured that if the insurgents were going to launch an ambush or try and attack us, they would come down that road. Meanwhile, I watched the team on the ground. The assault began smoothly, with the soldiers taking first one house and then another. They moved quickly, without a snag.

Suddenly, shots flew through our position. I ducked down as

a round hit the cement nearby, splattering chips everywhere. This was an everyday occurrence in Ramadi, something that happened not once a day but several times.

I waited a second to make sure the insurgents were done firing, then got back up.

"You guys all right?" I yelled, looking down the street toward the soldiers on the ground, making sure they were okay.

"Yeah," grunted the other sniper.

Ryan didn't answer. I glanced back and saw him, still down.

"Hey, get up," I told him. "They stopped firing. Come on."

He didn't move. I went over.

"What the hell?" I yelled at him. "Get up. Get up."

Then I saw the blood.

I knelt down and looked at him. There was blood all over. The side of his face had been smashed in. He'd taken a bullet.

We had pounded into him the fact that you have to always have your weapon up and ready; he'd had it up and scanning when the bullet hit. It apparently got the rifle first, then ricocheted into his face.

I grabbed the radio. "Man down!" I yelled. "Man down!"

I dropped back and examined his wounds. I didn't know what to do, where to start. Ryan looked as if he'd been hit so bad that he was going to die.

His body shook. I thought it was a death spasm.

Two of our platoon guys, Dauber and Tommy, ran up. They were both corpsmen. They slipped down between us and started treating him.

Marc Lee came up behind them. He took the 60 and began laying down fire in the direction the shots had come from, chasing the insurgents back so we could carry Ryan down the stairs.

I picked him up and held him up over my shoulder, then started to run. I reached the stairs and started going down quickly.

About halfway, he started groaning loudly. The way I was holding him, the blood had rushed into his throat and head; he was having trouble breathing.

I set him down, even more worried, knowing in my heart he was going to die, hoping that somehow, some way, I might do something to keep him going, even though it was hopeless.

Ryan began spitting blood. He caught his breath—he was breathing, a miracle in itself.

I reached out to grab him and pick him up again.

"No," he said. "No, no I'm good. I got this. I'm walking."

He put an arm around me and walked himself down the rest of the way.

Meanwhile, the Army rolled a tracked vehicle, a personnel carrier, up to the front door. Tommy went in with Ryan and they pulled away.

I ran back upstairs, feeling as if I'd been shot and wishing that it had been me, not him, who was hit. I was sure he was going to die. I was sure I'd just lost a brother. A big, goofy, lovable, great brother.

Biggles.

Nothing I'd experienced in Iraq had ever affected me like this.

PAYBACK

We collapsed back to Shark Base.

As soon as we got there, I shed my gear and put my back against the wall, then slowly lowered myself to the ground.

Tears started flowing from my eyes.

I thought Ryan was dead. Actually, he was still alive, if just barely. The docs worked like hell to save him. Ryan would eventually be medevac'd out of Iraq. His wounds were severe—he'd never see again, not only out of the eye that had been hit but the other as well. It was a miracle that he lived.

But at that moment at base, I was sure he was dead. I knew it in my stomach, in my heart, in every part of me. I'd put him in the spot where he got hit. It was my fault he'd been shot.

A hundred kills? Two hundred? More? What did they mean if my brother was dead?

Why hadn't I put myself there? Why hadn't I been standing there? I could have gotten the bastard—I could have saved my boy.

I was in a dark hole. Deep down.

How long I stayed there, head buried, tears flowing, I have no idea.

"Hey," said a voice above me, finally.

I looked up. It was Tony, my chief.

"You wanna go get some payback?" he asked.

"Fuck yeah I do!" I jumped to my feet.

A FEW GUYS WEREN'T SURE WHETHER WE SHOULD GO OR NOT. We talked about it, and planned out the mission.

I didn't hardly have time for it, though. I just wanted blood for my guy.

MARC

THE INTEL PUT THE BAD GUYS IN A HOUSE NOT TOO FAR FROM where Ryan had been hit. A couple of Bradleys drove us over to a field near the house. I was in a second vehicle; some of the other guys had already gone into the house by the time we arrived.

As soon as the ramp dropped on our Bradley, bullets started

flying. I ran to join the others; and found them stacking to go up the stairs to the second floor. We were huddled together, facing downward, waiting to move up.

Marc Lee was at the lead, above us on the steps. He turned, glancing out a window on the staircase. As he did, he saw something and opened his mouth to shout a warning.

He never got the words out. In that split second, a bullet passed right through his open mouth and flew out the back of his head. He dropped down in a pile on the steps.

We'd been set up. There was a savage on the roof of the house next door, looking down at the window from the roof there.

Training took over.

I scrambled up the steps, stepping over Marc's body. I sent a hail of bullets through the window, flushing the neighboring roof. So did my teammates.

One of us got the insurgent. We didn't stop to figure out who it was. We went on up to the roof, looking for more of our ambushers.

Dauber, meanwhile, stopped to check Marc. He was hurt pretty bad; Dauber knew there was no hope.

THE TANK CAPTAIN CAME AND GOT US. THEY WERE ENGAGED the whole way, driving in under heavy contact. He brought two tanks and four Bradleys, and they went Winchester, firing all their ammo. It was shit-hot, a fierce hail of lead covering our retreat.

On the way back, I looked out the port on the back ramp of my Bradley. All I could see was black smoke and ruined buildings. They'd suckered us, and their entire neighborhood had paid the price.

For some reason, most of us thought Marc was going to live; we thought Ryan was going to die. It wasn't until we got back to camp that we heard their fates were reversed.

Having lost two guys in the space of a few hours, our officers and Tony decided it was time for us to take a break. We went back to Shark Base and stood down. (Standing down means you're out of action and unavailable for combat. In some ways, it's like an official timeout to assess or reassess what you're doing.)

It was August: hot, bloody, and black.

Taya:

Chris broke down when he called me with the news. I hadn't heard anything about it until he called, and it took me by surprise.

I felt grateful that it wasn't him, yet incredibly sad that it was any of them.

I tried to be as quiet as possible as he talked. I wanted just to listen. There have been very few times in his life, if ever, that I've seen Chris in that much pain.

There was nothing I could do, aside from telling his relatives for him.

We sat on the phone for a long time.

A few days later, I went to the funeral at the cemetery overlooking San Diego Bay.

It was so sad. There were so many young guys, so many young families. . . . It was emotional to be at other SEAL funerals, but this was even more so.

You feel so bad, you cannot imagine their pain. You pray for them and you thank God for your husband being spared. You thank God you are not the one in the front row.

People who've heard this story tell me my description gets bare, and my voice faraway. They say I use less words to describe what happened, give less detail, than I usually do.

I'm not conscious of it. The memory of losing my two boys burns hot and deep. To me, it's as vivid as what is happening around me at this very moment. To me, it's as deep and fresh a wound as if those bullets came into my own flesh this very moment.

STANDING DOWN

We had a memorial service at Camp Ramadi for Marc Lee. SEALs from every part of Iraq came in for it. And I believe the entire Army unit we'd been working with showed up. They had a lot of concern for us; it was unbelievable. I was very moved.

They put us on the front row. We were his family.

Marc's gear was right there, helmet and Mk-48. Our task unit commander gave a short but powerful speech; he teared up and I doubt there was a dry eye in the audience—or the camp, for that matter.

As the service ended, each unit left a token of appreciation—a unit patch or coin, something. The captain of the Army unit left a piece of brass from one of the rounds he'd fired getting us out.

Someone in our platoon put together a memorial video with some slides of him, and played it that night with the movie showing on a white sheet we had hung over a brick wall. We shared some drinks, and a lot of sadness.

Four of our guys accompanied his body back home. Meanwhile, since we were on stand-down and not doing anything, I tried to go see Ryan in Germany, where he was being treated. Tony or someone else in the head shed arranged to get me on a flight, but by the time everything was set up, Ryan was already being shipped back to the States for treatment.

Brad, who'd been evac'd earlier because of the frag wound in his knee, met Ryan in Germany and went back to the States with him. It was lucky in a way—Ryan had one of us to be with him and help him deal with everything he had to face.

WE ALL SPENT A LOT OF TIME IN OUR ROOMS.

Ramadi had been hot and heavy, with an op tempo that was pretty severe, worse even than Fallujah. We'd spend several days, even a week out, with barely a break in between. Some of us were starting to get a little burned out even before our guys got hit.

We stayed in our rooms, replacing bodily fluids, keeping to ourselves mostly.

I spent a lot of time praying to God.

I'm not the kind of person who makes a big show out of religion. I believe, but I don't necessarily get down on my knees or sing real loud in church. But I find some comfort in faith, and I found it in those days after my friends had been shot up.

Ever since I had gone through BUD/S, I'd carried a Bible with me. I hadn't read it all that much, but it had always been with me. Now I opened it and read some of the passages. I skipped around, read a bit, skipped around some more.

With all hell breaking loose around me, it felt better to know I was part of something bigger.

MY EMOTIONS SHOT UP WHEN I HEARD THAT RYAN HAD SURVIVED. But my overriding reaction was: Why wasn't it me?

Why did this have to happen to a new guy?

I'd seen a lot of action; I'd had my achievements. I had my war. I should have been the one sidelined. I should have been the one blinded.

Ryan would never see the look on his family's face when he came home. He'd never see how much sweeter everything is when you get back—see how much better America looks when you've been gone from it for a while.

You forget how beautiful life is, if you don't get a chance to see things like that. He never would.

And no matter what anybody told me, I felt responsible for that.

REPLACEMENTS

WE'D BEEN IN THAT WAR FOR FOUR YEARS, THROUGH COUNTless hairy situations, and no SEAL had ever died. It had looked like the action in Ramadi, and all Iraq, was starting to wind down, and now we'd been hit terribly hard.

We thought we would be shut down, even though our deployment still had a couple of months to run. We all knew the politics—my first two commanders had been ultra-cautious pussies, who got ahead because of it. So we were afraid that the war was over for us.

Plus, we were seven men short, cut nearly in half. Marc was dead. Brad and Ryan were out because of their wounds. Four guys had gone home to escort Marc's body home.

A WEEK AFTER LOSING OUR GUYS, THE CO CAME AROUND TO talk to us. We gathered in the chow hall at Shark Base and listened as he talked. It wasn't a long speech.

"It's up to you," he said. "If you want to take it easy now, I understand. But if you want to go out, you have my blessing."

"Fuck yeah," we all said. "We want to go out."

I sure did.

HALF OF A PLATOON JOINED US FROM A QUIETER AREA TO help fill us out. We also got some guys who had graduated training but hadn't been assigned to a platoon yet. Real new guys. The idea was to give them a little exposure to the war, a little taste of what they were getting into before they trained up for the main event. We were pretty careful with them—we didn't allow them to go out on ops.

Being SEALs, they were chomping at the bit, but we held them back, treating them like gofers at first: *Hey, go line the Hummers up so we can go.* It was a protection thing; after all we'd just been through, we didn't want them getting hurt out in the field.

We did have to haze them, of course. This one poor fella, we shaved his head and his eyebrows, then spray-glued the hair back on his face.

While we were in the middle of that, another new guy walked into the outer room.

"You don't want to go in there," warned one of our officers.

The new guy peeked in and saw his buddy getting pummeled.

"I gotta."

"You don't want to go in there," repeated the officer. "It's not going to end well."

"I have to. He's my buddy."

"Your funeral," said the officer, or words to that effect.

New guy number two ran into the room. We respected the fact that he was coming to his friend's rescue, and showered him with affection. Then we shaved him, too, taped them together, and stood them in the corner.

Just for a few minutes.

WE ALSO HAZED A NEW-GUY OFFICER. HE GOT ABOUT WHAT everyone got, but didn't take it too well.

He didn't like the idea of being mishandled by some dirty enlisted men.

RANK IS A FUNNY CONCEPT IN THE TEAMS. IT'S NOT DISRE-spected exactly, but it's clearly not the full measure of the man.

In BUD/S, officers and enlisted are all treated the same: like shit. Once you make it through and join the Teams, you're a new guy. Again, all new guys are treated the same: like shit.

Most officers take it fairly well, though obviously there are exceptions. The truth is, the Teams are run by the senior enlisted. A guy who's a chief has twelve to sixteen years of experience. An officer joining a platoon has far less, not just in SEALs but in the Navy as well. Most of the time he just doesn't know shit. Even an OIC might have only four or five years' experience.

That's the way the system works. If he's lucky, an officer might get as many as three platoons; after that, he's promoted to task unit commander (or something similar) and no longer works directly in the field. Even to get there, much of what he's done has been admin work and things like de-confliction (making sure a unit doesn't get fired on by another one). Those are important tasks, but they're not quite the same as hands-on combat. When it comes to door-kicking or setting up a sniper hide, the officer's experience generally doesn't run too deep.

There are exceptions, of course. I worked with some great officers with good experience, but as a general rule, an officer's knowledge of down-and-dirty combat is just nowhere near the same as the guy with many years of combat under his belt. I used to tease LT that when we did a DA, he would be in the stack, ready to go in, not with a rifle but his tactical computer.

Hazing helps remind everybody where the experience lies—and who you better look to when the shit hits the fan. It also shows the people who have been around a little bit what to expect from the new guys. Compare and contrast: who do you want on your back, the guy who ran in to save his buddy or the officer who shed tears because he was being mistreated by some dirty enlisted men?

Hazing humbles all the new guys, reminding them that they don't know shit yet. In the case of an officer, that dose of humility can go a long way.

I've had good officers. But all the great ones were humble.

BACK IN THE MIX

WE WORKED BACK INTO THINGS SLOWLY, STARTING WITH brief overwatches with the Army. Our missions would last for an overnight or two in Injun country. A tank got hit by an IED, and we went out and pulled security on it until it could be recovered. The work was a little lighter, easier than it had been. We didn't go as far from the COPs, which meant that we didn't draw as much fire.

With our heads back in the game, we started to extend. We went deeper into Ramadi. We never actually went to the house where Marc had been shot, but we were back in that area.

Our attitude was, we're going out there and we're getting the guys who did this back. We're going to make them pay for what they did to us.

WE WERE AT A HOUSE ONE DAY, AND AFTER TAKING DOWN some insurgents who'd been trying to plant IEDs, we came under fire ourselves. Whoever was shooting at us had something heavier than an AK—maybe a Dragunov (the Russian-made sniper rifle), because the bullets flew through the walls of the house.

I was up on the roof, trying to figure out where the gunfire was coming from. Suddenly, I heard the heavy whoop of Apache helicopters approaching. I watched as they circled placidly for a second, then tipped and fell into a coordinated attack dive.

In our direction.

"VS panels!" someone shouted.

That might have been me. All I know is, we hustled out every VS or recognition panel we had, trying to show the pilots we were friendly. (VS panels are bright orange pieces of cloth, hung or laid out by friendly forces.) Fortunately, they figured it out and broke off at the last moment.

Our com guy had been talking to the Army helos just before the attack and gave them our location. But, apparently, their maps were labeled differently than ours, and when they saw men on the roof with guns, they drew the wrong conclusions.

We worked with Apaches quite a bit in Ramadi. The aircraft were valuable, not just for their guns and rockets but also for their ability to scout around the area. It's not always clear in a city where gunfire is coming from; having a set of eyes above you, and being able to talk to the people who own those eyes, can help you figure things out.

(The Apaches had different ROEs than we did. These especially came into play when firing Hellfire missiles, which could only be used against crew-served weapons at the time. This was part of the strategy for limiting the amount of collateral damage in the city.)

Air Force AC-130s also helped out with aerial observation from time to time. The big gunships had awesome firepower, though, as it happened, we never called on them to use their howitzers or cannons during this deployment. (Again, they had restrictive ROEs.) Instead, we relied on their night sensors, which gave them a good picture of the battlefield even in the pitch black.

One night we hit a house on a DA while a gunship circled above protectively. While we were going in, they called down and told us that we had a couple of "squirters"—guys running out the back.

I peeled off with a few of my boys and started following in the direction the gunship gave us. It appeared that the insurgents had ducked into a nearby house. I went in, and was met inside by a young man in his early twenties.

"Get down," I yelled at him, motioning with my gun.

He looked at me blankly. I gestured again, this time pretty emphatically.

"Down! Down!"

He looked at me dumbfounded. I couldn't tell whether he was planning to attack me or not, and I sure couldn't figure out why he wasn't complying. Better safe than sorry—I punched him and slapped him down to the ground.

His mother jumped out from the back, yelling something. By now there were a couple of guys inside with me, including my terp. The interpreter finally got things calmed down and started asking questions. The mother eventually explained that the boy was mentally handicapped, and didn't understand what I'd been doing. We let him up.

Meanwhile, standing quietly to one side, was a man we thought was the father. But once we settled her concerns about her son, the mother made it clear she didn't know who the asshole was. It turned out that he had just run in, only pretending to live there. So we had one of our squirters, courtesy of the Air Force.

I SUPPOSE I SHOULDN'T TELL THAT STORY WITHOUT GIVING myself up.

The house where the men ran from was actually the third house we hit that night. I'd led the boys to the first. We were all lined up outside, getting ready to breach in, when our OIC raised his voice.

"Something doesn't look right," he said. "I'm not feeling this."

I craned my head back and glanced around.

"Shit," I admitted. "I took you all to the wrong house."

We backed out and went to the right one.

Did I ever hear the end of that?

Rhetorical question.

TWOFER

ONE DAY WE WERE OUT ON AN OP NEAR SUNSET AND ANOTHER street, which came off on a T intersection. Dauber and I were up on a roof, watching to see what the locals were up to. Dauber had just gone off the gun for a break. As I pulled up my scope, I spotted two guys coming down the street toward me on a moped.

The guy on the back had a backpack. As I was watching, he dropped the backpack into a pothole.

He wasn't dropping the mail; he was setting an IED.

"Y'all gotta watch this," I told Dauber, who picked up his binoculars.

I let them get to about 150 yards away before I fired my .300 Win Mag. Dauber, watching through the binos, said it was like a scene from *Dumb and Dumber*. The bullet went through the first guy and into the second. The moped wobbled, then veered into a wall.

Two guys with one shot. The taxpayer got good bang for his buck on that one.

THE SHOT ENDED UP BEING CONTROVERSIAL. BECAUSE OF THE IED, the Army sent some people over to the scene. But it took them something like six hours to get there. Traffic backed up, and it was impossible for me, or anyone else, to watch the pothole for the entire time. Further complicating things, the Marines took down a dump truck suspected of being a mobile IED on the same road. Traffic backed up all over the place, and naturally the IED disappeared.

Ordinarily, that wouldn't have been a problem. But a few days earlier we had noticed a pattern: mopeds would ride past a COP a few minutes before and after an attack, obviously scouting the place and then getting intel on the attack. We requested to be cleared hot to shoot anyone on a moped. The request was denied.

The lawyers or someone in the chain of command probably thought I was blowing them off when they heard about my double shot. The JAG—Judge Advocate General, kind of like a military version of a prosecuting attorney—came out and investigated.

Fortunately, there were plenty of witnesses to what had happened. But I still had to answer all the JAG's questions.

Meanwhile, the insurgents kept using mopeds and gathering intelligence. We watched them closely, and destroyed every parked moped we came across in houses and yards, but that was the most we could do.

Maybe legal expected us to wave and smile for the cameras.

IT WOULD HAVE BEEN TOUGH TO GO AND JUST BLATANTLY shoot people in Iraq. For one thing, there were always plenty of witnesses around. For another, every time I killed someone in Ramadi I had to write a shooter's statement on it.

No joke.

This was a report, separate from after-action reports, related only to the shots I took and kills I recorded. The information had to be very specific.

I had a little notebook with me, and I'd record the day, the time, details about the person, what he was doing, the round I used, how many shots I took, how far away the target was, and who witnessed the shot. All that went into the report, along with any other special circumstances.

The head shed claimed it was to protect me in case there was ever an investigation for an unjustified kill, but what I think I was really doing was covering the butts of people much further up the chain of command.

We kept a running tally of how many insurgents we shot, even during the worst firefights. One of our officers was always tasked with getting his own details on the shooting; he, in turn, would relay it back by radio. There were plenty of times when I was still engaging insurgents and giving details to LT or another officer at the same time. It got to be such a pain in the ass that one time when the officer came to ask the details on my shot, I told him it was a kid waving at me. It was just a sick joke I made. It was my way of saying, "Fuck off."

The red tape of war.

I'M NOT SURE HOW WIDESPREAD THE SHOOTER STATEMENTS were. For me, the process began during my second deployment when I was working on Haifa Street. In that case, someone else filled them out for me.

I'm pretty sure it was all CYA—cover your ass, or, in this case, cover the top guy's ass.

We were slaughtering the enemy. In Ramadi, with our kill total becoming astronomical, the statements became mandatory and elaborate. I'd guess that the CO or someone on his staff saw the numbers and said that the lawyers might question what was going on, so let's protect ourselves.

Great way to fight a war—be prepared to defend yourself for winning.

What a pain in the ass. I'd joke that it wasn't worth shooting someone. (On the other hand, that's one way I know exactly how many people I "officially" killed.)

CLEAR CONSCIENCE

SOMETIMES IT SEEMED LIKE GOD WAS HOLDING THEM BACK until I got on the gun.

"Hey, wake up."

I opened my eyes and looked up from my spot on the floor.

"Let's rotate," said Jay, my LPO. He'd been on the gun for about four hours while I'd been catching a nap.

"All right."

I unfolded myself from the ground and moved over to the gun.

"So? What's been going on?" I asked. Whenever someone came on the gun, the person he was relieving would brief him quickly, describing who'd been in the neighborhood, etc.

"Nothing," said Jay. "I haven't seen anyone."

"Nothing?"

"Nothing."

We swapped positions. Jay pulled his ball cap down to catch some sleep.

I put my eye near the sight, scanning. Not ten seconds later, an insurgent walked fat into the crosshairs, AK out. I watched him move tactically toward an American position for a few seconds, confirming that he was within the ROEs.

Then I shot him.

"I fuckin' hate you," grumbled Jay from the floor nearby. He didn't bother moving his ball cap, let alone get up.

I NEVER HAD ANY DOUBTS ABOUT THE PEOPLE I SHOT. MY guys would tease me: *Yeah, I know Chris. He's got a little gun cut on the end of his scope. Everybody he sees is in the ROEs.*

But the truth was, my targets were always obvious, and I, of course, had plenty of witnesses every time I shot.

The way things were, you couldn't chance making a mistake. You'd be crucified if you didn't strictly obey the ROEs.

Back in Fallujah, there was an incident involving Marines clearing a house. A unit had gone into a house, stepping over some bodies as they moved to clear the rooms. Unfortunately, one of the bastards on the ground wasn't dead. After the Marines were in the house, he rolled over and pulled the pin on a grenade. It exploded, killing or wounding some of the Marines.

From then on, the Marines started putting a round in anybody they saw as they entered a house. At some point, a newsman with a camera recorded this; the video became public and the Marines got in trouble. Charges were either dropped or never actually filed, since the initial investigation explained the circumstances. Still, even the potential for charges was something you were always aware of.

The worst thing that you could ever do for that war was having all these media people embedded in the units. Most Americans can't take the reality of war, and the reports they sent back didn't help us at all.

The leadership wanted to have the backing of the public for the war. But really, who cares?

The way I figure it, if you send us to do a job, let us do it. That's why you have admirals and generals—let them supervise us, not some fat-ass congressman sitting in a leather chair smoking a cigar back in DC in an air-conditioned office, telling me when and where I can and cannot shoot someone.

How would they know? They've never even been in a combat situation.

And once you decide to send us, let me do my job. War is war.

Tell me: Do you want us to conquer our enemy? Annihilate them? Or are we heading over to serve them tea and cookies?

Tell the military the end result you want, and you'll get it. But don't try and tell us how to do it. All those rules about when and under what circumstances an enemy combatant could be killed didn't just make our jobs harder, they put our lives in danger.

The ROEs got so convoluted and fucked-up because politicians were interfering in the process. The rules are drawn up by lawyers who are trying to protect the admirals and generals from the politicians; they're not written by people who are worried about the guys on the ground getting shot.

FOR SOME REASON, A LOT OF PEOPLE BACK HOME—NOT ALL people—didn't accept that we were at war. They didn't accept that war means death, violent death most times. A lot of people, not just politicians, wanted to impose ridiculous fantasies on us, hold us to some standard of behavior that no human being could maintain.

I'm not saying war crimes should be committed. I *am* saying that warriors need to be let loose to fight war without their hands tied behind their backs.

According to the ROEs I followed in Iraq, if someone came into my house, shot my wife, my kids, and then threw his gun down, I was supposed to NOT shoot him. I was supposed to take him gently into custody.

Would you?

You can argue that my success proves the ROEs worked. But I feel that I could have been more effective, probably protected more people and helped bring the war to a quicker conclusion without them.

IT SEEMED THE ONLY NEWS STORIES WE READ WERE ABOUT atrocities or how impossible it was going to be to pacify Ramadi.

Guess what? We killed all those bad guys, and what happened? The Iraqi tribal leaders *finally* realized we meant business, and they *finally* banded together not just to govern themselves, but to kick the insurgents out. It took force, it took violence of action, to create a situation where there could be peace.

LEUKEMIA

"OUR DAUGHTER IS SICK. HER WHITE BLOOD CELL COUNT IS very low."

I held the phone a little tighter as Taya continued to talk. My little girl had been sick with infections and jaundice for a while. Her liver didn't seem to be able to keep up with the disease. Now the doctors were asking for more tests, and things looked real bad. They weren't saying it was cancer or leukemia but they weren't saying it wasn't. They were going to test her to confirm their worst fears.

Taya tried to sound positive and downplay the problems. I could tell just from the tone of her voice that things were more serious than she would admit, until finally I got the entire truth from her.

I am not entirely sure what all she said, but what I heard was, leukemia. *Cancer.*

My little girl was going to die.

A cloud of helplessness descended over me. I was thousands of miles away from her, and there was nothing I could do to help. Even if I'd been there, I couldn't cure her.

My wife sounded so sad and alone on the phone.

The stress of the deployment had started to get to me well before that phone call in September 2006. The loss of Marc and Ryan's extreme injuries had taken a toll. My blood pressure had shot up and I couldn't sleep. Hearing the news about my daughter pushed me to my breaking point. I wasn't much good for anyone.

Fortunately, we were already winding down our deployment. And as soon as I mentioned my little girl's condition to my command, they started making travel arrangements to get me home. Our doctor put through the paperwork for a Red Cross letter. That's a statement that indicates a service member's family needs him for an emergency back home. Once that letter arrived, my commanders made it happen.

I ALMOST DIDN'T GET OUT. RAMADI WAS SUCH A HOT ZONE that there weren't a whole lot of opportunities for flights. There were no helos in or out. Even the convoys were still getting hit by insurgent attacks. Worried about me and knowing I couldn't afford to wait too long, my boys loaded up the Humvees. They set me in the middle, and drove me out of the city to TQ airfield.

When we got there, I nearly choked up handing over my body armor and my M-4.

My guys were going back to war and I was flying home. That sucked. I felt like I was letting them down, shirking my duty.

It was a conflict—family and country, family and brothers in arms—that I never really resolved. I'd had even more kills in Ramadi than in Fallujah. Not only did I finish with more kills than anyone else on that deployment, but my overall total made me the most prolific American sniper of all time—to use the fancy official language.

And yet I still felt like a quitter, a guy who didn't do enough.

12

HARD TIMES

HOME

I caught a military charter, first to Kuwait, then to the States. I was in civilian clothes, and with my longer hair and beard, I got hassled a bit, since no one could figure out why someone on active duty was authorized to travel in civilian clothes.

Which, looking back, is kind of amusing.

I got off the plane in Atlanta, then had to go back through security to continue on. It had taken me a few days to make it this far, and when I took my boots off, I swear half a dozen people in line nearby keeled over. I'm not sure I've ever gotten through security quite as fast.

Taya:

He would never tell me how dangerous things were, but I got to the point where I felt like I could read him.

And when he told me that his guys were taking him out in a convoy, just the way he told me about it made me fear not only for them but for him. I asked a couple questions and the careful responses told me how dangerous his extract was going to be.

I felt very strongly that the more people I had praying for him, the better his chances. So I asked if I could tell his parents to pray for him.

He said yes.

Then I asked if I could tell them why, about the fact that he was coming home and the danger in the city, and he said no.

So, I didn't.

I asked people for prayer, alluded to danger, and gave no further details other than to ask them to trust me. I knew it would be a tough pill to swallow for those few I was asking. But I felt strongly that people needed to pray—and at the same time that I had to adhere to my husband's desires about what was to be shared. I know it wasn't popular, but I felt the need for prayer overrode my need for popularity.

When he got home, it seemed to me Chris was so stressed he was numb to everything.

It was hard for him to pinpoint how he felt about anything. He was just wiped out and overwhelmed.

I felt sad for everything he'd been through. And I felt terribly torn about needing him. I did need him, tremendously. But at the same time, I had to get along without him so much that I developed an attitude that I didn't need him, or at least that I shouldn't need him.

I guess it may not make any sense to anyone else, but I felt this strange mixture of feelings, all across the spectrum. I was so mad at him for leaving the kids and me on our own. I wanted him home but I was mad, too.

I was coming off months of anxiety for his safety and frustration that he chose to keep going back. I wanted to count on him, but I couldn't. His Team could, and total strangers who happened to be in the military could, but the kids and I certainly could not.

It wasn't his fault. He would have been in two places at once if he could have been, but he couldn't. But when he had to choose, he didn't choose us.

All the while, I loved him and I tried to support him and show him love in every way possible. I felt five hundred emotions, all at the same time.

I guess I had had an undercurrent of anger that whole deployment. We'd have conversations where we talked and he realized something was wrong. He'd ask what was bothering me and I'd deny it. And then finally he'd press and I would say, "I'm mad at you for going back. But I don't want to hate you, and I don't want to be mad. I know you could be killed tomorrow. I don't want you to be distracted by this. I don't want to have this conversation."

Now finally he was back, and all of my emotions just exploded inside me, happiness and anger all mixed together.

GETTING BETTER

THE DOCTORS PERFORMED ALL SORTS OF TESTS ON MY LITTLE girl. Some of them really pissed me off.

I remember especially when they took blood, which they had

to do a lot. They'd hold her upside down and prick her foot; a lot of times it wouldn't bleed and they'd have to do it again and again. She'd be crying the whole time.

These were long days, but eventually the docs figured out that my daughter didn't have leukemia. While there was jaundice and some other complications, they were able to get control of the infections that had made her sick. She got better.

One of the things that was incredibly frustrating was her reaction to me. She seemed to cry every time I held her. She wanted Mommy. Taya said that she reacted that way to all men—whenever she heard a male voice, she would cry.

Whatever the reason, it hurt me badly. Here I had come all this way and truly loved her, and she rejected me.

Things were better with my son, who remembered me and now was older and more ready to play. But once again, the normal troubles that parents have with their kids and with each other were compounded by the separation and stress we'd all just gone through.

Little things could really be annoying. I expected my son to look me in the eye when I was scolding him. Taya was bothered by this, because she felt he wasn't accustomed to me or my tone and it was too much to ask a two-year-old to look me in the eye in that situation. But my feeling was just the opposite. It was the right thing for him to do. He wasn't being corrected by a stranger. He was being disciplined by someone who loved him. There's a certain two-way road of respect there. You look me in the eye, I look you in the eye—we understand each other.

Taya would say, "Wait a minute. You've been gone for how long? And now you want to come home and be part of this family and make the rules? No sir, because you're leaving again in another month to go back on training."

We were both right, from our perspectives. The problem was trying to see the other's, and then live with it.

I WASN'T PERFECT. I WAS WRONG ON A FEW THINGS. I HAD to learn how to be a dad. I had my idea of how parenting should be, but it wasn't based on any reality. Over time, my ideas changed.

Somewhat. I still expect my kids to look me in the eye when I'm talking to them. And vice versa. And Taya agrees.

MIKE MONSOOR

I'D BEEN HOME FOR ROUGHLY TWO WEEKS WHEN A SEAL friend of mine called and asked what was up.

"Nothing much," I told him.

"Well, who did y'all lose?" he asked.

"Huh?"

"I don't know who it was, but I heard you lost another."

"Damn."

I got off the phone and started calling everyone I knew. I finally got a hold of someone who knew the details, though he couldn't talk about them at the moment, because the family had not been informed yet. He said he'd call me back in a few hours.

They were long hours.

Finally I found out Mike Monsoor, a member of our sister platoon, had been killed saving the lives of some of his fellow platoon members in Ramadi. The group had set up an overwatch in a house there; an insurgent got close enough to toss a grenade.

Obviously, I wasn't there, but this is the description of what happened from the official summary of action:

The grenade hit him in the chest and bounced onto the deck [here, the Navy term for floor]. He immediately leapt to his feet and yelled "grenade" to alert his teammates of impending danger, but they could not evacuate the sniper hide-sight in time to escape harm. Without hesitation and showing no regard for his own life, he threw himself onto the grenade, smothering it to protect his teammates who were lying in close proximity. The grenade detonated as he came down on top of it, mortally wounding him.

Petty Officer Monsoor's actions could not have been more selfless or clearly intentional. Of the three SEALs on that rooftop corner, he had the only avenue of escape away from the blast, and if he had so chosen, he could have easily escaped. Instead, Monsoor chose to protect his comrades by the sacrifice of his own life. By his courageous and selfless actions, he saved the lives of his two fellow SEALs.

He was later awarded the Medal of Honor.

A lot of memories about Mikey came back as soon as I found out he'd died. I hadn't known him all that well, because he was in the other platoon, but I was there for his hazing.

I remember us holding him down so his head could be shaved. He didn't like that at all; I may still have some bruises.

I DROVE A VAN TO PICK UP SOME OF THE GUYS FROM THE AIRport and helped arrange Mikey's wake.

SEAL funerals are kind of like Irish wakes, except there's a lot more drinking. Which begs the question, how much beer do you need for a SEAL wake? That is classified information, but rest assured it is more than a metric ass-ton.

I stood on the tarmac in dress blues as the plane came in. My arm went up in a stiff salute as the coffin came down the ramp, then, with the other pallbearers, I carried it slowly to the waiting hearse.

We attracted a bit of a crowd at the airport. People nearby who realized what was going on stopped and stared silently, paying their respects. It was touching; they were honoring a fellow countryman even though they didn't know him. I was moved at the sight, a last honor for our fallen comrade, a silent recognition of the importance of his sacrifice.

THE ONLY THING THAT SAYS WE'RE SEALS ARE THE SEAL TRIdents we wear, the metal insignia that show we're members. If you don't have that on your chest, you're just another Navy puke.

It's become a sign of respect to take it off and hammer it onto the coffin of your fallen brother at the funeral. You're showing the guy that you'll never forget, that he remains part of you for the rest of your life.

As the guys from Delta Platoon lined up to pound their tridents into Mikey's coffin, I backed off, head bowed. It happened that Marc Lee's tombstone was just a few yards from where Monsoor was going to be buried. I'd missed Marc's funeral because I'd still been overseas, and still hadn't had a chance to pay my respects. Now it suddenly seemed appropriate to put my trident on his tombstone.

I walked over silently and laid it down, wishing my friend one last good-bye.

ONE OF THE THINGS THAT MADE THAT FUNERAL BITTERSWEET was the fact that Ryan was released from the hospital in time to attend it. It was great to see him, even though he was now permanently blind.

Before passing out from blood loss after he'd been shot, Ryan had been able to see. But as his brain swelled with internal bleeding, bone or bullet fragments that were in his eye severed his optic nerves. There was no hope for restoring sight.

When I saw him, I asked him why he'd insisted on walking out of the building under his own power. It struck me as a remarkably brave thing—characteristic of him. Ryan told me he knew that our procedures called for at least two guys to go down with him if he couldn't move on his own. He didn't want to take more guys out of the fight.

I think he thought he could have gotten back on his own. And probably he would have if we'd let him. He might even have picked up a gun and tried to continue the fight.

Ryan left the service because of his injury, but we remained close. They say friendships forged in war are strong ones. Ours would prove that truism.

PUNCHING OUT SCRUFF FACE

AFTER THE FUNERAL WE WENT TO A LOCAL BAR FOR THE WAKE proper.

As always, there were a bunch of different things going on at our favorite nightspot, including a small party for some older SEALs and UDT members who were celebrating the anniversary of their graduation. Among them was a celebrity I'll call Scruff Face.

Scruff served in the military; most people seem to believe he was a SEAL. As far as I know, he was in the service during the Vietnam conflict but not actually in the war.

I was sitting there with Ryan and told him that Scruff was holding court with some of his buddies.

"I'd really like to meet him," Ryan said.

"Sure." I got up and went over to Scruff and introduced myself. "Mr. Scruff Face, I have a young SEAL over here who's just come back from Iraq. He's been injured but he'd really like to meet you."

Well, Scruff kind of blew us off. Still, Ryan really wanted to meet him, so I brought him over. Scruff acted like he couldn't be bothered.

All right.

We went back over to our side of the bar and had a few more drinks. In the meantime, Scruff started running his mouth about the war and everything and anything he could connect to it. President Bush was an asshole. We were only over there because Bush wanted to show up his father. We were doing the wrong thing, killing men and women and children and murdering.

And on and on. Scruff said he hates America and that's why he moved to Baja California. 9/11 was a conspiracy.

And on and on some more.

The guys were getting upset. Finally, I went over and tried to get him to cool it.

"We're all here in mourning," I told him. "Can you just cool it? Keep it down."

"You deserve to lose a few," he told me.

Then he bowed up as if to belt me one.

I was uncharacteristically level-headed at that moment.

"Look," I told him, "why don't we just step away from each other and go on our way?"

Scruff bowed up again. This time he swung.

Being level-headed and calm can last only so long. I laid him out.

Tables flew. Stuff happened. Scruff Face ended up on the floor.

I left.

Quickly.

I have no way of knowing for sure, but rumor has it he showed up at the BUD/S graduation with a black eye.

FIGHTING IS A FACT OF LIFE WHEN YOU'RE A SEAL. I'VE BEEN in a few good ones.

In April '07, we were in Tennessee. We ended up across the state line in a city where there'd been a big UFC mixed-martial-arts fight earlier that evening. By coincidence, we happened into a bar where there were three fighters who were celebrating their first victories in the ring. We weren't looking for trouble; in fact, I was in a quiet corner with a buddy where there was hardly anyone else around.

For some reason, three or four guys came over and bumped into my friend. Words were said. Whatever they were, the wannabe UFC fighters didn't like them, so they went after him.

Naturally, I wasn't going to let him fight alone. I jumped in. Together, we beat the shit out of them.

This time, I didn't follow Chief Primo's advice. In fact, I was still pounding one of the fighters when the bouncers came to break us up. The cops came in and arrested me. I was charged with assault. (My friend had slipped out the back. No bad wishes on him; he was only following Primo's second rule of fighting.)

I got out on bail the next day. I had a lawyer come in and work out a plea bargain with the judge. The prosecutor agreed to drop the charges, but to make it all legal I had to get up there in front of the judge.

"Mr. Kyle," she said, in the slow drawl of justice, "just because you're trained to kill, doesn't mean you have to prove it in my city. Get out and don't come back."

And so I did, and haven't.

THAT LITTLE MISHAP GOT ME IN A BIT OF TROUBLE AT HOME. No matter where I was during training, I would always give Taya a call before I went to sleep. But having spent the night in the drunk tank, there was no call home.

I mean, I only had one call, and she couldn't get me out, so I put it to good use.

There might not have been a real problem, except that I was supposed to go home for one of the kids' birthday parties. Because of the court appearance, I had to extend my stay in town.

"Where are you?" asked Taya when I finally got a hold of her.

"I got arrested."

"All right," she snapped. "Whatever."

I can't say I blamed her for being mad. It wasn't the most responsible thing I'd ever done. Coming when it did, it was just one more irritant in a time filled with them—our relationship was rapidly going downhill.

Taya:

I didn't fall in love with a frickin' Navy SEAL, I fell in love with Chris.

Being a SEAL is cool and everything, but that's not what I loved about him.

If I'd known what to expect, that would have been one thing. But you don't know what to expect. No one does. Not really—not in real life. And not every SEAL does multiple back-to-back wartime deployments, either.

As time went on, his job became more and more

important to him. He didn't need me for family, in a way—he had the guys.

Little by little, I realized I wasn't the most important thing in his life. The words were there, but he didn't mean it.

FIGHTS AND MORE FIGHTS

I AM BY NO MEANS A BAD-ASS, OR EVEN AN EXTREMELY SKILLED fighter, but several instances have presented themselves. I would rather get my ass beat than look like a pussy in front of my boys.

I have had other run-ins with fighters. I like to think I've held my own.

While I was serving with my very first platoon, the whole SEAL team went to Fort Irwin in San Bernardino out in the Mojave Desert. After our training sessions, we headed into town and found a bar there, called the Library.

Inside, a few off-duty police officers and firemen were having a party. A few of the women turned their attention to our guys. When that happened, the locals got all jealous and started a fight.

Which really showed some truly poor judgment, because there had to be close to a hundred of us in that little bar. A hundred SEALs is a force to be reckoned with, and we did the reckoning that day. Then we went outside and flipped over a couple of cars.

Somewhere around there, the cops came. They arrested twenty-five of us.

YOU'VE PROBABLY HEARD OF CAPTAIN'S MAST—THAT'S WHERE the commanding officer listens to what you've done and hands out what is called a nonjudicial punishment if he thinks it's warranted. The punishments are prescribed by military law and can be anything from a stern "tsk, tsk, don't do that again" to an actual reduction in grade and even "correctional custody," which pretty much means what you think it means.

There are similar hearings with less critical consequences, heard by officers below the CO. In our case, we had to go before the XO (executive officer, the officer just below the commander) and listen while he told us in extremely eloquent language how truly fucked up we were. In the process, he read off all the legal charges, all the destruction—I forget how many people got hurt and how much money's worth of damage we caused, but it took a while for him to catalog. He finished by telling us how ashamed he was.

"All right," he said, lecture over. "Don't let it happen again. Get the hell out of here."

We all left, duly chastised, his words ringing in our ears for . . . a good five seconds or so.

But the story doesn't end there.

Another unit heard of our little adventure, and they decided that they should visit the bar and see if history would repeat itself.

It did.

They won that fight, but from what I understand the conditions were a little more difficult. The outcome wasn't quite so lopsided.

A little after that, yet another military group soon had to train in the same area. By now, there was a competition. The only problem was that the folks who lived there knew there would be a competition. And they prepared for it.

They got their collective asses kicked.

From then on, the entire town was placed off limits for SEALs.

You might think it'd be tough to get into a drunken brawl in Kuwait, since there really aren't any bars where you can drink alcohol. But it just so happened that there was a restaurant where we liked to eat, and where, not so coincidentally, it was easy to sneak in alcohol.

We were there one night and started to get a little loud. Some of the locals objected; there was an argument, which led to a fight. Four of us, including myself, were detained.

The rest of my boys came over and asked the police to release us.

"No way," said the police. "They're going to jail and stand trial."

They emphasized their position. My boys emphasized theirs.

If you've read this far, you've caught on that SEALs can be persuasive. The Kuwaitis finally saw it their way and released us.

I was arrested in Steamboat Springs, Colorado, though I think in that case the circumstances may speak well of me. I was sitting in the bar when a waitress passed with a pitcher of beer. A guy at a table nearby pushed his chair back and bumped into her, not knowing she was there; a little bit of beer spilled on him.

He got up and slapped her.

I went over and defended her honor the only way I know how. That got me arrested. Those granolas are tough when it comes to fighting with women.

Those charges, like all the others, were dismissed.

THE SHERIFF OF RAMADI

The Ramadi offensive would eventually be considered an important milestone and turning point in the war, one of the key events that helped Iraq emerge from utter chaos. Because of that, there was a good deal of attention on the fighters who were there. And some of that attention eventually came to focus on our Team.

As I hope I've made clear, I don't feel SEALs should be singled out publicly as a force. We don't need the publicity. We are silent professionals, every one of us; the quieter we are, the better able we are to do our job.

Unfortunately, that's not the world we live in. If it were, I wouldn't have felt it necessary to write this book.

Let me say for the record that I believe the credit in Ramadi and in all of Iraq should go to the Army and Marine warriors who fought there as well as the SEALs. It should be fairly proportioned out. Yes, SEALs did a good job, and gave their blood. But as we told the Army and Marine officers and enlisted men we fought beside, we're no better than those men when it comes to courage and worth.

BUT BEING IN THE MODERN WORLD, PEOPLE WERE INTERESTED in knowing about SEALs. After we got back, command called us together for a briefing so we could tell a famous author and former SEAL what had happened in battle. The author was Dick Couch.

The funny thing was, he started out not by listening but by talking.

Not even talking. Mr. Couch came and lectured us about how wrong-headed we were.

I have a lot of respect for Mr. Couch's service during the Vietnam War, where he served with Navy Underwater Demolition and SEAL Teams. I honor and respect him greatly for that. But a few of the things he said that day didn't sit all that well with me.

He got up in front of the room and started telling us that we were doing things all wrong. He told us we should be winning their hearts and minds instead of killing them.

"SEALs should be more SF-like," he claimed, referring (I guess) to one of Special Forces' traditional missions of training indigenous people.

Last time I checked, they think it's okay to shoot people who shoot at you, but maybe that's beside the point.

I was sitting there getting furious. So was the entire team, though they all kept their mouths shut. He finally asked for comments.

My hand shot up.

I made a few disparaging remarks about what I thought we might do to the country, then I got serious.

"They only started coming to the peace table after we killed enough of the savages out there," I told him. "That was the key."

I may have used some other colorful phrases as I discussed what was really going on out there. We had a bit of a back-and-forth before my head shed signaled that I ought to leave the room. I was glad to comply.

Afterward, my CO and command chief were furious with me. But they couldn't do too much, because they knew I was right.

Mr. Couch wanted to interview me later on. I was reluctant. Command wanted me to answer his questions. Even my chief sat me down and talked to me.

So I did. Yup, nope. That was the interview.

In fairness, from what I've heard his book is not quite as negative as I understood his lecture to be. So maybe a few of my fellow SEALs did have some influence on him.

HARD TIMES

YOU KNOW HOW RAMADI WAS WON?

We went in and killed all the bad people we could find.

When we started, the decent (or potentially decent) Iraqis didn't fear the United States; they did fear the terrorists. The U.S. told them, "We'll make it better for you."

The terrorists said, "We'll cut your head off."

Who would you fear? Who would you listen to?

When we went into Ramadi, we told the terrorists, "We'll cut *your* head off. We will do whatever we have to and eliminate you."

Not only did we get the terrorists' attention—we got *everyone's* attention. We showed *we* were the force to be reckoned with.

That's where the so-called Great Awakening came. It wasn't from kissing up to the Iraqis. It was from kicking butt.

The tribal leaders saw that we were bad-asses, and they'd better get their act together, work together, and stop accommodating the insurgents. Force moved that battle. We killed the bad guys and brought the leaders to the peace table.

That is how the world works.

KNEE SURGERY

I'D FIRST HURT MY KNEES IN FALLUJAH WHEN THE WALL FELL on me. Cortisone shots helped for a while, but the pain kept coming back and getting worse. The docs told me I needed to have my legs operated on, but doing that would have meant I would have to take time off and miss the war.

So I kept putting it off. I settled into a routine where I'd go to the doc, get a shot, go back to work. The time between shots became shorter and shorter. It got down to every two months, then every month.

I made it through Ramadi, but just barely. My knees started

locking and it was difficult to get down the stairs. I no longer had a choice, so, soon after I got home in 2007, I went under the knife.

The surgeons cut my tendons to relieve pressure so my kneecaps would slide back over. They had to shave down my kneecaps because I had worn grooves in them. They injected synthetic cartilage material and shaved the meniscus. Somewhere along the way they also repaired an ACL.

I was like a racing car, being repaired from the ground up.

When they were done, they sent me to see Jason, a physical therapist who specializes in working with SEALs. He'd been a trainer for the Pittsburgh Pirates. After 9/11, he decided to devote himself to helping the country. He chose to do that by working with the military. He took a massive pay cut to help put us back together.

I DIDN'T KNOW ALL THAT THE FIRST DAY WE MET. ALL I WANTED to hear was how long it was going to take to rehab.

He gave me a pensive look.

"This surgery—civilians need a year to get back," he said finally. "Football players, they're out eight months. SEALs—it's hard to say. You hate being out of action and will punish yourselves to get back."

He finally predicted six months. I think we did it in five. But I thought I would surely die along the way.

JASON PUT ME INTO A MACHINE THAT WOULD STRETCH MY knee. Every day I had to see how much further I could adjust it. I would sweat up a storm as it bent my knee. I finally got it to ninety degrees.

"That's outstanding," he told me. "Now get more."

"More?"

"*More!*"

He also had a machine that sent a shock to my muscle through electrodes. Depending on the muscle, I would have to stretch and point my toes up and down. It doesn't sound like much, but it is clearly a form of torture that should be outlawed by the Geneva Convention, even for use on SEALs.

Naturally, Jason kept upping the voltage.

But the worst of all was the simplest: the exercise. I had to do more, more, more. I remember calling Taya many times and telling her I was sure I was going to puke if not die before the day was out. She seemed sympathetic but, come to think of it in retrospect, she and Jason may have been in on it together.

There was a stretch where Jason had me doing crazy amounts of ab exercises and other things to my core muscles.

"Do you understand it's my knees that were operated on?" I asked him one day when I thought I'd reached my limit.

He just laughed. He had a scientific explanation about how everything in the body depends on strong core muscles, but I think he just liked kicking my ass around the gym. I swear I heard a bullwhip crack over my head any time I started to slack.

I always thought the best shape I was ever in was straight out of BUD/S. But I was in far better shape after spending five months with him. Not only were my knees okay, the rest of me was in top condition. When I came back to my platoon, they all asked if I had been taking steroids.

ROUGH TIMES

I'D PUSHED MY BODY AS FAR AS I COULD BEFORE GETTING THE operations. Now the thing that was deteriorating was even more important than my knees—my marriage.

This was the roughest of a bunch of rough spots. A lot of resentment had built up between us. Ironically, we didn't actually fight all that much, but there was always a lot of tension. Each of us would put in just enough effort to be able to say we were trying—and imply that the other person was not.

After years of being in war zones and separated from my wife, I think in a way I'd just forgotten what it means to be in love—the responsibilities that come with it, like truly listening and sharing. That forgetting made it easier for me to push her away. At the same time, an old girlfriend happened to get in contact with me. She called the home phone first, and Taya passed the message along to me, assuming I wasn't the type of guy she had to worry about straying.

I laughed off the message at first, but curiosity got the best of me. Soon my old girlfriend and I were talking and texting regularly.

Taya figured out that something was up. One night I came home and she sat me down and laid everything out, very calmly, very rationally—or at least as rational as you can be in that kind of situation.

"We have to be able to trust each other," she said at one point. "And in the direction we're going, that's not going to work. It just won't."

We had a long, heartfelt talk about that. I think we both cried. I know I did. I loved my wife. I didn't want to be separated from her. I wasn't interested in getting divorced.

I KNOW: IT SOUNDS CORNY AS SHIT. A FUCKING SEAL TALKING about love?

I'd rather get choked out a hundred times than do that in public, let alone here for the whole world to see.

But it was real. If I'm going to be honest, I have to put it out there.

WE SET UP A FEW RULES THAT WE WOULD LIVE BY. AND WE both agreed to go to counseling.

TAYA:

Things just got to the point where I felt as if I was looking down into a deep pit. It wasn't just arguments over the kids. We weren't relating to each other. I could tell his mind had strayed from our marriage, from us.

I remember talking to a girlfriend who'd been through an awful lot. I just unloaded.

She said to me, "Well this is what you have to do. You have to lay it all on the line. You have to tell him that you love him, and you want him to stay, but if he wants to go, he is free to do so."

I took her advice. It was a hard, hard conversation.

But I knew several things in my heart. First, I knew I loved Chris. And second, and this was very important to me, I knew that he was a good dad. I'd seen him with our son, and with our daughter. He had a strong sense of discipline and respect, and at the same time had so much fun with the kids that by the time they were done playing they all ached from laughing. Those two things

> *really convinced me that I had to try to keep our marriage together.*
>
> *From my side, I hadn't been the perfect wife, either. Yes, I loved him, truly, but I'd been a real bitch at times. I had pushed him away.*
>
> *So both of us had to want the marriage and we both had to come together to make it work.*

I'd like to say that things instantly got better from that point on. But life really isn't like that. We did talk a lot more. I started to become more focused on the marriage—more focused on my responsibilities to my family.

One issue that we didn't completely resolve had to do with my enlistment, and how it would fit with our family's long-term plans. My earlier reenlistment was going to be up in roughly two years; we had already begun discussing that.

Taya made it clear that our family needed a father. My son was growing in leaps and bounds. Boys do need a strong male figure in their lives; there was no way I could disagree.

But I also felt as if I had a duty to my country. I had been trained to kill; I was very good at it. I felt I had to protect my fellow SEALs, and my fellow Americans.

And I liked doing it. A lot.

But . . .

I went back and forth. It was a very difficult decision.

Incredibly difficult.

In the end, I decided she was right: others could do my job protecting the country, but no one could truly take my place with my family. And I had given my country a fair share.

I told her I would not reenlist when the time came.

I still wonder sometimes if I made the right decision. In my mind, as long as I am fit and there is a war, my country needs me.

Why would I send someone in my place? A part of me felt I was acting like a coward.

Serving in the Teams is serving a greater good. As a civilian, I'd just be serving *my* own good. Being a SEAL wasn't just what I did; it became who I was.

A FOURTH DEPLOYMENT

IF THINGS HAD WORKED ACCORDING TO "NORMAL" PROCEdures, I would have been given a long break and a long stretch of shore duty after my second deployment. But for various reasons, that didn't happen.

The Team promised that I'd have a break after this deployment. But that didn't work either. I wasn't real happy about it. I lost my temper talking about it, as a matter of fact. I'd guess more than once.

Now, I like war, and I love doing my job, but it rankled me that the Navy wasn't keeping its word. With all the stress at home, an assignment that would have kept me near my family at that point would have been welcome. But I was told that the needs of the Navy came first. And fair or not, that's the way it was.

MY BLOOD PRESSURE WAS STILL ELEVATED.

The doctors blamed it on coffee and dip. According to them, my blood pressure was as high as if I were drinking ten cups of coffee right before the test. I was drinking coffee, but not nearly that much. They strongly urged me to cut back, and to stop using dip.

Of course I didn't argue with them. I didn't want to get kicked out of the SEALs, or go down a road that might lead to a medical discharge. I suppose, in retrospect, some might wonder why I didn't do that, but it would have seemed like a cowardly thing to do. It would never have felt right.

In the end, I was all right with being scheduled for another deployment. I still loved war.

DELTA PLATOON

Usually, when you come home, a few guys will rotate out of the platoon. Officers will usually change out. A lot of times the chief leaves, the LPO—lead petty officer—becomes the chief, and then someone else becomes LPO. But other than that, you stay pretty tight-knit. In our case, most of the platoon had been together for many years.

Until now.

Trying to spread out the experience in the Team, command decided to break up Charlie/Cadillac Platoon and spread us out. I was assigned to Delta, and put in as LPO of the platoon. I worked directly with the new chief, who happened to be one of my BUD/S instructors.

We worked out our personnel selections, making assignments and sending different people off to school. Now that I was LPO, I not only had more admin crap to deal with, but couldn't be point man anymore.

That hurt.

I drew the line when they talked about taking my sniper rifle away. I was still a sniper, no matter what else I did in the platoon.

Besides finding good point men, one of the toughest personnel decisions I had to make involved choosing a breacher. The breacher is the person who, among other things, is in charge of the explosives, who sets them and blows them (if necessary) on the DA. Once the platoon is inside, the breacher is really running things. So the group is entirely in his hands.

There are a number of other important tasks and schools I haven't mentioned along the way, but which do deserve attention. Among them is the JTAC—that's the guy who gets to call in air support. It's a popular position in the Teams. First of all, the job is kind of fun: you get to watch things blow up. And secondly, you're often called away for special missions, so you get a lot of action.

Comms and navigation are a lot further down the list for most SEALs. But they're necessary jobs. The worst school you can send someone to has to do with intel. People hate that. They joined the SEALs to kick down doors, not to gather intelligence. But everyone has a role.

Of course, some people like to fall out of planes, and swim with the sharks.

Sickos.

The dispersal of talent may have helped the Team in general, but as platoon LPO I was concerned about getting the best guys over to Delta with me.

The master chief in charge of the personnel arrangements was working everything out on an organizational chart that had been set up on a big magnetic board. One afternoon, while he was out, I snuck into his office and rearranged things. Suddenly, everyone who was anyone in Charlie was now assigned to Delta.

My changes had been a little too drastic, and as soon as the master chief got back, my ears started ringing even more than normal.

"Don't *ever* go into my office when I am not here," he told me as soon as I reported to him. "Don't touch my board. *Ever.*"

Well, truth is, I did go back.

I knew he'd catch anything drastic, so I made one little switch and got Dauber into my platoon. I needed a good sniper and corpsman. The master chief apparently never noticed it, or at least didn't change it.

I had my answer ready in case I was caught: "I did it for the good of the Navy."

Or at least Delta Platoon.

STILL RECOVERING FROM KNEE SURGERY, I COULDN'T ACTUally take part in a lot of the training for the first few months the platoon was together. But I kept tabs on my guys, watching them when I could. I hobbled around the land warfare sessions, observing the new guys especially. I wanted to know who I was going to war with.

I was just about back into shape when I got into a pair of fights, first the one in Tennessee I mentioned earlier, where I was arrested, and then another near Fort Campbell where, as my son put it, "some guy decided to break his face on my daddy's hand."

"Some guy" also broke my hand in the process.

My platoon chief was livid.

"You've been out with knee surgery, we get you back, you get arrested, now you break your hand. What the fuck?"

There may have been a few other choice words thrown in there as well. They may also have continued for quite a while.

THINKING BACK, I DID SEEM TO GET INTO A NUMBER OF FIGHTS during this training period. In my mind, at least, they weren't my fault—in that last case, I was on my way out when the idiot's girlfriend tried picking a fight with my friend, a SEAL. Which was absolutely as ridiculous in real life as it must look on the printed page.

But taken together, it was a bad pattern. It might even have been a disturbing trend. Unfortunately, I didn't recognize it at the time.

PUNCHED OUT

THERE'S A POSTSCRIPT TO THE STORY ABOUT "SOME GUY" AND my broken hand.

The incident happened while we were training in an Army town. I knew pretty much when I punched him that I'd broken my hand, but there was no way in hell that I was going to the base hospital; if I did, they'd realize I was (a) drunk and (b) fighting, and the MPs would be on my ass. Nothing makes an MP's day like busting a SEAL.

So I waited until the next day. Now sober, I reported to the hospital and claimed I had broken my fist by punching out my gun before I actually cleared the doorjamb. (Theoretically possible, if unlikely.)

While I was getting treated, I saw a kid in the hospital with his jaw wired shut.

Next thing I knew, some MPs came over and started questioning me.

"This kid is claiming you broke his jaw," said one of them.

"What the hell is he talking about?" I said, rolling my eyes. "I just came in off a training exercise. I broke my damn hand. Ask the SF guys; we're training with them."

Not so coincidentally, all of the bouncers at the bar where we'd been were Army SF; they would surely back me up if it came to that.

It didn't.

"We thought so," said the MPs, shaking their heads. They went back over to the idiot soldier and started bitching him out for lying and wasting their time.

Serves him right for getting into a fight started by his girlfriend.

I CAME BACK WEST WITH A SHATTERED BONE. THE GUYS ALL made fun of me for my weak genes. But the injury wasn't all that funny for me, because the doctors couldn't figure out whether they should operate or not. My finger set a little deeper in my hand, not quite where it should be.

In San Diego, one of the doctors took a look and decided they might be able to fix it by pulling it and resetting it in the socket.

I told him to give it a go.

"You want some painkiller?" he asked.

"Nah," I said. They'd done the same thing at the Army hospital back East, and it hadn't really hurt.

Maybe Navy doctors pull harder. The next thing I knew I was lying flat back on a table in the cast room. I'd passed out and pissed myself from the pain.

But at least I got away without surgery.

And for the record, I've since changed my fighting style to accommodate my weaker hand.

READY TO GO

I HAD TO WEAR A CAST FOR A FEW WEEKS, BUT MORE AND more I got into the swing of things. The pace built up as we got ready to ship out. There was only one down note: we had been assigned to a western province in Iraq. From what we had heard, nothing was going on there. We tried to get transferred to Afghanistan, but we couldn't get released by the area commander.

That didn't sit too well with us, certainly not with me. If I was going back to war, I wanted to be in the action, not twiddling my (broken) fingers in the desert. Being a SEAL, you don't want to sit around with your thumb up your ass; you want to get in the action.

Still, it felt good to be getting back to war. I'd been burned out when I came home, completely overwhelmed and emotionally drained. But now I felt recharged and ready to go.

I was ready to kill some more bad guys.

13

MORTALITY

BLIND

It seemed like every dog in Sadr City was barking.

I scanned the darkness through my night vision, tense as we made our way down one of the nastiest streets in Sadr City. We walked past a row of what might have been condos in a normal city. Here they were little better than rat-infested slums. It was past midnight in early April 2008, and, against all common sense but under direct orders, we were walking into the center of an insurgent hellhole.

Like a lot of the other drab-brown buildings on the street, the house we were heading to had a metal grate in front of the door. We lined up to breach it. Just then, someone appeared from behind the grate at the door and said something in Arabic.

Our interpreter stepped over and told him to open up.

The man inside said he didn't have a key.

One of the other SEALs told him to go get it. The man disappeared, running up the stairs somewhere.

Shit!

"Go!" I yelled. "Break the grate the fuck in."

We rushed in and started clearing the house. The two bottom levels were empty.

I raced up the stairs to the third floor and moved to the doorway of a room facing the street, leaning back against the wall as the rest of my guys stacked to follow. As I started to take a step, the whole room blew up.

By some miracle, I hadn't been hit, though I sure felt the force of the blast.

"Who the fuck just threw a frag!" I yelled.

Nobody. And the room itself was empty. Someone had just fired an RPG into the house.

Gunfire followed. We regrouped. The Iraqi who'd been inside had clearly escaped to alert the nearby insurgents where we were. Worse, the walls in the house proved pretty flimsy, unable to stand up to the rocket grenades that were being fired at us. If we stayed here, we were going to get fried.

Out of the house! *Now!*

The last of my guys had just cleared out of the building when the street shook with a huge force: the insurgents had set off an IED down the street. The blast was so powerful it knocked a few of us off our feet. Ears ringing, we ran to another building nearby. But as we were fixing to enter it, all hell broke loose. We got gunfire from every direction, including above.

A shot flew into my helmet. The night went black. I was blind.

It was my first night in Sadr City, and it looked like it was soon going to be my last on earth.

OUT WEST

Until that point, I had spent an uneventful, even boring fourth deployment in Iraq.

Delta Platoon had arrived roughly a month before, traveling out to al-Qa'im in western Iraq, near the Syrian border. Our mission was supposed to involve long-range desert patrols, but we'd spent our time building a base camp with the help of a few Seabees. Not only was there no action to speak of, but the Marines who owned the base were in the process of shutting it down, meaning that we'd have to move out soon after we set it up. I have no idea what the logic was.

Morale had hit rock bottom when my chief risked his life early one morning—by that I mean he entered my room and shook me awake.

"What the hell?" I yelled, jumping up.

"Easy," said my chief. "You need to get dressed and come with me."

"I just got to sleep."

"You'll want to come with me. They're putting together a task unit over in Baghdad."

A task unit? *All right!*

It was like something out of the movie *Groundhog Day*, but in a good way. The last time this had happened to me, I was in Baghdad heading west. Now I was west, and heading east.

Why exactly, I wasn't sure.

According to the chief, I had been chosen for the unit partly because I was qualified to be an LPO, but mostly because I was a sniper. They were pulling snipers from all over the country for the operation, though he had no details of what was being planned. He didn't even know whether I was going to a rural or urban environment.

Shit, I thought, *we're going to Iran.*

It was an open secret that the Iranians were arming and training insurgents and in some cases even attacking Western troops themselves. There were rumors that a force was being formed to stop the infiltrators on the border.

I was convoyed over to al-Asad, the big airbase in al-Anbar Province, where our top head shed was located. There, I found out we weren't going to the border, but a place much worse: Sadr City.

Located on the outskirts of Baghdad, Sadr City had become even more of a snake pit since the last time I'd been with the GROMs a few years before. Two million Shiites lived there. The rabidly anti-American cleric Muqtada al-Sadr (the city had been named for his father) had been steadily building his militia, the Mahdi Army (known in Arabic as the *Jaish al-Mahdi*). There were other insurgents operating in the area, but the Mahdi Army was by far the biggest and most powerful.

With covert help from Iran, the insurgents had gathered arms and started launching mortars and rockets into Baghdad's Green Zone. The entire place was a vipers' nest. Like Fallujah and Ramadi, there were different cliques and varying levels of expertise among the insurgents. The people here were mostly Shiites, whereas my earlier battles in Iraq had been primarily with Sunnis. But otherwise it was a very familiar hellhole.

This was all fine with me.

THEY PULLED SNIPERS AND JTACS, ALONG WITH SOME OFFI-
cers and chiefs, from Teams 3 and 8 to create a special task unit.
There were about thirty of us altogether. In a way it was an all-star
team, with some of the best of the best guys in the country. And it
was very sniper-heavy, because the idea was to implement some of
the tactics we'd used in Fallujah, Ramadi, and elsewhere.

There was a lot of talent, but because we were drawn from all
different units, we needed to spend a bit of time getting used to
each other. Small differences in the way East Coast and West Coast
teams typically operated could make for a big problem in a firefight. We also had a lot of personnel decisions to make, selecting
point men and the like.

THE ARMY HAD DECIDED TO CREATE A BUFFER ZONE TO PUSH
the insurgents far enough away that their rockets would not reach
the Green Zone. One of the keys to this was erecting a wall in Sadr
City—basically, a huge cement fence called a "T-wall" that would
run down a major thoroughfare about a quarter of the way into the
slum. Our job was to protect the guys building that wall—and take
down as many bad guys as possible in the process.

The boys building that wall had an insanely dangerous job. A
crane would take one of the concrete sections off the back of a flat-
bed and haul it into place. As it was set down, a private would have
to climb up and unhook it.

Under fire, generally. And not just pop shots—the insurgents
would use any weapon they had, from AKs to RPGs. Those Army
guys had serious balls.

A Special Forces unit had already been operating in Sadr City, and they gave us some pointers and intel. We took about a week getting things all worked out and figuring out how we were going to skin this cat. Once everything was settled, we were dropped off at an Army FOB (forward operating base).

At this point, we were told we were going to foot patrol into Sadr City at night. A few of us argued that it didn't make much sense—the place was crawling with people who wanted to kill us, and on foot we'd be easy targets.

But someone thought it would be smart if we walked in during the middle of the night. Sneak in, they told us, and there won't be trouble.

So we did.

SHOT IN THE BACK

They were wrong.

There I was, shot in the head and blind. Blood streamed down my face. I reached up to my scalp. I was surprised—not only was my head still there, but it was intact. But I knew I'd been shot.

Somehow I realized that my helmet, which hadn't been strapped, had been pushed back. I pulled it forward. Suddenly I could see again. A bullet had struck the helmet, but with incredible luck had ricocheted off my night vision, slamming the helmet backward but otherwise not harming me. When I pulled it forward, I brought the scope back down in front of my eyes, and could see again. I hadn't been rendered blind at all, but in the confusion I couldn't tell what was going on.

A few seconds later, I got hit in the back with a heavy round. The bullet pushed me straight to the ground. Fortunately, the round hit one of the plates in my body armor.

Still, it left me dazed. Meanwhile, we were surrounded. We called to each other and organized a retreat to a marketplace we'd passed on the way in. We started laying down fire and moving together.

By this time, the blocks around us looked like the worst scenes in *Black Hawk Down*. It seemed like every insurgent, maybe every occupant, wanted a piece of the idiot Americans who'd foolishly blundered into Sadr City.

We couldn't get into the building we retreated to. By now we'd called for QRF—a quick response force, a fancy name for the cavalry. We needed backup and extraction—"HELP" in capital letters.

A group of Army Strykers came in. Strykers are heavily armed personnel carriers, and they were firing everything they had. There were plenty of targets—upward of a hundred insurgents lined the roofs on the surrounding streets, trying to get us. When they saw the Strykers, they changed their aim, trying to take out the Army's big personnel carriers. There they were overmatched. It started looking like a video game—guys were falling off the rooftops.

"Motherfucker, thank you," I said aloud when the vehicles reached our building. I swear I could hear a cavalry horn somewhere in the background.

They dropped their ramps and we ran inside.

"Did you see how many motherfuckers were up there?" said one of the crewmen as the vehicle sped back to the base.

"No," I answered. "I was too busy shooting."

"They were all over the place." The kid was stoked. "We were dropping them and that wasn't even half of them. We were just laying it down. We thought y'all were fuckin' done."

That made more than two of us.

THAT NIGHT SCARED THE SHIT OUT OF ME. THAT'S WHEN I came to the realization that I'm not superhuman. I can die.

All through everything else, there had been points where I thought, *I'm going to die.*

But I never did die. Those thoughts were fleeting. They evaporated.

After a while, I started thinking, they can't kill me. They can't kill us. We're fucking undefeatable.

I have a guardian angel and I'm a SEAL and I'm lucky and whatever the hell it is: *I cannot die.*

Then, all of a sudden, within two minutes I was nailed twice.

Motherfucker, my number is up.

BUILDING THE WALL

WE FELT HAPPY AND GRATEFUL TO HAVE BEEN RESCUED. We also felt like total asses.

Trying to sneak into Sadr City was not going to work, and command should have known that from the start. The bad guys would always know we were there. So we would just have to make the most of it.

Two days after getting our butts kicked out of the city, we came back, this time riding in Strykers. We took over a place known as the banana factory. This was a building four or five stories high, filled with fruit lockers and assorted factory gear, most of it wrecked by looters long before we got there. I'm not sure exactly what it had to do with bananas or what the Iraqis might have done there; all I knew at the time was that it was a good place for a sniper hide.

Wanting a little more cover than I would have had on the roof, I set up in the top floor. Around nine o'clock in the morning, I realized the number of civilians walking up and down the street had started to thin. That was always a giveaway—they spotted something and knew they didn't want to end up in the line of fire.

A few minutes later, with the street now deserted, an Iraqi came out of a partially destroyed building. He was armed with an AK-47. When he reached the street he ducked down, scouting in the direction of the engineers who were working down the road on the wall, apparently trying to pick one out to target. As soon as I was sure what he was up to, I aimed center-mass and fired.

He was forty yards away. He fell, dead.

An hour later, another guy poked his head out from behind a wall on another part of the street. He glanced in the direction of the T-wall, then pulled back.

It may have seemed innocent to someone else—and certainly didn't meet the ROEs—but I knew to watch more carefully. I'd seen insurgents follow this same pattern now for years. They would peek out, glance around, then disappear. I called them "peekers"—they "peeked" out to see if anyone was watching. I'm sure they knew they couldn't be shot for glancing around.

I knew it, too. But I also knew that if I was patient, the guy or whoever he was spotting for would most likely reappear. Sure enough, the fellow reappeared a few moments later.

He had an RPG in his hand. He knelt quickly, bringing it up to aim.

I dropped him before he could fire.

Then it became a waiting game. The rocket was valuable to them. Sooner or later, I knew, someone would be sent to get it.

I watched. It seemed like forever. Finally, a figure came down the street and scooped up the grenade launcher.

It was a kid. A child.

I had a clear view in my scope, but I didn't fire. I wasn't going to kill a kid, innocent or not. I'd have to wait until the savage who put him up to it showed himself on the street.

TARGET-RICH

I ENDED UP GETTING SEVEN INSURGENTS THAT DAY, AND MORE the next. We were in a target-rich environment.

Because of the way the streets were laid out and the number of insurgents, we were getting close shots—a number were as close as 200 yards. My longest during this time was only about 880; the average was around 400.

The city around us was schizophrenic. You'd have ordinary civilians going about their business, selling things, going to market, whatever. And then you'd have guys with guns trying to sneak up on the side streets and attack the soldiers putting up the wall. After we began engaging the insurgents, we would become the targets ourselves. Everyone would know where we were, and the bad guys would come out of their slug holes and try and take us down.

It got to the point where I had so many kills that I stepped back to let the other guys have a few. I started giving them the best spots in the buildings we took over. Even so, I had plenty of chances to shoot.

One day we took over this house and, after letting my guys choose their places, there were no more windows to fire from. So I took a sledgehammer and broke a hole in the wall. It took me quite a while to get it right.

When I finally set up my place, I had about a three-hundred-yard view. Just as I got on my gun, three insurgents came out right across the street, fifteen yards away.

I killed all of them. I rolled over and said to one of the officers who'd come over, "You want a turn?"

AFTER A FEW DAYS, WE FIGURED OUT THAT THE ATTACKS WERE concentrating when the work crews reached an intersection. It made sense: the insurgents wanted to attack from a place where they could easily run off.

We learned to bump up and watch the side streets. Then we started pounding these guys when they showed up.

FALLUJAH WAS BAD. RAMADI WAS WORSE. SADR CITY WAS THE worst. The overwatches would last two or three days. We'd leave for a day, recharge, then go back out. It was balls-to-the-wall firefights every time.

The insurgents brought more than just their AKs to a fight. We were getting rocketed every fight. We responded by calling in air cover, Hellfires and what-have-you.

The surveillance network overhead had been greatly improved over the past several years, and the U.S. was able to make pretty good use of it when it came to targeting Predators and other assets. But in our case, the bastards were right out in the open, extremely easy to spot. And very plentiful.

THERE WERE CLAIMS BY THE IRAQI GOVERNMENT AT ONE point that we were killing civilians. That was pure bullshit. While just about every battle was going down, Army intelligence analysts were intercepting insurgent cell phone communications that were giving a blow-by-blow account.

"They just killed so-and-so," ran one conversation. "We need more mortarmen and snipers. . . . They killed fifteen today."

We had only counted thirteen down in that battle—I guess we should have taken two out of the "maybe" column and put them in the "definite" category.

GET MY GUN

As always, there were moments of high anxiety mixed with bizarre events and random comic relief.

One day at the tail end of an op, I hustled back to the Bradley with the rest of the guys. Just as I reached the vehicle, I realized my sniper rifle had been left behind—I'd put it down in one of the rooms, then forgotten to bring it with me when I'd left.

Yeah. Stupid.

I reversed course. LT, one of my officers, was just running up.

"Hey, we gotta go back," I said. "My gun's in the house."

"Let's do it," said LT, following me.

We turned around and raced back to the house. Meanwhile, insurgents were sweeping toward it—so close we could hear them. We cleared the courtyard, sure we would run into them.

Fortunately, there was no one there. I grabbed the rifle and we raced back to the Bradleys, about two seconds ahead of a grenade attack. The ramp shut and the explosions sounded.

"What the hell?" demanded the officer in charge as the vehicle drove off.

LT smirked.

"I'll explain later," he said.

I'm not sure he ever did.

VICTORY

It took about a month to get the barriers up. As the Army reached its objective, the insurgents started to give up.

It was probably a combination of them realizing the wall was going to be finished whether they liked it or not, and the fact that we had killed so many of the bastards that they couldn't mount much of an attack. Where thirty or forty insurgents would gather with AKs and RPGs to fire on a single fence crew at the beginning of the op, toward the end the bad guys were putting together attacks with two or three men. Gradually, they faded into the slums around us.

Muqtada al-Sadr, meanwhile, decided it was time for him to try and negotiate a peace with the Iraqi government. He declared a ceasefire and started talking to the government.

Imagine that.

Taya:

People always told me I didn't really know Chris or what he was doing, because he was a SEAL. I remember going to an accountant one time. He said he knew some SEALs and those guys told him no one ever really knew where they went.

"My husband's on a training trip," I said. "I know where he is."

"You don't know that."

"Well, yes I do. I just talked to him."

"But you don't know really what they're doing. They're SEALs."

"I—"

"You can never know."

"I know my husband."

"You just can't know. They're trained to lie."

People would say that a lot. It irritated me when it was someone I didn't know well. The people I did know well respected that I might not know every detail but I knew what I needed to know.

IN THE VILLAGES

WITH THINGS RELATIVELY CALM IN SADR CITY, WE WERE given a new area to target. IED-makers and other insurgents had set up shop in a series of villages near Baghdad, trying to operate under the radar as they supplied weapons and manpower to fight Americans and the loyal Iraqi forces. The Mahdi army was out there, and the area was a virtual no-go zone for Americans.

We had worked with members of 4-10 Mountain Division during much of the Sadr City battle. They were fighters. They wanted to be in the shit—and they certainly got their wish there. Now as we bumped out into the villages outside the city, we were happy to have a chance to work with them again. They knew the area. Their snipers were especially good, and having them along improved our effectiveness.

OUR JOBS ARE THE SAME, BUT THERE ARE A FEW DIFFERENCES between Army and SEAL snipers. For one thing, Army snipers use spotters, which we don't, as a general rule. Their weapon set is a bit smaller than ours.

But the bigger difference, at least at first, had to do with tactics and the way they were deployed. Army snipers were more used to going out in three- or four-man groups, which meant they couldn't stay out for very long, certainly not all night.

The SEAL task unit, on the other hand, moved in heavy and locked down an area, basically looking for a fight and having the enemy provide us with one. It wasn't so much an overwatch anymore as a dare: *Here we are; come and get us.*

And they did: village after village, the insurgents would come and try and kill us; we'd take them down. Typically, we'd spend at least one night and usually a few, going in and extracting after sunset.

In this area, we ended up going back to the same village a few times, usually taking a different house each time. We'd repeat the process until all the local bad guys were dead, or at least until they understood that attacking us was not very smart.

It was surprising how many idiots you had to kill before they finally got that point.

COVERED WITH CRAP

THERE WERE LIGHTER MOMENTS, BUT EVEN SOME OF THOSE were shitty. Literally.

Our point man, Tommy, was a great guy but, as it turned out, a terrible point in a lot of ways.

Or maybe I should say sometimes he was more of a duck than a point man. If there was a puddle between us and the objective, Tommy took us through it. The deeper the better. He was always having us walk through the worst possible terrain.

It got so ridiculous that finally I told him, "One more time, I'm going to whup your ass, and you're fired."

On the very next mission, he found a path to a village that he was sure would be dry. I had my doubts. In fact, I pointed them out to him.

"Oh, no, no," he insisted, "it's good, it's good."

Once we were out in the field, we followed him across some farmland on a narrow path that led to a pipe across a path of mud. I was at the back at the group, one of the last to come across the pipe. As I stepped off, I sunk right through the mud and into crap up to my knee. The mud was actually just a thin crust atop a deep pool of sewage.

It stunk even worse than Iraq usually stunk.

"Tommy," I yelled, "I'm going to whip your ass as soon as we get to the house."

We pushed on to the house. I was still in the rear. We cleared the house and, once all the snipers were deployed, I went to find Tommy and give him the thrashing I'd promised.

Tommy was already paying for his sins: when I found him downstairs, he was hooked up to an IV and puking his brains out. He had fallen into the muck and was completely covered with shit. He was sick for a day, and he smelled for a week.

Every article of clothing he'd been wearing was disposed of, probably by a hazmat unit.

Served him right.

I SPENT SOMEWHERE BETWEEN TWO AND THREE MONTHS IN the villages. I had roughly twenty confirmed kills while I was there. The action on any particular op could be fierce; it could also be slow. There was no predicting.

Most of the houses we took over belonged to families who at least pretended to be neutral; I'd guess that the majority of them hated the insurgents for causing trouble and would have been even happier than we were to have the bad guys leave. But there were exceptions, and we were plenty frustrated when we couldn't do anything about it.

We went into one house and saw police uniforms. We knew instantly that the owner was muj—the insurgents were stealing uniforms and using them to disguise themselves in attacks.

Of course he gave us a BS line about having just gotten a job as a part-time police officer—something he'd mysteriously forgotten to mention when we first interrogated him.

We called it back to the Army, gave them the information, and asked what to do.

They had no intelligence on the guy. In the end, they decided the uniforms weren't evidence of anything.

We were told to turn him loose. So we did.

It gave us something to think about every time we heard of an attack by insurgents dressed as policemen, over the next few weeks.

EXTRACTED

ONE NIGHT WE ENTERED ANOTHER VILLAGE AND TOOK OVER A house at the edge of some large open fields, including one used for soccer. We set up without a problem, surveying the village and preparing for any trouble we might face in the morning.

The tempo of the ops had slowed quite a bit over the past week or two; it looked as if things were slacking down, at least for us. I started thinking about going back west and rejoining my platoon.

I set up in a room on the second floor with LT. We had an Army sniper and his spotter in the room next to us, and a bunch of guys on the roof. I'd taken the .338 Lapua with me, figuring that most of my shots would be on the long side, since we were on the edge of the village. With the area around us quiet, I started scanning out farther, to the next village, a little more than a mile away.

At some point I saw a one-story house with someone moving on the roof. It was about 2,100 yards away, and even with a twenty-five power scope I couldn't make out much more than an outline. I studied the person, but at that point he didn't seem to have a weapon, or at least he wasn't showing it. His back was to me, so I could watch him, but he couldn't see me. I thought he was suspicious, but he wasn't doing anything dangerous, so I let him be.

A little while later an Army convoy came down the road beyond the other village, heading in the direction of the COP we had staged out of. As it got closer, the man on the roof raised a weapon to his shoulder. Now the outline was clear: he had a rocket launcher, and he was aiming it at Americans.

RPG.

We had no way of calling the convoy directly—to this day I don't know exactly who they were, except that they were Army. But I put my scope on him and fired, hoping to at least scare him off with the shot or maybe warn the convoy.

At 2,100 yards, plus a little change, it would take a lot of luck to hit him.

A lot of luck.

Maybe the way I jerked the trigger to the right adjusted for the wind. Maybe gravity shifted and put that bullet right where it had to be. Maybe I was just the luckiest son of a bitch in Iraq. Whatever—I watched through my scope as the shot hit the Iraqi, who tumbled over the wall to the ground.

"Wow," I muttered.

"You dumb lucky fucker," said LT.

Twenty-one hundred yards. The shot amazes me even now. It was a straight-up luck shot; no way one shot should have gotten him.

But it did. It was my longest confirmed kill in Iraq, even longer than that shot in Fallujah.

The convoy started reacting, probably unaware of how close they'd come to getting lit up. I went back to scanning for bad guys.

As the day went on, we started taking fire from AKs and rocket-propelled grenades. The conflict ratcheted up quickly. The RPGs began tearing holes in the loose concrete or adobe walls, breaking through and starting fires.

We decided it was time to leave and called for extraction:

Send the RG-33s! (RG-33s are big, bulletproof vehicles designed to withstand IEDs and equipped with a machine-gun turret on the top.)

We waited, continuing the firefight and ducking the insurgents' growing spray of bullets. Finally, the relief force reported that it was five hundred yards away, on the other side of the soccer field.

That was as close as they were getting.

A pair of Army Hummers blew through the village and appeared at the doors, but they couldn't take all of us. The rest of us started to run for the RG-33s.

Someone threw a smoke grenade, I guess with the thought that it would cover our retreat. All it really did was make it impossible for us to see. (The grenades should be used to screen movement; you run behind the smoke. In this case, we had to run through it.) We ran from the house, through the cloud of smoke, ducking bullets and dodging into the open field.

It was like a scene from a movie. Bullets sprayed and plinked into the dirt.

The guy next to me fell. I thought he'd been hit. I stopped, but before I could grab him, he jumped to his feet—he'd only tripped.

"I'm good! I'm good!" he yelled.

Together we continued toward the trucks, bullets and turf flying everywhere. Finally, we reached the trucks. I jumped into the back of one of the RG-33s. As I caught my breath, bullets splashed against one of the bulletproof windows on the side, spiderwebbing the glass.

MORTALITY

A FEW DAYS LATER, I WAS WESTWARD-BOUND, BACK TO DELTA Platoon. The transfer I'd asked for earlier was granted.

The timing was good. Things were starting to get to me. The stress had been building. Little did I know it was going to get a lot worse, even as the fighting got a lot less.

CHIEF PETTY OFFICER KYLE

BY NOW, MY GUYS HAD LEFT AL-QA'IM AND WERE AT A PLACE called Rawah, also out west near the Syrian border. Once again they'd been put to work building barracks and the rest.

I got lucky; I missed the construction work. But there wasn't much going on when I arrived, either.

I was just in time for a long-range desert patrol out on the border. We drove out there for a few days hardly seeing a person, let alone insurgents. There had been reports of smuggling across the desert, but if it was going on, it wasn't going on where we were.

Meanwhile, it was *hot*. It was 120 degrees at least, and we were driving in Hummers that had no air-conditioning. I grew up in Texas, so I know warm; this was worse. And it was constant; you couldn't get away from it. It hardly cooled off at night—it might fall to 115. Rolling down the windows meant taking a risk if there was an IED. Almost worse was the sand, which would just blow right in and cover you.

I decided I preferred the sand and IED danger to the heat. I rolled down the windows.

Driving, all you saw was desert. Occasionally, there would be a nomad settlement or a tiny village.

We linked up with our sister platoon, then the next day we stopped at a Marine base. My chief went in and did some business; a little while later he came out and found me.

"Hey," he told me, grinning. "Guess what—you just made chief."

I HAD TAKEN THE CHIEF'S EXAM BACK IN THE STATES BEFORE we deployed.

In the Navy, you usually have to take a written test to get promoted. But I'd lucked out. I got a field promotion to E5 during my second deployment and made E6 thanks to a special merit program before my third deployment. Both came without taking written tests.

(In both cases I had been doing a lot of extra work within the Team, and had made a reputation on the battlefield. Those were the important factors in awarding the new ranks.)

That didn't fly for the chief's exam. I took the written test and barely passed.

I SHOULD EXPLAIN A BIT MORE ABOUT WRITTEN TESTS AND promotions. I'm not unusually adverse or allergic to tests, at least no more than anyone else. But the tests for SEALs added an extra burden.

At the time, in order to get promoted, you had to take an exam in your job area—not as a SEAL, but in whatever area you had selected before being a SEAL. In my case, that would have meant being evaluated in the intelligence area.

MORTALITY

Obviously, I wasn't in a position to know anything about that area. I was a SEAL, not an intelligence analyst. I didn't have a clue what sort of equipment and procedures intel used to get their jobs done.

Considering the accuracy of the intel we usually got, I would have guessed dartboard, maybe. Or just a fine pair of dice.

In order to get promoted, I would have had to study for the test, which would have involved going to a secure reading area, a special room where top-secret material can be reviewed. Of course, I would have had to do this in my spare time.

There weren't any secure reading areas in Fallujah or Ramadi where I fought. And the literature in the latrines and heads wouldn't have cut it.

(The tests are now in the area of special operations, and pertain to things SEALs actually do. The exams are incredibly detailed, but at least it has to do with our job.)

BECOMING A CHIEF WAS A LITTLE DIFFERENT. THIS TEST WAS on things SEALs should know.

That hurdle cleared, my case had to be reviewed by a board and then go through further administrative review by the upper echelon. The board review process included all these chief petty officers and master chiefs sitting down and reviewing a package of my accomplishments. The package is supposed to be a long dossier of everything you've done as a SEAL. (Minus the bar fights.)

The only thing in my package was my service record. But that had not been updated since I graduated BUD/S. My Silver Stars and Bronze Medals weren't even in there.

I wasn't crazy about becoming a chief. I was happy where I was. As chief, I would have all sorts of administrative duties, and I wouldn't get as much action. Yes, it was more money for our family, but I wasn't thinking about that.

Chief Primo was on the review board back at our base in the States. He was sitting next to one of the chiefs when they began reviewing my case.

"Who the hell is this dipshit?" said the other chief when he saw my thin folder. "Who does he think he is?"

"Why don't you and I go to lunch?" said Primo.

He agreed. The other chief came back with a different attitude.

"You owe me a Subway sandwich, fucker," Primo told me when I saw him later on. Then he told me the story.

I owe him all that and more. The promotion came through, and, to be honest, being chief wasn't near as bad as I thought it would be.

TRUTH IS, I NEVER CARED ALL THAT MUCH ABOUT RANK. I never tried to be one of the highest-ranking guys. Or even, back in high school, to be one of the students with the highest average.

I'd do my homework in the truck in the morning. When they stuck me in the Honor Society, I made sure my grades dipped just enough the next semester to get kicked out. Then I brought them up again so my parents wouldn't get on me.

Maybe the rank thing had to do with the fact that I preferred being a leader on the ground, rather than an administrator in a back room. I didn't want to have to sit at a computer, plan everything, then tell everyone about it. I wanted to do my thing, which was being a sniper—get into combat, kill the enemy. I wanted to be the best at what I wanted to do.

I think a lot of people had trouble with that attitude. They naturally thought that anyone who was good should have a very high rank. I guess I'd seen enough people with high rank who weren't good not to be swayed.

TOO MUCH THINKING

"ON THE ROAD AGAIN..."

Willie Nelson cranked through the speaker system of our Hummer as we set out for our base the next day. Music was about the only diversion we had out here, outside of the occasional stop in a village to talk to the locals. Besides the old-school country my buddy behind the wheel preferred, I listened to a bit of Toby Keith and Slipknot, country and heavy metal vying for attention.

I'm a big believer in the psychological impact of music. I've seen it work on the battlefield. If you're going into combat, you want to be pumped up. You don't want to be stupid crazy, but you do want to be psyched. Music can help take the fear away. We'd listen to Papa Roach, Dope, Drowning Pool—anything that amped us up. (They're all in heavy rotation on my workout mix now.)

But nothing could amp me up on the way back to base. It was a long, hot ride. Even though I'd just gotten some good news about my promotion, I was in a dark mood, bored on the one hand, and tense on the other.

Back at base, things were incredibly slow. Nothing was going on. And it started to get to me.

As long as I had been in action, the idea of my being vulnerable, being mortal, had been something I could push away. There was too much going on to worry about it. Or rather, I had so much else to do, I didn't really focus on it.

But now, it was practically all I could think of.

I had time to relax, but I couldn't. Instead, I'd lie on my bed thinking about everything I'd been through—getting shot especially.

I relived the gunshot every time I lay down to rest. My heart thumped hard in my chest, probably a lot harder than it had that night in Sadr City.

Things seemed to go downhill in the few days after we got back from our border patrol. I couldn't sleep. I felt very jumpy. Extremely jumpy. And my blood pressure shot up again, even higher than before.

I felt like I was going to explode.

Physically, I was beat up. Four long combat deployments had taken their toll. My knees felt better, but my back hurt, my ankle hurt, my hearing was screwed up. My ears rang. My neck had been injured, my ribs cracked. My fingers and knuckles had been broken. I had floaters and decreased vision in my right eye. There were dozens of deep bruises and an assortment of aches and pains. I was a doctor's wet dream.

But the thing that really bothered me was my blood pressure. I sweated buckets and my hands would even shake. My face, pretty white to begin with, became pale.

THE MORE I TRIED TO RELAX, THE WORSE THINGS GOT. IT WAS as if my body had started to vibrate, and thinking about it only made it buzz more.

Imagine climbing a tall ladder out over a river, a thousand miles up, and there you're struck by lightning. Your body becomes electric, but you're still alive. In fact, you're not only aware of everything that's happening, but you know you can deal with it. You know what you have to do to get down.

So you do. You climb down. But when you're back on the ground, the electricity won't go away. You try to find a way to discharge the electricity, to ground yourself, but you can't find the damn lightning rod to take the electricity away.

U̲n̲a̲b̲l̲e̲ ̲t̲o̲ ̲e̲a̲t̲ ̲o̲r̲ ̲s̲l̲e̲e̲p̲,̲ ̲I̲ ̲f̲i̲n̲a̲l̲l̲y̲ ̲w̲e̲n̲t̲ ̲t̲o̲ ̲t̲h̲e̲ ̲d̲o̲c̲s̲ ̲a̲n̲d̲ told them to check me out. They took a look at me, and asked if I wanted medication.

Not really, I told them. But I did take the meds.

They also suggested that, since the mission tempo was practically nonexistent and we were only a few weeks from going home anyway, it made sense for me to go home.

Not knowing what else to do, I agreed.

14

HOME AND OUT

DUCKING OUT

It was late August when I left. As usual, it was almost surreal—one day I was in the war; the next I was home. I felt bad about leaving. I didn't want to tell anyone about the blood pressure, or anything else. I kept it to myself as best I could.

To be honest, it felt a little like I was ducking out on my boys, running away because my heart was pounding funny or whatever the hell it was doing.

Nothing that I had accomplished earlier could erase the feeling that I was letting my boys down.

I know it doesn't make sense. I know I had accomplished a huge amount. I needed a rest, but felt I shouldn't take one. I thought I should be stronger than was possible.

To top things off, some of the medication apparently didn't agree with me. Trying to help me sleep, a doctor back home in San

HOME AND OUT

Diego prescribed a sleeping pill. It put me out—so much so that when I really woke up I was on base with no recollection of working out at home and driving myself to base. Taya told me about my workout and I knew I had driven to work, because my truck was there.

I never took that one again. It was nasty.

Taya:

It's taken me years to get my head around some of this stuff. On the surface, Chris wants to just go and have a good time. When people really need him though—when lives are on the line—he is the most dependable guy. He's got a situational sense of responsibility and caring.

I saw this in his promotions in the military: he didn't care. He didn't want the responsibility of the higher rank, even though it would mean providing better for his family. And yet if a job needed to be done, he was there. He will always rise to the challenge. And he's prepared, because he's been thinking about it.

It was a real dichotomy, and I don't think a lot of people understood it. It was even hard for me to reconcile at times.

PROTECTING PEOPLE

WHILE I WAS HOME, I GOT INVOLVED IN A FAIRLY INTERESTING scientific program relating to stress and combat situations.

It used virtual reality to test what sorts of effects battle has on your body. In my case, specifically, they monitored my blood pressure, or at least that was the one measurement that really interested

359

me. I wore a headpiece and special gloves while viewing a simulation. It was basically a video game, but it was still pretty cool.

Well, in the simulations, my blood pressure and heart rate would start out steady. Then, once we got into a firefight, they would drop. I would just sit there and do everything I had to do, real comfortable.

As soon as it was over and things were peaceful, my heart rate would just zoom.

Interesting.

The scientists and doctors running the experiment believe that during the heat of the battle, my training would take over and would somehow relax me. They were really intrigued, because apparently they hadn't seen that before.

Of course, I'd lived it every day in Iraq.

THERE WAS ONE SIMULATION THAT LEFT A DEEP IMPRESSION on me. In this one, a Marine was shot and he went down screaming. He'd been gut-shot. As I watched that scene, my blood pressure spiked even higher than it had been.

I didn't need a scientist or a doctor to tell me what that was about. I could just about feel that kid dying on my chest in Fallujah again.

PEOPLE TELL ME I SAVED HUNDREDS AND HUNDREDS OF people. But I have to tell you: it's not the people you saved that you remember. It's the ones you couldn't save.

Those are the ones you talk about. Those are the faces and situations that stay with you forever.

IN OR OUT?

MY ENLISTMENT WAS COMING TO AN END. THE NAVY KEPT trying to entice me to stay, making different offers: handle training, work in England, anything I wanted just so I would stay in the Navy.

Even though I had told Taya I wouldn't reenlist, I wasn't ready to quit.

I wanted to go back to the war. I felt I'd been cheated on my last deployment. I struggled, trying to decide what to do. Some days, I was through with the Navy; other days, I was ready to tell my wife the hell with it, and reenlist.

We talked about it a lot.

TAYA:

I told Chris that both our kids needed him, especially, at that particular time, our son. If he wasn't going to be there, then I would move closer to my father so that at least he would grow up with a strong grandfather very close to him.

I didn't want to do that at all.

And Chris really loved us all. He really wanted to have and nurture a strong family.

Part of it came down to the conflict we'd always had—where were our priorities: God, family, country (my version), or God, country, family (Chris's)?

To my mind, Chris had already given his country so much, a tremendous amount. The previous ten years had been filled with constant war. Heavy combat deployments were combined with extensive training workups that kept him away from home. It was more heavy action—and absence—than any other SEAL I knew of. It was time to give his family some of himself. But as always, I couldn't make the decision for him.

The Navy suggested that they could send me to Texas as recruiter. That sounded pretty good, since the job would allow me to have regular hours and come home at night. It looked to me like a possible compromise.

"You have to give me a little time to work this out," said the master chief I was dealing with. "This isn't the sort of thing that we can do overnight."

I agreed to extend my enlistment a month while he worked on it.

I waited and waited. No orders came in.

"It's coming, it's coming," he said. "You have to extend again." So I did.

A few more weeks passed—we were almost through October by now—and no orders came through. So I called him up and asked what the hell was going on.

"It's a Catch-22," he explained. "They want to give it to you, but it's a three-year billet. You don't have any time."

In other words, they wanted me to enlist first, then they would give me the job. But there were no guarantees, no contract.

I'd been there before. I finally told them thanks, but no thanks—*I'm getting out.*

Taya:

He always says, "I feel like a quitter." I think he's done his job, but I know that's how he feels. He thinks if there are people out there fighting, it should be him. And a lot of other SEALs feel that way about themselves, as well. But I believe not one of them would blame him for getting out.

RYAN GETS MARRIED

Ryan and I remained close after he returned to the States; in fact, our friendship grew even stronger, which I wouldn't have thought possible. I felt drawn to him by his tremendous spirit. He'd been a warrior in combat. Now he was an even greater warrior in life. You never completely forgot that he was blind, but you also never, ever got the impression that his disability defined him.

He had to get a prosthetic eye made, because of his wounds. According to LT, who went with him to pick it up, he actually had two—one was a "regular" eye; the other had a golden SEAL trident where the iris ordinarily would be.

Once a SEAL, *always* a SEAL.

I'd been with Ryan a lot before he got hurt. A lot of the guys on the team had a wicked sense of humor, but Ryan was in a class by himself. He'd get you in stitches.

He wasn't any different after he got shot. He just had a very dry sense of humor. One day a young girl came up to him, looked at his face, and asked, "What happened to you?"

He bent down and said, in a very serious voice, "Never run with scissors."

Dry, droll, and a heart of gold. You couldn't help but love him.

We were all prepared to hate his girlfriend. We were sure she would leave him after he was torn up. But she stood by him. He finally proposed, and we were all happy about it. She is one awesome lady.

If there is a poster child for overcoming disabilities, Ryan was it. After the injury, he went to college, graduated with honors, and had an excellent job waiting for him. He climbed Mount Hood, Mount Rainer, and a bunch of other mountains; he went hunting and shot a prize trophy elk with the help of a spotter and a gun with some bad-ass technology; he competed in a triathlon. I remember one night Ryan said that he was glad it was he who got shot instead of any of the other guys. Sure he was angry at first, but he felt he was at peace and living a full life. He felt he could handle it and be happy no matter what. He was right.

When I think about the patriotism that drives SEALs, I am reminded of Ryan recovering in a hospital in Bethesda, Maryland. There he was, freshly wounded, almost fatally, and blind for life. Many reconstructive surgeries to his face loomed ahead. You know what he asked for? He asked for someone to wheel him to a flag and give him some time.

He sat in his wheelchair for close to a half-hour saluting as the American flag whipped in the wind.

That's Ryan: a true patriot.

A genuine warrior, with a heart of gold.

Of course we all gave him shit and told him somebody probably wheeled him in front of a Dumpster and just told him it was a flag. Being Ryan, he dished out as many blind jokes as he took and had us all rolling every time we talked.

When he moved away, we would chat on the phone and get together whenever we could. In 2010, I found out he and his wife were expecting their first child.

Meanwhile, the injuries he'd had in Iraq required further surgeries. He went into the hospital one morning; later that afternoon I got a call from Marcus Luttrell, asking if I had heard about Ryan.

"Yeah. I just talked to him yesterday," I told him. "He and his wife are having a baby. Isn't it great?"

"He died just a little while ago," said Marcus, his voice quiet.

Something had gone wrong at the hospital. It was a tragic end to a heroic life. I'm not sure any of us who knew him have gotten over it. I don't think I ever will.

The baby was a beautiful girl. I'm sure her father's spirit lives on in her.

MIGHTY WARRIORS

AFTER HER SON'S DEATH, MARC LEE'S MOM, DEBBIE, BECAME almost a surrogate mother to the other members of our platoon. A very courageous woman, she has dedicated herself to helping other warriors as they have made the transition from the battlefield. She's now president of America's Mighty Warriors (www.AmericasMightyWarriors.org) and has done a lot personally for veterans through what she calls "random acts of kindness" inspired by Marc's life and a letter he wrote to her before he passed away.

There's nothing random about Debbie; she's a dedicated and hardworking woman, as devoted to her cause as Marc was to his.

Before he died, Marc wrote an incredible letter home. Available at the site, it told a moving story about some of the things he saw in Iraq—a terrible hospital, ignorant and despicable people. But it was also an extremely positive letter, full of hope and encouraging all of us to do some small part for others.

To my mind, though, whatever he wrote home doesn't adequately describe the Marc we all knew. There was a lot more to him. He was a real tough guy with a great sense of humor. He was a gung-ho warrior and a great friend. He had unshakable faith in

God and loved his wife with might. Heaven is surely a better place because he's there, but earth has lost one of its best.

CRAFT

Deciding to leave the Navy was hard enough. But now I was going to be out of a job. It was time to figure out what to do with the rest of my life.

I had a number of options and possibilities. I'd been talking with a friend of mine named Mark Spicer about starting a sniper school in the States. After twenty-five years in the British Army, Mark retired as a sergeant major. He was one of the foremost snipers in their army, and had served over twenty years as a sniper and sniper platoon commander. Mark has written three books on sniping and is one of the world's leading experts on the subject.

We both realized there was and is a need for certain types of very specific training for military and police units. No one was providing the sort of hands-on instruction that would help prepare their personnel for the different situations they might find. With our experience, we knew we could tailor courses and provide enough range time to make a difference.

The problem was getting everything together to do it.

Money, of course, was a pretty big consideration. Then, partly by chance, I happened to meet someone who realized the company could be a good investment, and who also had faith in me: J. Kyle Bass.

Kyle had made a lot of money investing, and when we met, he was looking for a bodyguard. I guess he figured, "Who better than a SEAL?" But when we got talking and he asked where I saw myself in a few years, I told him about the school. He was intrigued, and rather than hiring me as his bodyguard, he helped provide the financing for our company. And just like that, Craft International was born.

ACTUALLY, IT WASN'T "JUST LIKE THAT"—WE BUSTED BUTT TO get it going, working long hours and sweating out all the details the way any entrepreneurs do. Two other guys joined Mark and me to form the ownership team: Bo French and Steven Young. Their areas of expertise have more to do with the business side of things, but they're both knowledgeable about weapons and the tactics that we teach.

Today, Craft International's corporate offices are in Texas. We have training sites in Texas and Arizona and work internationally on security measures and other special projects. Mark can occasionally be seen on the History channel. He's pretty comfortable in front of the cameras, so at times he'll relax into a real thick British accent. The History channel is kind enough to translate his thick accent into good 'ol boy English with subtitles. We have yet to need subtitles for any Craft courses, but we haven't ruled out the possibility.

We've assembled a team we believe is the best of the best in their given areas for all the areas of training we provide. (You can find more information at www.craftintl.com.)

Building a company involves a lot of different skills I didn't think I had. It also includes a ton of admin work.

Damn.

I don't mind hard work, even if it is at a desk. One of the pullbacks on this job is that it's given me "Dell hand"—I spend a lot of time pounding a computer keyboard. And every blue moon I have to wear a suit and tie. But otherwise, it's a perfect job for me. I may not be rich, but I enjoy what I do.

THE LOGO FOR CRAFT CAME FROM THE PUNISHER SYMBOL, with a crusader crosshair in the right eye in honor of Ryan Job. He also inspired our company slogan.

In April 2009, after Somali pirates had taken over a ship and were threatening the captain with death, SEAL snipers killed them from a nearby destroyer. Someone from the local media asked Ryan what he thought.

"Despite what your mama told you," he quipped, "violence does solve problems."

That seemed a pretty appropriate slogan for snipers, so it became ours.

BACK IN TEXAS

I WAS STILL CONFLICTED ABOUT LEAVING THE NAVY, BUT knowing that I was going to start Craft gave me more incentive. When the time finally came, I couldn't wait.

After all, I was going back home. Was I in a hurry? I got out of the Navy November 4; on November 6, I was kicking Texas dust.

While I was working on Craft International, my family stayed back in the San Diego area, the kids finishing up with school and Taya getting the house ready to sell. My wife planned to have everything wrapped up in January so we could be reunited in Texas.

They came out at Christmas. I'd been missing the kids and her terribly.

I pulled her into the room at my parent's place and said, "What do you think about going back by yourself? Leave the kids with me."

She was tickled. She had a lot to do, and while she loved our children, taking care of them and getting the house ready to sell was exhausting.

I loved having my son and daughter with me. I had a big assist from my parents, who helped watch them during the week. Friday afternoons I'd take the kids and we'd have Daddy vacations for three and sometimes four days at a shot.

People have an idea in their heads that fathers aren't able to spend comfortable time with very young children. I don't think that's true. Hell, I had as much fun as they did. We'd mess around on a trampoline and play ball for hours. We'd visit the zoo, hit the playgrounds, watch a movie. They'd help Dad grill. We all had a great time.

WHEN MY DAUGHTER WAS A BABY, IT TOOK A BIT OF TIME FOR her to warm up to me. But gradually, she came to trust me more, and got used to having me around. Now she is all about her daddy.

Of course, she had him wrapped around her little finger from day one.

I BEGAN TEACHING MY SON HOW TO SHOOT WHEN HE WAS TWO, starting with the basics of a BB rifle. My theory is that kids get into trouble because of curiosity—if you don't satisfy it, you're asking for big problems. If you inform them and carefully instruct them on safety when they're young, you avoid a lot of the trouble.

My son has learned to respect weapons. I've always told him, if you want to use a gun, come get me. There's nothing I like better than shooting. He already has his own rifle, a .22 lever-action, and he shoots pretty good groups with it. He's amazing with a pistol, too.

My daughter is still a little young, and hasn't shown as much interest yet. I suspect she will soon, but in any event, extensive firearms training will be mandatory before she is allowed to date . . . which should be around the time she turns thirty.

Both kids have gone out hunting with me. They're still a little young to focus for long periods of time, but I suspect they'll get the hang of it before too long.

TAYA:

Chris and I have gone back and forth about how we would feel if our children went into the military. Of course we don't want them to be hurt, or for anything to happen to them. But there are also a lot of positives to military service. We'll both be proud of them no matter what they do.

If my son was to consider going into SEALs, I would tell him to really think about it. I would tell him that he has to be prepared.

I think it's horrible for family. If you go to war, it does change you, and you have to be prepared for that, too. I'd tell him to sit down and talk to his father about the reality of things.

Sometimes I feel like crying just thinking about him in a firefight.

I think Chris has done enough for the country so that we can skip a generation. But we'll both be proud of our children no matter what.

Settling in Texas got me closer to my parents on a permanent basis. Since I've been back with them, they tell me some of the shell that I built up during the war has melted away. My father says that

I closed off parts of myself. He believes they've come back, somewhat at least.

"I don't think you can train for years to kill," he admits, "and expect all that to disappear overnight."

DOWN IN THE DEPTHS

WITH ALL THIS GOOD STUFF GOING ON, YOU'D THINK I WAS living a fairy tale or a perfect life. And maybe I should be.

But real life doesn't travel in a perfect straight line; it doesn't necessarily have that "all lived happily ever after" bit. You have to work on where you're going.

And just because I had a great family and an interesting job didn't mean things were perfect. I still felt bad about leaving the SEALs. I still resented my wife for presenting me with what felt like an ultimatum.

So even though life should have been sweet, for some months after getting out of the service, it felt like it was plunging down a mineshaft.

I started drinking a lot, pounding back beers. I'd say I went into a depression, feeling sorry for myself. Pretty soon drinking was all I did. After a while, it was hard liquor, and it was all through the day.

I don't want to make this sound more dramatic than it really is. Other people have faced more difficult problems. But I was certainly headed in the wrong direction. I was going downhill and gathering speed.

Then one night I turned a corner too fast in my truck. Now, maybe there were extenuating circumstances, maybe the road was slippery or something else was out of whack. Or maybe that guardian angel that had saved me back in Ramadi decided to intervene.

Whatever. All I know is I totaled my truck and came out without a scratch.

On my body. My ego was something else again.

The accident woke me up. I'm sorry to say that I needed something like that to get my head back straight.

I still drink beer, though not nearly to excess.

I think I realize everything I have, and everything I could lose. And I also understand not just where my responsibilities are but how to fulfill them.

GIVING BACK

I'M STARTING TO UNDERSTAND THE CONTRIBUTIONS I CAN make to others. I realize that I can be a complete man—taking care of my family and helping in a small way to take care of others.

Marcus Luttrell started an organization called Lone Survivor Foundation. It gets some of our wounded warriors out of the hospital and into situations where they can enjoy themselves a little. After being wounded in Afghanistan, Marcus said he healed twice as fast at his mom's ranch than he had in the hospital. Something about the open air and being able to roam around naturally helped the process. That's one of the inspirations for his foundation, and it's become one of my guiding principles as I try to do my small share.

I've gotten together with some people I know around Texas who have ranches and asked if they could donate their places for a few days at a time. They've been more than generous. We've had small groups of servicemen disabled in the war come in and spend time there hunting, shooting guns on a range, or just hanging out. The idea is to have a good time.

I should mention that my friend Kyle—the same guy who was a

driving force behind getting Craft afloat—is also extremely patriotic and supportive of the troops. He graciously allows us to use his beautiful Barefoot Ranch for many of our retreats for the wounded troops. Rick Kell and David Feherty's organization, Troops First, also works with Craft to help as many wounded guys as we can.

Hell, I've had a bunch of fun myself. We go hunting a couple of times a day, shoot a few rounds on the range, then at night trade stories and beers.

It's not so much the war stories as the funny stories that you remember. Those are the ones that affect you. They underline the resilience of these guys—they were warriors in the war, and they take that same warrior attitude into dealing with their disabilities.

As you'd expect if I'm involved, there's a lot of bustin' going on back and forth, giving each other hell. I don't always get the last laugh, but I do take my shots. The first time I had some of them out to one of the ranches, I took them out on the back porch before we started shooting and gave them a little orientation.

"All right," I told them, picking up my rifle, "since none of you are SEALs, I better give you some background. This here is a trigger."

"Screw you, Squid!" they shouted, and we had a good time from there on out, pushing each other and making fun.

WHAT WOUNDED VETERANS DON'T NEED IS SYMPATHY. THEY need to be treated like the men they are: equals, heroes, and people who still have tremendous value for society.

If you want to help them, start there.

In a funny way, bustin' back and forth shows more respect than asking "Are you okay?" in a sickly sweet voice.

We've only just begun, but we've had good enough success that the hospitals are very cooperative. We've been able to expand the program to include couples. We're aiming to do maybe two retreats a month going forward.

Our work has gotten me thinking bigger and bigger. I wouldn't mind doing a reality hunting show with these guys—I think it could inspire a lot of other Americans to really give back to their veterans and their present military families.

Helping each other out—that's America.

I think America does a lot to support people. That's great for those truly in need. But I also think we create dependency by giving money to those who don't want to work, both in other countries and our own. Help people help themselves—that's the way it should be.

I'd like us to remember the suffering of those Americans who were injured serving this country before we dole out millions to slackers and moochers. Look at the homeless: a lot are vets. I think we owe them more than just our gratitude. They were willing to sign a blank check for America, with the cost right up to their life. If they were willing to do that, why shouldn't we be taking care of them?

I'm not suggesting we give vets handouts; what people need are hand-ups—a little opportunity and strategic help.

One of the wounded vets I met at the ranch retreats has an idea to help homeless vets by helping build or renovate housing. I think it's a great idea. Maybe this house won't be where they live forever, but it'll get them going.

Jobs, training—there's an enormous amount that we can do.

I know some people will say that you'll have a bunch just taking advantage. But you deal with that. You don't let it ruin things for everyone.

There's no reason someone who has fought for their country should be homeless or jobless.

WHO I AM

IT'S TAKEN A WHILE, BUT I HAVE GOTTEN TO A POINT WHERE being a SEAL no longer defines me. I need to be a husband and a father. Those things, now, are my first calling.

Being a SEAL has been a huge part of me. I still feel the pull. I certainly would have preferred having the best of both worlds—the job *and* the family. But at least in my case, the job wouldn't allow it.

I'm not sure I would have either. In a sense, I had to step away from the job to become the fuller man my family needed me to be.

I don't know where or when the change came. It didn't happen until I got out. I had to get through that resentment at first. I had to move through the good things and the bad things to reach a point where I could really move ahead.

Now I want to be a good dad and a good husband. Now I've rediscovered a real love for my wife. I genuinely miss her when I'm on a business trip. I want to be able to hug her and sleep next to her.

TAYA:

What I loved about Chris in the beginning was the way he unabashedly wore his heart on his sleeve. He didn't play games with my heart or my head. He was a straight shooter who seemed to back up his feelings in actions: spending an hour and a half to drive up to see me, then leaving in time for work at five a.m.; communicating; putting up with my moods.

His sense of fun balanced out my serious side and brought out the youthful side of me. He was up for anything and completely supportive of anything I wanted or dreamed of. He got along famously with my family and I did with his.

When our marriage reached a crisis, I said I wouldn't love him the same if he reenlisted again. It wasn't that I didn't love him, but I felt that his decision would confirm what I thought was becoming increasingly evident. In the beginning, I believed he loved me more than anything. Slowly the Teams started to become his first love. He continued to say the words and tell me what he felt I needed to hear and what he had always said in the past to express his love. The difference is, the words and actions were no longer meshing. He still loved me but it was different. He was consumed by the Teams.

When he was away, he would tell me things like "I would do anything to be home with you," and "I miss you," and "You are the most important thing in the world to me." I knew if he joined up again that all of what he had been telling me over the past years were mostly words or feelings in theory, rather than feelings expressed in actions.

How could I love with the same reckless abandon if I knew I was not what he said I was? I was second fiddle at best.

He would die for strangers and country. My challenges and pain seemed to be mine alone. He wanted to live his life and have a happy wife to come home to.

At the time, it meant everything I loved in the beginning was changing and I would have to love him differently. I thought it might be less, but it turns out it was just different.

Just like in any relationship, things changed. We

changed. We both made mistakes and we both learned a lot. We may love each other differently, but maybe that is a good thing. Maybe it is more forgiving and more mature, or maybe it is just different.

It is still really good. We still have each other's backs and we've learned that even through the tough times, we don't want to lose each other or the family we've built.

The more time that goes by the more we are each able to show each other love in ways the other one understands and feels.

I feel like my love for my wife has gotten deeper over the past few years. Taya bought me a new wedding ring made of tungsten steel—I don't think it's a coincidence that it's the hardest metal she could find.

It has crusader crosses on it, too. She jokes that it's because marriage is like a crusade.

Maybe for us it has been.

Taya:

I feel something coming from him that I hadn't felt before.

He's definitely not the person he was before the war, but there are a lot of the same qualities. His sense of humor, his kindness, his warmth, his courage, and a sense of responsibility. His quiet confidence inspires me.

Like any couple, we still have our day-to-day life things we have to work through, but most importantly, I feel loved. And I feel the kids and I are important.

WAR

I'M NOT THE SAME GUY I WAS WHEN I FIRST WENT TO WAR.

No one is. Before you're in combat, you have this innocence about you. Then, all of a sudden, you see this whole other side of life.

I don't regret any of it. I'd do it again. At the same time, war definitely changes you.

You embrace death.

As a SEAL, you go to the Dark Side. You're immersed in it. Continually going to war, you gravitate to the blackest parts of existence. Your psyche builds up its defenses—that's why you laugh at gruesome things like heads being blown apart, and worse.

Growing up, I wanted to be military. But I wondered, how would I feel about killing someone?

Now I know. It's no big deal.

I did it a lot more than I'd ever thought I would—or, for that matter, more than any American sniper before me. But I also witnessed the evil my targets committed and wanted to commit, and by killing them, I protected the lives of many fellow soldiers.

I DON'T SPEND A LOT OF TIME PHILOSOPHIZING ABOUT KILLING people. I have a clear conscience about my role in the war.

I am a strong Christian. Not a perfect one—not close. But I strongly believe in God, Jesus, and the Bible. When I die, God is going to hold me accountable for everything I've done on earth.

He may hold me back until last and run everybody else through the line, because it will take so long to go over all my sins.

"Mr. Kyle, let's go into the backroom...."

Honestly, I don't know what will really happen on Judgment

Day. But what I lean toward is that you know all of your sins, and God knows them all, and shame comes over you at the reality that He knows. I believe the fact that I've accepted Jesus as my savior will be my salvation.

But in that backroom or whatever it is when God confronts me with my sins, I do not believe any of the kills I had during the war will be among them. Everyone I shot was evil. I had good cause on every shot. They all deserved to die.

MY REGRETS ARE ABOUT THE PEOPLE I COULDN'T SAVE— Marines, soldiers, my buddies.

I still feel their loss. I still ache for my failure to protect them.

I'm not naive and I'm beyond romanticizing war and what I had to do there. The worst moments of my life have come as a SEAL. Losing my buddies. Having a kid die on me.

I'm sure some of the things I went through pale in comparison to what some of the guys went through in World War II and other conflicts. On top of all the shit they went through in Vietnam, they had to come home to a country that spat on them.

When people ask me how the war changed me, I tell them that the biggest thing has to do with my perspective.

You know all the everyday things that stress you here?

I don't give a shit about them. There are bigger and worse things that could happen than to have this tiny little problem wreck your life, or even your day. I've seen them.

More: I've lived them.

ACKNOWLEDGMENTS

THIS BOOK WOULD NEVER HAVE BEEN POSSIBLE WITHOUT MY brother SEALs, who supported me in battle and throughout my career in the Navy. And I wouldn't be here without the SEALs, sailors, Marines, airmen, and soldiers who had my back during the war.

I'd also like to thank my wife, Taya, for helping me write this book and making her own contributions. My brother and my parents supplied their memories as well as their support. Several of my friends also kindly provided information that was invaluable. Among those who were especially helpful were one of my lieutenants and a fellow sniper who appear as LT and Dauber in this book, respectively. Marc Lee's mom also helped with some key insights.

Special thanks and appreciation go to Jim DeFelice for his patience, wit, understanding, and writing ability. Without his help, this book would not be what it is today. I also want to express my sincere appreciation to Jim's wife and son for opening their home to Taya and me as this book developed.

We worked on this book in a variety of places. None matched

ACKNOWLEDGMENTS

the comfort of Marc Myers's ranch, which he very generously allowed us to use while we worked.

Scott McEwen recognized the value of my story before I did, and played a critical role in bringing it to print.

I'd like to thank my editor, Peter Hubbard, who contacted me directly about writing this book and connected us with Jim DeFelice. Thanks also to the entire staff at William Morrow/HarperCollins.

IN MEMORIAM

INTRODUCTION

WHEN OUR EDITOR FIRST CONTACTED US ABOUT PUTTING together a memorial edition as a tribute to Chris, we were overwhelmed. While Chris certainly deserved such an honor, we worried about how to adequately sum up what he meant to people. What more could be said about him that hadn't been told, either in *American Sniper* itself or the more recent *American Gun*, which at that point was going to press?

As we thought about it, though, we realized that while those books have Chris's voice, both miss the voices of those around him. We knew the best tribute would be to include the words of others, with their own unique perspectives on who Chris was. And so we started contacting his fellow SEALs, veterans, friends, relatives, neighbors, and others to ask for help.

These are the memories of everyday people loving each other the best they can and unknowingly blessing each other along the way. As humble as Chris was, the people in his life were also humble. In writing about Chris, not one of them drew attention to

AMERICAN SNIPER: MEMORIAL EDITION

In Memory of Chris Kyle

Memorial Ceremony
Cowboys Stadium
Arlington, Texas

In Memory of Chris Kyle

Procession
National Anthem

Prayer
Opening Remarks
Photo Tribute
SEAL creed/wreath laying
Message from high school friend
"Valor"
Message from teammates
"Navy Hymn"
Letter from the family
Message from Taya Kyle
Love Song
"Amazing Grace"

TAPS
Recession

Psalm 91:1-2
1. He that dwelleth in the secret place of the most High shall abide under the shadow of the Almighty.
2. I will say of the Lord, He is my refuge and my fortress: my God; in him will I trust.

Chief Chris Kyle (USN) tragically died on Saturday, February 2, 2013. Chris lived and died by his personal creed, "It is our duty to serve those who serve us." Chris was one of a kind in so many ways. You could tell the difference between those who knew Chris, even if briefly, and those who knew OF Chris. The difference was simple, if they only talked about a fun-loving, humble warrior who loved his family, they heard of him. If they talked about his heart of gold and his ability to give without end, they were touched by him. If they talked about the twinkle in his eye, his hearty laugh, his ability to make you feel like you were important, and that mischievous grin where you just knew he was "fixin' to do something", they really KNEW him.

Chris was a father who was able to bring an unparalleled playful spirit to his family's home while he taught respect and honor. Every day he felt "blessed and blown away" by the gift God gave him in his children. He was a husband who loved deeply and never stopped trying. He felt his family deserved the best of him and he fought tooth and nail to give them everything he had. He succeeded. He was a son and brother who brought laughter and love from the beginning. They have always been, and always will be, proud of the boy he was and the man he became.

A devout Christian, a teammate and friend, Chris had a profound effect on the lives of many. He was publicly known for being the President of Craft International, LLC and the author of the best-selling book American Sniper. He was a Navy SEAL who served four combat tours in Operation Iraqi Freedom and elsewhere. He was awarded several medals for combat bravery, including two silver stars and five bronze stars with valor among many others. Chris was a true American hero

The program from Chris's memorial, held at Cowboys Stadium in Arlington, Texas, on February 11, 2013.

IN MEMORIAM

themselves. So please allow us a moment to thank them, as well as all of his friends and family and the many supporters we've met and have yet to meet, readers and well-wishers in general.

The list of contributors here is nowhere near an exhaustive list of Chris's closest friends, let alone a list of those he touched with his life. It is merely a cross-section, a taste, of those he meant a lot to. Some of his closest and dearest friends are not represented. The contributions were unfortunately limited by time and space. Please accept that they are meant to be representative rather than exhaustive. Taken together, they provide one more glimpse not just of who Chris was or how others saw him when he was alive, but of the legacy that he has left behind. He lives on not just in our hearts, but in the deeds and actions of those who knew him in the short time God shared him with us.

We start with some messages from the memorial service at Cowboys Stadium in Arlington, Texas, on February 11, 2013, read by Chris's parents and Taya.

—TAYA KYLE AND JIM DeFELICE

WAYNE AND DEBY KYLE
CHRIS'S MOM AND DAD

Chris with his parents at his and Taya's wedding.

Chris was a son who was strong enough to know when he was weak and brave enough to face himself when afraid. One who could stand proud, even in defeat, but humble and gentle in victory.

Chris was a son whose heart was true and whose goals were high. He never asked anything of anyone that he had not already asked of himself.

IN MEMORIAM

Chris always kept his sense of humor, so he could be serious and yet never take himself too seriously.

Chris put action to the quote, "It's our duty to serve those who serve us." He would not allow words to take the place of deeds.

Chris's chosen path in life was not easy but stressful, laden with difficulties and challenges. He stood tall in the storms, but showed compassion for those who failed.

Chris, there are not enough words to describe how proud we are of you! We believe in your courage, compassion, and strength of character. We believe in your goodness. We believe in YOU!

The following is the letter we wrote to Chris that was read at his memorial:

> We shared Chris's laughter, smile, pranks, jokes, and stories. He always had a story to be told, and only in the way Chris could express so vividly. There were so many laughs; even the two o'clock April Fool's calls and New Year's wake-up surprises were funny, at least after the fact.
>
> As parents we have such dreams for our sons—they're unlimited. We encouraged Chris to dream big. He did, and he achieved those dreams, even more than he could imagine.
>
> Chris, God had a plan for your life much bigger than we can even comprehend. You have touched so many lives with your infectious laughter, your side grin, your great sense of humor, your compassion and tenderheartedness, and of course that twinkle in your eye. You loved life and lived it full blast. We stand here today brokenhearted, knowing that death may end a life, but your spirit will live on for eternity. It will never end our immense love for you. You have been an

example of standing up for your convictions, pride in your country, and true love for Texas.

Our hearts ache to feel, once more, those all-engulfing and loving bear hugs you always gave; to hear you say, "I love you, Dad," or "I love you, Mom." To see you smile, hear you laugh, and watch you with your family.

As parents all we could give you was love, direction, and courage to succeed and believe in yourself. You took that and lived life to the fullest. You had a passion for everything you did.

God anointed you with your name: "The Protector." Your life embodied the full meaning of the word. You were tender to the young, compassionate with the wounded, and sympathetic with the less fortunate. The Lord had his hand on you the moment you were born. You were destined for greatness.

We could not be any more proud of you, son. Not in your medals, honors, or notoriety, but in the loving son, committed husband and father, the truly amazing man you became. Your courage of conviction, your strength to persevere, and the hope that survives disappointments are the keys to your success in life. You embraced and lived the slogan, "Courage is being scared to death but saddling up anyway." You knew that a successful life is not measured in how well known you were but in how well respected you were; not in your power to take but in your willingness to give. Your success is measured by the height of your aspirations, the width of your vision, and the depths of your convictions.

Chris, you define the true meaning of a successful life. Until you spread your wings, you will not know

IN MEMORIAM

how far you can fly. Son, heaven has no limits. Soar to heaven and keep watch over us.

Son, we are so thankful for having you in our life for the years that God gave us. We are so blessed to have shared your happiness and your sorrow. We are so proud that we watched you achieve your goals. You were and will always be a true blessing.

Son, you will live in our hearts forever. We will rejoice in the memories that you have given us. We are so brokenhearted, but we will persevere as we grasp onto your strength. We will stand at ease because we know that you are standing guard.

We have loved you and we will continue to love you even more.

TAYA KYLE

When you think you cannot do something, think again.

Chris always said, "The body will do whatever the mind tells it to." I am counting on that now.

I stand before you a broken woman, but I am now and always will be the wife of a man who is a warrior both on the battlefield and off.

Some people along the way have told Chris that through it all, he was lucky I stayed with him. I am standing before you now to set the record straight. Remember this: I am the one who is literally, in every sense of the word, blessed that Chris stayed with me.

I feel compelled to tell you that I am not a fan of people romanticizing their loved ones in death. I don't need to romanticize Chris, because our reality is messy, passionate, full of every extreme emotion known to man, including fear, compassion, anger, pain, laughing so hard we doubled over and hugged it out, laughing when we were irritated with each other, and laughing when we were so in love it felt like someone hung the moon for only us.

All of it, the messy, painful, constantly changing, crazy ride, was rolled up into the deepest, most soul-changing experience that only one man, Chris Kyle, could bring.

Chris was all in, no matter what he did in life. If he loved you, and I mean really loved you, he did it without judgment.

I will relate one of my clearest memories to you now in an attempt to explain how he put me, and others in his life, at ease. The backstory is this: Chris and I fell in love quickly. He was like a kid in a candy store and jumped into loving me with both feet and no looking back. It made me feel like pure gold, because I thought he was the most uniquely idealistic, fun, loving, intelligent, intuitive, and sensitive man I had ever met. It was starting to weigh heavily on my heart that this amazing man had a "love is blind" thing going on. A couple of months into our relationship, we were in the car in Coronado, California, and I got up the courage to tell Chris something I felt was very important for him to know. As happy as I was with Chris when we were physically together, we lived in different cities, and my real life, meaning the time I was not physically in his company, was full of stress and anxiety for many different reasons.

"Chris, I think you need to know something," I confessed. "I am really messed up. I really struggle with a lot of things."

Without batting an eye, and without pausing, he gently said in a way only Chris could, "You're a package deal, babe. I love you. All of you."

He grabbed my hand, and that was it. That was Chris for me through good and tough times. When I was hard on myself, he was the gentle force telling me that sum of me—failures, successes, love, joy, anxiety, and pain, were all rolled up into a package that was just fine by him. Thank you, Chris. Thank you for loving me, all of me.

I want to take a minute and honor Chad Littlefield. Because loving without judgment is what Chad gave to Chris also.

Chad and Chris started with a clean slate. Chad met Chris as just another father on the ball field trying to love his family. In the craziness of life, Chad came along with his quiet, large presence and easy smile, rugged beard and dimples. He blessed Chris with a friendship that was the one thing Chris needed more than anything. It was effortless. Chad would just show up and share some laughs, or show up and not say a word, depending on Chris's mood that day.

Chad helped Chris get back into his workouts by doing one

thing—he showed up. It was good for both of them. Chris used to tell me some mornings after a 5 A.M. workout with Chad, "Well, Chad and I were real chatty this morning."

I would start laughing. "Oh yeah?" I would say. "Did y'all say one sentence or two?"

A couple times Chris shocked me by saying there were maybe a couple short bursts of conversations. But it was 5 A.M. Neither one of them wanted to be there at 5 A.M. They were there because Chris needed it.

If Chris had had a particularly rough day, there were times he would mention it to Chad, and I have a feeling those conversations were as short as the 5 A.M. ones, plus or minus some. On those days, after the kids were in bed, it was common for Chad to just pop over for a visit. Chad and Leanne told us once they were Chris and my "FBBs"—that stood for "Friends Before the Book." That was absolutely true and we all knew it. That didn't mean that Chad didn't appreciate "The Legend" and the SEAL in Chris, though.

A little over a week ago, Chad showed up as he often did, just after the kids had gone to bed. He sauntered in, Sonic bag and large soda in hand, with his usual smile, nod, and a "Whassup girl?" to me. That evening he showed Chris a new rifle and scope he had just invested in. He asked Chris to fix up the scope for him.

Chris began asking Chad all kinds of technical questions about what he wanted and needed with it. Chad just cocked his head sideways and laughed, "You tell me, brother." Chris went to work. Chad looked at me and said, "Chris Kyle is fixin' up my scope, what?" In that tone he knew would crack us all up—and it did.

The bottom line is this: If it was a workout Chris needed, Chad was in. If it was a quiet night of hanging out, Chad was in. Thank you, Chad. Thank you for being that effortless, no expectations, comforting friend Chris needed. Chris and I both knew you loved him, and the feeling was mutual, my friend. I think you know that, too.

Kids, I will cherish the look on your dad's face when you would both come running across the house just to take a flying leap into his arms and tell him how much you missed him when he was gone. He loved that! I hope you know with all your heart that being your dad was the highlight of your father's life. He would always shake his head and wonder how he got so lucky to be with you. I honestly don't remember a night where Daddy and I would tuck you in and he wouldn't say, "Man, we are so blessed to have you two kids."

Bubba, your dad was so impressed by your intelligence, your kind heart, and your athletic ability, among many other things. He loved to make you laugh; if it was inappropriate and it made you laugh, he did it more, just to see you laugh longer. He loved the way you hugged him and sat cuddled up next to him on the couch. You made him feel like the best dad in the world. He called you his little man because in so many ways he already saw the man in you and was proud. He loved you beyond measure.

Baby Girl, Daddy had no idea what having a daughter would be like. He soon found out that you would soften and melt his heart with your many kisses and hugs. You would squeeze him and not let go, or if the way to his lap was empty, you would crawl up there and fill it up. You loved him in a way that is different than anything he had ever known and it always has and always will delight him to no end. He loved your jokes and loved the way you would be his sweet little girl with a no-holds-barred attitude. Like the time you told him off in the sweetest, most sincere way after the Six Flags ride scared you. Above all else, he loved you wholly and completely and he knew you also thought he was the best dad in the world.

So, my sweet angels, we will put one foot in front of the other and remember how silly Dad was, and how we all made fun of his Texas twang. We will laugh at how we would "poke the bear," and we will hug each other tightly just like Dad would do with us. We will pray the prayers he prayed with us.

We will remember that your dad had so much pride in your manners, good sportsmanship, and friendship to each other, and we will continue them all. We will remember that his Baby Girl and his Bubba meant the world to him and that he didn't just talk about that, he loved you and he lived his life to show you.

Chris, there isn't enough time to tell you everything you mean to me and everything you taught me. I know you had no idea you were teaching me. There is something only God and I have known for a long time: God worked through you to make me into the woman I am supposed to be. I almost feel sorry for you, babe, because God knew it would take the toughest and softest-hearted man on earth to get a hardheaded, cynical, hard-loving woman like me to see what God needed me to see. He chose you for the job. He chose well. You taught me innocent, reckless love without abandon. You taught me how to turn a life full of fear into a life full of faith. You taught me that I could be more independent than I ever wanted to be.

You taught me how to raise children with love and softness and proved it could be done with a high standard of respect and old-fashioned values. You taught me that I could forgive more deeply than I thought I could. You taught me that I was actually able to hold my tongue in anger. (By the way, I am sorry that took so long.)

You taught me that even as a Yankee, I could learn to have a conversation with my slow-talking Texas man without interrupting. I swear I never thought that was possible, and I know you thought that, too. You taught me that I am okay just the way I am.

IN MEMORIAM

You taught me that no matter what life lays in front of you, it's unwise to worry or overthink it, because even in the worst of times, life has a way of working out. And you have showed me that in life and even in death some people are always with you.

I love you, Chris. I love you, I love you, I love you.

AMERICAN SNIPER: MEMORIAL EDITION

"BUBBA,"
CHRIS'S SON

> Dad, I miss you a lot. One of the best things that has happened to me is you. I love you Dad. I always will.
>
> Love, Bubba

"BABY GIRL,"
CHRIS'S DAUGHTER

> Daddy, I love you Dad. you are the best dad ever. I never wanted you to die. I will miss your heart. I will love you even if you died.
>
> love you forever, Baby Girl

IN MEMORIAM

AMERICAN SNIPER: MEMORIAL EDITION

JEFF KYLE
CHRIS'S BROTHER

Seeing Jeff off before his deployment as a Marine. 29 Palms military base, 2006.

It's extremely difficult to squeeze a lifetime's worth of memories into a few words.

Chris was my mentor as well as my brother and friend. Like a lot of brothers, we went through a phase where we wanted to kill

IN MEMORIAM

each other every second. We were constantly fighting and at each other's throats. Then, suddenly, we weren't. I don't know what turned it around. After he graduated from high school and went to college, I went to see him and we hung out like friends. Being together was suddenly easy. Oh, we still had our disagreements and arguments, but it was different. We got pretty tight.

Even through that little time of conflict, I'd watch what he did. He was my example, my mentor. We shared the values of how we were raised, and I saw him put them into action. As we grew older, we had more and more in common. Chris joined the military; I joined a year later. We both went to Iraq, both fought for our country. We came home, started raising families.

The kids loved him. It was the little things Chris did with the kids that I remember. My oldest daughter called him Uncle Kiss. She still asks for him. My youngest was born a few weeks prematurely—thankfully, just in time for Chris to meet her before he died. I'll always remember how happy he was for us all. He'd do anything for the kids—even eat olives.

When my oldest was two, she became the pickiest eater in the world. And if someone made so much as a face when she was eating something, she decided that it was terrible and she wouldn't touch it. It didn't matter what it was—it could be Cheerios, her favorite. It was suddenly unfit for consumption.

We were all at a family dinner one day and my little girl got a plate of olives, at this point about the only vegetable she was still willing to eat. Uncle Kiss made a face, and just like that, olives were no longer edible.

"Thanks," I told my brother, half thinking that now she'd never eat any vegetable at all until she was in her twenties.

Chris decided he was going to fix that. He looked at my daughter. "Olives are good," he told her. "Look, I'll show you."

Now you have to understand—when I say Chris hated olives, I

mean he *hated* olives. A half sliver of one buried in a pizza somewhere would turn his stomach in the worst way. But he picked one up from her plate and ate it whole. And just like that, she was back to eating olives. I'm sure if we'd had them there, he'd've had her eating the entire vegetable kingdom by the end of the night, no matter what the effect on his stomach.

I want my kids to know he was an outstanding man before he was a military hero. He stuck up for people. He was inspirational and fun, and always a teacher—something always rubbed off on you, one way or another, when you were with him.

Not long after he died, a television interviewer asked me how I thought Chris would want to be remembered. I told them that he didn't care about the hype. He just wanted to be known as Chris Kyle, a good ol' country boy, a guy who was wired to help other people, but at the end of the day, just a regular guy.

IN MEMORIAM

ANDREW ALEXANDER
FRIEND

Andrew Alexander and Chris in 2012. To his friends, Chris was a gentle giant and an inspiration to do something worthwhile with their lives.

It goes without saying that Chris Kyle was one of the most heroic war fighters our country has ever seen. A man not afraid to fight a nasty battle for his country so that you and I could live in "the land of the free."

Chris created countless memories for me over the years during hunting and fishing trips. I will never forget how he was *always* a gentleman to everyone who crossed his path.

Chris had a spirit that was positive, warm, kind, and inviting. I cannot recall a time that he ever met a stranger—everyone was instantly a friend. Never did he pass by someone who wanted to say hello, shake his hand, or thank him for his service. He always stopped and offered up a smile and a handshake or a hug. Chris was a true gentleman.

He taught me and others by example. This gentlemanly spirit will live on forever. His actions have created long-lasting and memorable reactions. I will do better, work harder, push further, give more, love more, and be more because of my friend, the gentleman, Chris Kyle!

IN MEMORIAM

BO PHARR
FRIEND

Bo and Chris posing in Chris's living room. Their friendship covered many years and many miles, but always remained solid.

> God sent an angel with the name of Chris Kyle
> Guess he thought we needed one with some country style.
> I was lucky enough to meet him when we were in the
>   third grade.
> Wasn't long after that best friends had been made.
> I can remember soccer, video games, playing outside and
>   more, and who could forget the annual birthday BB
>   gun war!
> It wasn't long before our parents sent us off to college.
> That's where we were supposed to gain all of our knowledge.
> A little school, lots of parties, and rodeo too—those were
>   the days of TSU.

After college, when life took us different ways, we would try to stay in touch and remember the glory days.
You would enlist in the Navy, take a bride, and fight for our nation; with honor and courage you would defend our salvation.
Because of your skill you would be nationally known but still would remain humble, a seed your parents had sown.
I was always proud that you weren't blinded by the Hollywood light but stayed true to yourself with the end goal in sight.
To help your fellow soldiers with their struggles after war: it was something that you were called for and couldn't ignore.
How tragic that is what took you away.
Thoughts of you pass through me every single day.
I know in time that my heart will start to mend
but God, please help me . . .
I'VE LOST MY BEST FRIEND!

I will always remember the boy that you were and the man that you became, but most of all I will remember your friendship!

MISS YA, BUDDY,
"THE MOOSE"

IN MEMORIAM

"W," WRITING ON BEHALF OF "THE TEAMS" AND CHRIS'S FELLOW SEALS

Chris Kyle was and is a true American hero.

He was a hero because of the way he conducted himself in battle. Chris was that guy who always put the mission and his teammates above himself and his own safety. He did this out of instinct. Consequently he found himself acting, in the face of grave danger, more valorously than all but a few American soldiers in the great history of our nation. Chris's legacy as a warrior lies not at the end of the rounds that he sent to the enemy, but in his uncanny courage to stand in front of those around him when the chips were down.

Chris Kyle is a hero because of the way he conducted himself after he completed his overseas battles. The hero that Chris was on the battlefield did not matter much after his role overseas was done. He, like many others in his generation, found it hard to leave that life—and especially his Teammates—behind. But, because of his uncanny instinct to protect others, and with the exceptional love and support from his wife, kids, parents, and brother, Chris was able to endure the challenge of transition.

It was only in the last year that Chris truly found his new calling: he put others above himself, standing with fellow veterans to help them deal with the struggles of returning home from war. He wanted to encourage kids with severe illness. He wanted to help local law enforcement officers make things better for their communities. All of these things make him a true hero, even today, as his legacy lives on.

Chris Kyle and his family sacrificed everything to make this country, the state of Texas, and their hometown a better place. The courage to face grave danger in order to help those around him was Chris's greatest asset, and he turned it into a great calling. His family supported and endured that calling. Now, it is our turn. We must stand beside those around us to prove that the United States of America is truly the land of the free and the home of the brave. We must show the courage Chris showed in our communities, our own states, our own country.

IN MEMORIAM

BRYAN RURY
LIFELONG FRIEND

There's no way to single out in a few words the entire lifetime of a man, of a friend, like Chris. He so completely understood friendship and what it meant to be a friend that you just can't explain it simply.

Chris and I went to school together. He didn't have any enemies growing up. It seems funny to say, but it's completely true. He was always looking out for other people. He was involved in a few fights, but he was never the one who started them. He was always sticking up for other kids, including me.

His protective nature went beyond bullies and fights. He only got mad at me once. I was on the track team. We were at a party and, well, kids being kids, for some reason I took a cigarette and was smoking it.

He saw me. He didn't say anything, but he gave me a look. A real hard, Chris Kyle look.

Later on, he straightened me out. "What do you think you're doing?" he said, in the sternest voice I ever heard him use. "You better straighten yourself up."

And I did.

We didn't see each other for quite a while during his military service. When he came home, I was worried that he would be different, that our friendship would change somehow. But it didn't change at all, not one bit. We picked up exactly where we left off.

He was just as generous with other people as he was with me. As a friend, as a father—if you needed something, he'd lay it down for you. A year or so ago, there was a bad storm in our area. It knocked down a lot of trees and did some other damage to houses and the like. Well, I went out of the house at 6 A.M., just looking around to check what had happened. Chris drove up in his pickup not a minute later, a chain saw in the back.

We must have worked for several hours clearing the trees that had come down on my property. We hauled three full loads away. Finally, we were done.

"You tired?" he asked.

"A little," I admitted.

"Why don't we go see who else needs help?"

How could I refuse that? We spent the rest of the day working around town.

I could tell a million stories—the time he blew off George W. Bush just to be with us at a family event that meant a lot to my wife, the day he hung my Christmas lights because he knew I was stuck at work.

He was a hero on the battlefield. He saved lives there. But when he returned home, he was a superhero to his friends. He lived the meaning of friendship every day.

IN MEMORIAM

MARCUS LUTTRELL
FELLOW SEAL, FRIEND

Chris and Marcus Luttrell relaxing in 2012 before a speaking appearance. The two Texas boys were good friends before fame touched each one.

Chris Kyle is not a man I ever thought I would refer to in the past tense. No matter how much danger he faced, we always knew Chris would come out alive with an awesome story filled with close calls. To say I lost a friend this year does not say enough. I lost someone I looked up to as a frogman and Texan brother. He exemplified each word of the SEAL creed, and he deserves the highest honor and respect for what he put on the line to keep his brothers safe from the enemy. I know there are mothers and fathers out there right now who are grateful their son or daughter returned home from war thanks to Chris Kyle. He saved countless lives. Whether he sat high on a rooftop taking out the enemy threatening his teammates, or if he was fighting side by side with a Marine platoon, his mission was always clear: "draw on every remaining ounce of strength to protect his brothers."

Chris gave a piece of his life to the SEAL Teams, but there came a time when he needed to refocus on his family. No matter how difficult his decision to leave the military, he knew he was doing the right thing for his wife and two children. He became well known after the much-deserved success of his first book, *American Sniper*. The ways he handled himself under the spotlight and shared his passions are a testament to the man he was. Chris gave away the proceeds of his book to veterans and families of fallen teammates. He was the founder of a security company that was dedicated to teaching fine skills to law enforcement and other security details. He was committed to his family, he was committed to helping veterans, he was committed to several charities, he was committed to serving others. That was Chris. He lived by his own rules, and I couldn't respect him more.

I have to pay tribute to Chris's wife, Taya. Taya is carrying the torch for Chris, their kids, and those he fought to defend. She has promised to see through all of the projects Chris left behind (including the excellent book *American Gun: A History of the U.S. in Ten Firearms*), as well as to ensure that Chris's memory is honored as it should be. I think Chris married a person who may be stronger than even he was—that's saying something. With Chris's spirit beside her, she is never out of the fight.

IN MEMORIAM

ASHLEY PURVIS SMITH
FAMILY FRIEND

Before I even met Chris, I knew him through Taya. I was curious, of course, but not overly so until the first time I heard her talking to him on the phone.

Taya was very guarded at that stage in her life. She had a successful career, a confident air, and a brilliant ability to make people laugh with her quick wit and charismatic ways. But there was a whole other side to her—a deeply loving, nurturing, vulnerable side that very few were allowed to see. I remember her sitting in the backseat of my car, talking quietly on the phone in gentle, almost giggling tones to this new man she had met. She sounded so young, so happy. Her reaction to him made me *very* curious.

When I first met Chris, I had to laugh. He was a mix of gentleman and instigator with a twist of overgrown puppy. He was youthful then—playful, polite, and unhindered by political correctness. Taya and Chris both had a happy flush in their faces when they were together. He was smart enough to keep up with her, gentle enough to gain her trust, and playful enough to make her life fun.

Chris was also very observant. I remember being impressed when Taya told me that Chris had delivered the perfect coffee to her one morning early in their relationship. She had never told him how she took her coffee, so she asked how he knew. He had simply paid attention. He was like that; he had a keen eye for detail.

He was also a lot smarter than most people recognized. He didn't flaunt it, but you could see it in the way he processed things. And he loved crossword puzzles. Whenever he came to stay with our family during the holidays, they were a staple by the bedside—and all around the house, for that matter.

I loved to tease Chris about being my punk little brother. He was great to tease—always laughing and happy to give it back. He was fantastic with my kids. We all have fond memories of him hog-tying my then eight-year-old stepson and challenging him to find his way out of the knots. He knew how to empower through rough play, yet somehow the nurturer in him always knew when to quit so that it remained fun for everyone.

I remember early glimpses of the deeper side of Chris. I especially remember the stricken look on his face when he took a very brief break from Taya's side as she went through labor with their son. It was a horrific experience, and Taya was passing in and out of consciousness as she attempted to give birth. Chris had been with her nonstop, hour after hour. At one point he came out to the hospital lobby. His father stood and Chris walked straight to him in long strides, his face tight and etched with pain, and embraced him. The emotion was palpable. It was pure, raw, barely restrained, and I'll never forget it.

Over time, the need to survive day-to-day life hardened them both. I remember Chris coming back from war, still joking and laughing, but no longer an innocent youth. He was a man trying to reintegrate, and although he was a loving father and husband, his fuse was shorter. There were still times, though, when I was struck by his softer, less jaded side. He was playful and gentle when he interacted with children, he was patient and kind with horses, and more than once I saw him hold a puppy with a tenderness that I have rarely seen in a full-grown man.

I never respected Chris more than when he made the decision to leave the military. It was not something he wanted to do, but he chose to be a father and husband to a family that needed him to take a bigger part in their lives. For me, that is the selfless act that has meant the most. He was very blunt in saying that it was a choice he was struggling with, and yet he was able to stand by his choice and work to make that choice a positive one for everyone.

IN MEMORIAM

He never stopped remaining open to his family and he was ultimately an amazing husband and father who cherished those roles.

Even after his book, his notoriety always caught me by surprise. He still preferred a quiet holiday with his family or an evening on the porch swing, surrounded by family and longtime friends. It was easy to forget that there were so many looking up to him.

I knew Chris over the course of many years, but I didn't know him as well as I would have liked. In the days surrounding Chris's memorial, I had the extraordinary privilege of spending time with some of the people Chris valued. They were amazing, accomplished, thoughtful, and strong. His loss affected them all so deeply.

The public response honoring him was overwhelming and awe inspiring. It is something I will never forget—and it made me even more aware of how many people he touched in the time he spent on earth. There were a lot of layers to him—and the more I know, the more I wish I would have known.

AL HEMMLE
PRINCIPAL, MIDLOTHIAN HIGH SCHOOL

When people do for our country what Chris Kyle did, it elevates them to a special status. But what truly impressed me about Chris was his unassuming, matter-of-fact heroism in everyday life.

I'd known Chris when he was a student, even though I never had him in a class. When he was a senior, I coached the freshman football team, and I became acquainted with him through that connection. He was a very well-balanced kid, involved in FFA (Future Farmers of America) as well as sports, a really good kid and in a lot of ways typical of the sort of well-rounded young men we hope to graduate from Midlothian.

Once he went into the military, he took himself to a new level. I think he really found himself there. He decided he wanted to achieve, and he ended up doing that. He became one of the elite.

When he came home, though, he didn't act as if he was special. He didn't come off as a celebrity or someone "too good" for us. It was just the opposite. He remembered his roots, and he made himself available to help others on a very personal level.

I asked him one day to speak to our faculty and our graduating seniors, and he was very enthusiastic about it. He connected immediately with the kids as well as the adults. He talked for an hour and a half to our young people about the importance of an education and, I think more importantly, about how honesty and hard work set you up for success no matter what you do. I could see the kids making a connection.

I asked him back a few times, and he always came. In fact, I tried to pay him—he was spending so much time out of his busy schedule that I thought it only fair that we pay him like we would pay any outside speaker. He wouldn't have it, even when I insisted.

IN MEMORIAM

The best I could do was have him name a charity for us to send the fee to. That was the kind of guy he was.

We had a student who was involved in a little bit of trouble. The young man landed in our disciplinary program. This was a kid I knew could do better, but for some reason no one seemed able to reach him. I gave him my personal copy of *American Sniper,* and the young man really related to it. Chris heard about it, and the next thing I knew, he was insisting on talking to the young man himself. It made a very positive impact. I'm sure he helped plenty of other young people that way.

Out of the many things he told our students, one in particular really stands out. Chris believed that there is a time in people's lives when the opportunity comes along for them to make something of themselves, whether it's to achieve something important, or maybe to turn themselves around from a bad direction to a good one. Chris felt that if he could be there at that moment, he could have a big impact. If he thought investing his time could help a person, he did it.

That to me is what a hero is all about. To me, that's as big a hero as you can be. So, as important as what Chris Kyle did on the battlefield was, what he did one-on-one with our students was even bigger.

GLENN BECK*
TALK-SHOW HOST

I was trying to think last night: What do I take away from all of this? What is the story I will tell my eight-year-old son when I get home and kneel at his bedside?

Maybe it's this:

> *Son, there was once a boy whose daddy gave him a BB gun. He was little—he was about your age, and he learned to shoot it. And he got really, really good at shooting. It's one of those things that God gives you, but then he asks you in the end: What did you do with your talent?*
>
> *And I know what you're thinking, buddy: Shooting a gun can come from God? Yes, son, it can. Everybody gets their own talents from God, but that one has to come with another talent, because it comes with such responsibility. If God is going to give somebody the "gun gift," he has to make sure that another gift is already in place, and that's discernment. The gift of knowing good from bad in a second. I pray that you will never have to pull a trigger, son. But if you do, you'd better be right. Your head better be clear enough to ask God for an answer, and to trust what you feel.*
>
> *The little boy whose dad gave him a BB gun grew up to be a hero. Chris had discernment. He was crystal clear about the good guys and the bad guys. But killing bad guys was not all there was to Chris Kyle. He was a*

---

*Transcribed from a recent broadcast.

IN MEMORIAM

hero for how he loved as well. He gave away his chance to be rich so that his friend's mom could have a house and food. His friend had died in battle.

Once, in the car, his sweet wife confessed her weaknesses. She said, "I'm a mess, Chris." But her husband didn't make her pay for that. He loved her. He said, "Babe, you're a package deal."

His legend was growing as a warrior, but rather than build on it he left the military to be a dad. You see, Raphe, when God told Chris to shoot, he did. When God told him to sheathe his sword, learn how to love even better than he shot, he listened and obeyed, and he did that for her.

It's discernment. Knowing the difference between right and wrong. Having the courage to be honest. It's like Sir Galahad: his strength was as the strength of ten because his heart was pure.

And then, when my story is told and my little boy's eyes are closed, I will probably stay on my knees a little bit longer than usual and lay my head on that little boy's chest and thank God out loud that I've been given this gift of a son. And I will quietly, once again, ask God to help this dad be just a little more like Chris Kyle.

JEFF BURGE
DALLAS POLICE DEPARTMENT, FRIEND

On a wet, chilly January 2012 evening in Dallas, Texas, I was fortunate to have the opportunity to accompany Chris and Taya to the first of what would be many stops on the *American Sniper* book tour. The turnout for this event was beyond anyone's expectations and it was soon evident that the bookstore had seriously underestimated the volume of fans that would show up and stand for hours in the long line that snaked through the entire store.

Chris, though obviously blown away by the crowd, was not in the least bit deterred and made a point to engage each and every fan who came to see him. I watched as he signed books and posed for photographs. He thanked veterans for their service and families of servicemen and -women for their sacrifice. He shook hands, gave hugs, and, with genuine humility, addressed every man as "sir" and every lady as "ma'am" (ball cap removed, of course). He stood the entire time. That's the man he was. It's how he was raised—nice job, Wayne and Deby.

As the father of three boys, I realize that I bear the responsibility of teaching and modeling for my sons what it means to be a man. A real man: a man of faith, integrity, honor, discipline, patriotism, and self-sacrifice. Chris Kyle was the embodiment of all these virtues. Over the years, I have cautioned my boys about looking to public figures or celebrities as role models. All too often, we are left disappointed when we discover that the public persona is nothing like the person they are privately. Not so with Chris. He was the real deal. I am deeply honored to have called him friend and proud that my boys will forever look up to him for the role model and hero he was . . . and will forever be.

IN MEMORIAM

DR. KAREN HANTEN
PEDIATRICIAN, FRIEND

Karen Hanten and Chris share a good laugh after shoving birthday cake into each other's face at a party. It was a family ritual.

As the Kyle family pediatrician and Taya's dear friend, I knew Chris first and foremost as a husband and father. Speaking of legends! He made such an impact on Taya and his children's lives that I truly believe they are blessed with his memory and the undying love and devotion he gave them. I will never forget his deliberate, selfless, and complete love for them; it had no boundaries.

I loved the way Chris never tired of telling Taya (whom he almost always called "babe") how beautiful she was to him, even when she was soaked head to toe after a water fight with the kids. Or how he so wanted her to be happy that he'd bring home Chinese food time and time again, despite the fact that he really, really disliked Chinese food.

Because of Chris, the kids always answer, "Yes," never "Yeah"; they say "sir" and "ma'am" and treat their elders with respect. Their favorite thing was to run at full speed and jump on Chris while he was on the couch; even exhausted, he never tired of playing with them. They love to play and roughhouse, but they know when to stop and respect limits, even one of Chris's own: don't mess with another person's hat.

My family and I have always had great respect for our military. Chris's passionate dedication to his fellow soldiers and veterans has set a higher bar for the degree of commitment my family and I now have to them. Chris will always be a role model to our kids, demonstrating what we owe our military, and I am grateful to him for that.

Personally, I will miss his quick wit and incredible intelligence, his huge smile and laugh, and shoving cake in his face every birthday party, even though he always got me back worse. Before every deployment, I always promised Chris I would care for Taya and the kids as I would my own. That commitment remains steadfast.

IN MEMORIAM

KELLY JOB
WIFE OF CHRIS'S SEAL TEAMMATE RYAN JOB

Ryan in October, 2008, shooting a record-setting elk with the help of a computer-assisted scope and a close friend.

Chris was one of the few guys who really made an effort to keep in touch with my husband Ryan after he was seriously wounded. Chris was part of Ryan's healing process, supporting him as he went through many difficult operations and gradually overcame his disabilities. Ryan was blinded in the war; Chris was one of the people who helped Ryan realize he still had a lot to do with his life.

Then, when Ryan died during surgery, Chris became my friend as well. I'd known him, of course, but until then, he had always been more Ryan's friend than mine. With my husband gone, Chris and his wife Taya came into my life in a much more personal way. They showed me that it was still possible to have a good time—I remember being with them at a wedding, smiling and relaxing and just feeling very warm in their presence.

Chris would check in by phone whenever he could, to see if I needed anything.

"You're stuck with me now," he'd always say. "Don't forget that." He and Taya became part of my support network, always there if I needed to call on them.

His tragic death hurt us all. I was able to offer to support to Taya, finding strength I wasn't sure I had.

It's ironic: Sometimes you end up in friendships with people because of bad circumstances, and those friendships somehow become stronger and more meaningful than you ever could have imagined. You grow as a person, and you give something back. You do your share to help others and make the world a better place.

IN MEMORIAM

"DAUBER"
FELLOW SEAL, FRIEND

"Dauber" and Chris following a medal ceremony in San Diego. Afterward, Chris unceremoniously but characteristically tossed the medal into a drawer to gather dust.

I checked into SEAL Team Three in 2005 while they were finishing up their deployment. While I waited for my new platoon to return to the States, I went to sniper school. By the time I finished and finally met Charlie Platoon, Chris Kyle's legend had spread far and wide. I was excited to be one of a few snipers in his platoon, and a little anxious at the same time, especially as a new guy.

I learned quickly that working with Chris was nothing to be nervous about. He put others around him at ease while motivating them to perfect their craft. He made me want to be a better sniper. Despite setting the bar extremely high, he also made me feel that I could do as well as he did if I worked hard enough.

My most vivid memories of Chris are from our deployment to Ramadi, Iraq, in 2006. We often used a particular four-story apartment building for sniper overwatches. We'd been in-country for a couple months and had established a routine. One afternoon we set up to overwatch and provide security for an American patrol. To the west of us was a stretch of approximately one kilometer known for insurgent activity. The rest of the platoon snipers found spots to watch from inside while Chris and I settled in together on the rooftop. We stayed on the roof for twenty-four hours. Between the two of us, we killed twenty-three insurgents (the breakdown of kills favored Chris—heavily). That overwatch marked an important moment for me in my career as an operator. I realized my own potential and our incredible potential as a unit. Chris showed me what perseverance, attention to detail, and relentlessness can accomplish.

Chris's desire to protect others was most evident after Ryan Job was shot on August 2, 2006. After the incident, the platoon was back at our camp post attempting to regroup and make sense of what had happened. Despite six months of success on the battlefield, I was dazed by Ryan's injury. As we sat and contemplated our own mortality, there was a sense of uncertainty about how to move forward. While I sat quietly with the others around me, I noticed Chris. He was calmly and methodically refitting grenades, loading mags, and preparing to go back out. He felt no uncertainty about what the next step was—he planned to go out and get the ones responsible for taking Ryan from us. His calm and confidence provided an example for the rest of us. He became our leader when we ventured back into the streets to exact revenge on our enemies.

It was an honor to work with Chris in the SEAL teams and I am proud to have called him teammate. I am thankful that our relationship didn't end when our enlistments did, and even more proud that I called him friend.

IN MEMORIAM

KIM AND KENT STUDEBAKER
PARENTS-IN-LAW

Kent and Kim Studebaker, Taya and Chris. January 2013

We have so many memories of Chris. We really enjoyed getting to know him better and to spend time with him. We're just sorry we didn't get more time.

Kent remembers going out to play golf at the San Diego Naval Base golf course. Chris had not played golf before, so this was a real challenge to him. He made the usual mistakes—whiffing his drives and so on. But he also hit some really good shots. The wonderful thing was that he was able to laugh at the mistakes and really enjoy the good shots. His ability to laugh at himself and his genuine humility made it fun for the rest of the party to be out there with him.

Kim remembers watching Chris climb around on play equipment with the kids and tenderly watching out for their safety. She remembers birthday parties where he got smacked in the face with a cake and howled with laughter as a great cake fight began. She remembers the Christmas the kids got new low-rider bikes and Chris took them out to teach them how to ride them. She remembers him laughing and rolling in the snow up at Mount Hood, hanging on for dear life in the inner tube behind our boat, and riding a horse so comfortably it was clear he was a natural.

He always helped set the table when he visited—even if he had to ask what side the forks went on. And he always had a good helping of buttermilk pie—even though the lactose tended to upset his stomach.

The bedtime stories, the big warm hugs, the way he changed the kids' diapers, the way he laughed at his little girl's jokes, the way he picked up on his wife and children's moods, the way he just "got" people, the way he was a dad—they're all memories that flood back and say he was a real man, a loving husband and father.

But maybe our best memories of Chris have to do with him, his kids, and Texas. When his oldest was born, Chris had a bit of Texas dirt flown to him in California so the first thing his son's feet touched would be Texas soil. Chris made sure his son had a cowboy hat to wear from a very young age, and he confessed that he loved to hear his baby's laugh over the satellite phone when he was deployed to Iraq.

One of the last times we saw them all together was in December of 2012, when we went with them to Six Flags, the amusement park. Not everyone in the family was a big fan of roller coasters. Chris seemed to love them, even though he was actually afraid of heights. We'll always remember his raucous laughter watching his wife and son as they went on the ride, and the way he comforted his daughter when she was scared and annoyed during the day. As strong as he was, he was also a gentle, loving father. We'll all miss him very deeply.

IN MEMORIAM

ANONYMOUS
ACTIVE-DUTY SEAL, FRIEND

If you knew Chris well, you knew he was no "Legend." He was a son, a brother, a SEAL, a husband, and a father. Most of all, he was a friend.

In the Teams, we use the term *brotherhood* when referring to the bond all frogmen have with one another. It is a bond of blood and sweat. It starts in BUD/S and stays with you until you are carried to your final resting place; then it is passed to your family. Chris was a friend and "brotha" to me, and even though we did not talk every day, our bond allowed us to pick up where we left off with just a hug and a few words about how life was treating us. It was easy to love this Texas cowboy. He was the best the SEALs had to offer. He took care of the boys, loved the Teams, and loved his family.

Chris and I met after we assumed the position of leading petty officers (LPOs) for our platoons in Task Unit Bruiser. He was the Delta Platoon LPO and I was the Charlie Platoon LPO. We were the backbone of the Task Unit. At that time Bruiser's SEALs had a reputation as the toughest SOBs at SEAL Team Three and we both strived to continue that tradition.

During the first part of our training cycle, Chris and I spent considerable time at work together. We spent even more after hours, fixing the world's problems over many beers and whiskies. I don't think I've ever gained so much admiration for another man. So much so that without discussing it with my wife, I made up my mind that Chris would become the godfather of our firstborn.

My wife was taken aback that I would give such a large task to a man she knew little about and I had only known for a short time. I have a few lifelong friends from home as well as supportive older brothers and brothers-in-law who would also have been fine choices. But for me, the decision came down to picking a man I wanted my son to remember and who could tell him best about the man I was: a father, a husband, and a warrior.

I was no longer the boy from Indy that my friends and relatives knew. I was a SEAL. Chris knew that part of me best. I knew that he would love my son as I did, with a strong hand and an open heart.

When I told Chris my wishes, he was just as surprised as my wife. Still, he took on the responsibility without hesitation or question. He did it with his whole being and with conviction. Friends became family. Two men from totally different walks of life, a country boy from Texas and a city kid from Indiana, became lifelong friends and brothers, and our families became family.

But God works in mysterious ways, and our plans do not always follow his.

Chris's untimely death has taught me another valuable lesson about who I am, and who I have to be. When I met my wife I was in BUD/S. She only knows the SEAL, and has yet to truly find the man under all the armor and Kevlar. This is what Chris wanted to give back to Taya and the kids, "the man"; that's the reason he left the Navy. He gave them more of the man and less of the SEAL. They thrived because of it.

I understand that lesson now. Life is short and you never know when God will call his warriors home. So it's important to take advantage of what little time you do have.

The Teams and the country have lost a great warrior and a better man. His presence in our lives will be missed. He has fallen, but he is not forgotten.

I miss you, brotha.

IN MEMORIAM

KIM ESSARY
NEIGHBOR, FRIEND

"Team Kyle" with Chris—from left to right: Chris, Shelby Essary, Taya, Kim Essary, and Mike Essary. The Essary family joined the Kyles and other friends to wish Chris well during the airing of the television show Stars Earn Stripes.

I got my first glimpse of Chris when the moving van pulled up in front of the house Chris and Taya had just bought. I would peek out the window every little while, curious about our new neighbors. One can only imagine my thoughts when I saw our new neighbor carrying body targets out of the moving van!

I remember the first time my husband Mike and I met Chris. Taya and the kids were out of town, so we invited him over. As we sat on our back porch, there were the normal questions one asks someone they've just met. Chris briefly touched on the fact that he had been a sniper for the Navy. I have always been patriotic and have an enormous amount of respect for those who risk their lives and fight to keep us free, but until that time I had never had the pleasure of sitting and talking candidly with someone in the military service.

As we all talked, it was obvious Chris was what us Texans refer to as "a good ol' boy." I thought to myself, I like this guy—he seems genuine and down to earth.

Taya and I quickly became friends, and over time we formed a deep and close friendship. Mike and I had known some of Chris's background in the military, but we had no idea of the degree that he had touched people's lives over the years. It was obvious Chris was patriotic to the core and very passionate about what he believed in, but to us, Chris was just Chris: a neighbor and friend who wasn't any different than anyone else, other than the fact that he was an ex–Navy SEAL. While he loved deeply the men and women he served with, and had a passion and love for all vets, his main focus was now on the one thing he loved more than anything, his family.

One evening Chris opened up and shared with us how hard the decision had been to leave the military. He admitted that he felt he had let his military family down. He spoke of the deep bond formed when people fight together in combat. "There is no other friendship like it in the world," he told us. I will always remember that conversation; it allowed me to understand Chris more.

In many ways Chris was a no-nonsense type of guy; what you saw was what you got, and if you didn't like it—that was your problem, not his. But he was never arrogant. He had a healthy confidence about him; it complemented his gentle and loving side. To me, Chris was a man who had gone through hell and back, made some hard decisions in his life, and was now focusing his heart and soul into his family.

After Chris wrote *American Sniper,* I used to tease him that I would get around to reading it when I didn't have anything else better to do. It wasn't until months later, when Mike and I were

IN MEMORIAM

at the airport and saw it on the front table in a bookstore, that we decided to buy it.

Mike read it first. "You should read this," he told me when he was done. "There is a lot I never knew about Chris."

I have to admit that I didn't get to it right away. When I did, I was shocked. I remember calling Taya and telling her, "I can't quit crying!"

I have to admit that it was odd at first reading about our friends, but it definitely helped us to see a side of Chris that we knew very little about. My family and I had always respected him for what he had done for our country, but after reading the book, our respect grew immensely. After I finished, I put all teasing aside and marched across the street to their house. I looked Chris straight in the eyes and said, "I read your book and I had no idea. Thank you for all you have done and for all your sacrifice."

I had tears in my eyes. He smiled that Chris Kyle smile and didn't say a word. I slapped him on the arm and said, "By the way, your book made me cry!" I think Chris enjoyed that comment more than anything.

In the days after he died, my family saw an outpouring of love that was simply amazing. As we drove in the procession to Austin for the final services, we were in complete awe at the hundreds and hundreds of people who came out to pay their respects to Chris and his family. We had no idea of all the lives Chris had so deeply touched, and we were honored and privileged to call him our friend.

LARRY TOON
CHAIRMAN OF ELIZABETH TOON CHARITIES

I first met Chris and Taya shortly after Chris left the Navy. I met him through a mutual friend—former Dallas quarterback Roger Staubach. Chris had recently begun training military and police officers in a variety of tactical arts. We were looking for a unique fund-raising opportunity, and Chris offered to host a training session. It turned out to be a highly successful fund-raiser.

Chris was one of those guys who immediately got it. I admired his contributions as a member of the military, but it wasn't the military side of him that I saw. It was more a warm, giving side. He was one of those guys who flat give you the shirt off their back—then ask if you want another one.

My daughter had been gone for a few years at that point. I think Chris and I formed a connection in some way because of the grief that I had gone through and the things he had to endure in war. He had a sensitivity about him that touched me deeply.

Then came that terrible day when he died. It's hard to get my head around it even now. But suffering through my daughter's death taught me something very important. I used to spend my time asking God, Why did you take her? It was as if I was living in a very bad dream, each day hoping to wake up to a different reality but never quite getting there.

Then one day I realized I had my thinking backward. Rather than asking why God had taken her, I should instead be telling other people why God gave her to us. Her life was a gift to make us appreciate generosity and hope, what people can do when they are full of life and potential.

IN MEMORIAM

I feel exactly that way about Chris, and I'll be telling people about him for the rest of my life. His good works live on through dozens of organizations and hundreds of people, who are all taking his example and making the world a better place.

AMERICAN SNIPER: MEMORIAL EDITION

LEANNE LITTLEFIELD
FRIEND, NEIGHBOR

The Littlefield family with Chris during the airing of Stars Earn Stripes.

My husband Chad and I met the Kyle family through soccer. Our daughters were on the same team. I met Taya first; we hit it off immediately. We have been close friends since that first encounter, and now have a bond that is only shared between her and me, one that can never be broken.

Chad and Chris met later on, and they soon developed a close friendship as well. I was in the same grade as Chris's brother Jeff, so I knew of him, but I didn't know much about his military ser-

IN MEMORIAM

vice, and certainly nothing about the SEALs. We knew Chris as an ordinary dad. What we all did together, whether it was watching the kids play soccer, celebrating a birthday, or just hanging out, was ordinary stuff. Most Americans know Chris as a sniper and a hero; to me, he was a neighbor, a friend, a dad. Chad and Chris were such good friends because they had those things in common. They were dads, husbands, normal guys just doing what needed to be done to support their families.

Not knowing much about SEALs, I asked Chris once if what they did was anything like that movie *G.I. Jane*. Being a small-town country girl, I had no idea what Navy SEALs did, much less what snipers were, so that was the only thing I could relate to.

The look he gave me! That became a joke between us.

It's hard to single out one memory from the times we all spent together. There's not any one big event that stands out. But that was the way he wanted it—he wanted to be a normal dad, and do normal family things. He succeeded.

Chad and Chris really bonded. They worked out together as well. They held each other accountable and started out most days with a 5 A.M. workout. Though Chad had never served in the military, they had a lot of things in common. Sports, for example—they were both big Texas Ranger and Dallas Cowboy fans. They'd watch a game together and if things weren't going too well, Taya and I would slip away to the kitchen, giving them their space.

They were together at the end. It means they went to heaven together, not alone. I find great comfort in that. I picture them rising together, entering heaven's gates arm in arm, a bond shared between.

In the days that followed their deaths, one of Chad's coworkers sent me a picture of two doves that sat on Chad's office window all day long. Two sheep were randomly sitting in my yard just a couple of days after the boys died.

Coincidences?

I laughed then and I laugh now, because I picture Chad and Chris having a discussion that goes something like this:

>**Chris:** Hey, man, let's go sit in your yard as some random animal.
>**Chad:** That would be awesome! We just can't be cattle or something that would tear up my yard, though.

I know they are at peace with their Savior in heaven. They are heroes to my daughter and me, but daddies always are.

IN MEMORIAM

MARC MYERS
BUSINESSMAN, RANCH OWNER, FRIEND

In addition to opening their ranch to our family for relaxation, Marc and Jan Myers built a range for Chris to use in raising money for the Elizabeth Toon Foundation. The Myers also generously allowed us to use their ranch during the writing of American Sniper *as well as during the filming of Lester Holt's interviews with Chris in 2012 and Taya in 2013.*

A few years ago, my friend Larry Toon was hoping to raise money for the Elizabeth Toon Charities by hosting a weapons demonstration, and I volunteered my ranch. The idea of the event was simple: People would come to the ranch and get an advanced shooting lesson. In exchange, they would pay a fee, which would be donated to the charity. It was a great idea. The only problem was, I didn't have a proper rifle range for the event. I decided to build one, but naturally needed an expert to help lay it out.

Somehow, Chris Kyle got involved and came out to take a look and see what could be done. I knew a little bit about his background as a SEAL and a sniper, but whatever I expected was quickly contradicted. Here was the easiest-going, most casual guy ever. He was so easy to be around. Our ages were different—I am a year or two older, let's say—but he was instantly likable and we just got along very well. He came out to plan the rifle range and ended up being a good friend.

I remember watching him during the event. I thought it would start out with a half hour of lecture from him, all very technical and dry instruction. Not at all. He laid out his weapons on the bench, gave a few quick pointers on safety, and told everyone to have at it. He kept a watchful eye on everyone and helped people who weren't too familiar with the guns, but he was so casual about it that no one knew he was instructing them. He was adept and confident in a way that inspired other people to be confident.

That was Chris—an easygoing, regular guy. The Christmas before he died, he and Taya, the kids, and Taya's folks came out to the ranch to stay with us for a few days. Most of the time when I have company like that I can get a little nervous—you're always worried as a host about pleasing people, meeting their expectations, even if they're friends.

Not with Chris. He was just easy as easy could be. We did a little hunting, but mostly we just hung out. He never stressed, and neither did we.

To me, Chris was a John Wayne of the twenty-first century. He was a national hero. And yet was the easiest guy in the world to get along with. It's still hard to imagine he's gone.

IN MEMORIAM

MATHEW BULLINGER
FELLOW LITTLE LEAGUE COACH, FRIEND

Chris and I met because our children were friends from school. I didn't find out that he used to be a Navy SEAL sniper until much later. I got to know him as a family man, an amazing husband, dedicated father, and loyal friend. Besides baseball, we shared a passion for hunting and the outdoors. We could talk about those things for hours.

Chris and I coached together in Little League baseball, one season of T-ball and one of coach-pitch. He loved the game of baseball and was already signed up to coach another season when he was tragically taken from us. He was great coaching the kids. The boys didn't know of his military service or how many confirmed kills he had as a sniper. They looked up to him for being there and for his strict work ethic. Looking back, Chris always seemed drawn to the boys who were a little smaller or couldn't throw as far because he was always ready to help anyone in need. He would take the extra time and work individually with them to build up their confidence and baseball skills.

This season has been bittersweet. The boys are really developing into good ball players and I know he would have loved coaching them at this level.

On the way to one of our baseball games the other day, my five-year-old son told me that he missed Chris and that he cried because he was so sad that he won't ever see him again. He remembers Chris as the guy who he got to climb on like a jungle gym, who let him play games on his iPhone, and who always made him laugh by tickling him and lifting him up on his shoulders.

I consider myself lucky to have gotten to know the hometown dad and Little League coach. Hearing his SEAL brothers speak at his memorial service about the man, the myth, the legend, was an eye-opening experience for me and my wife. After his memorial service at Cowboys Stadium, my wife Jennifer wrote, "Today will be a day I will never forget. Such honor, truth, beauty, sadness, pain, rejoicing, tears, smiles, and respect. He wasn't Chris Kyle to my family. He was just Chris. Watching the tears fall down my young daughter's face said it all. He was her Mr. Chris. The man that hugged her, loved her, and always made her smile. Thank you for touching all our lives. We love you and miss you!"

Chris Kyle was a true warrior and an American hero. His legacy will live on through his family, his SEAL brothers, and all of us who were lucky enough to know him. Rest in peace, Chris.

IN MEMORIAM

OMAR AVILA
WOUNDED WARRIOR, FRIEND

Omar Avila and Chris share a smile. A long hour of conversation at a ranch retreat led to a close friendship.

I met Chris in 2010. It was a down time in my life. I'd been badly injured in Iraq three years before when our Humvee was hit by a massive IED. I stayed in the truck to provide cover fire with the .50-cal as the convoy regrouped, but stayed a bit too long—the fire started cooking off our spare grenades. I managed to get out, but ended up with burns over 75 percent of my body. The worst were fourth-degree burns, where the muscle kind of melts. Besides that, my legs were broken, my hands deformed, and my foot was so badly mangled I needed to get it amputated.

I was twenty-one.

That was 2007. Three years later, I was doing better physically, but mentally I was in a bad place. A hole. One day I was invited to a gathering at a ranch to spend a weekend hunting and hanging out with other disabled vets. I wasn't going to go. What was the sense? But then the idea of hunting tickled something. Hunting had been important to me before the war, and maybe the vague hope that I might do it again got me out.

I didn't end up doing much hunting that weekend. What I did do a lot of, starting from that first night, was talking to Chris. I'd never met him, and I had no idea who he was—this was before the book came out. We just started talking, ex-Army guy to former SEAL.

"So how are you doing?" he asked me after I told him about my injuries.

"I'm doing fine," I said. I thought the question was the kind of blow-off question people ask to be polite.

"No, no. How are you doing?" Chris insisted. He really wanted to know how I was mentally.

From that moment, I knew this was a person I could talk to. I opened up about survivor guilt—my best friend, a guy with a wife and a kid, had died on the mission. Chris knew exactly what I was talking about.

We talked for hours that weekend. Again and again, he told me I had to get my feelings out. "Write them down," he said. "If you can't share them with someone, at least write them down."

So I started to. I also started talking with him regularly, and hanging out. He kind of took me in, him and Taya and the kids. They made me feel like I was part of the extended family. He was there during my darkest days.

For a while there, I was drinking, smoking, not taking care of myself. Finally I caught myself and turned it around. Chris doesn't get all the credit—I have a strong family, and they were all there for me, along with some strong and important friends—but Chris Kyle was a big part of it. He made me come out of that negativity shell.

Today I'm paying it all back. I mentor other wounded warriors, talking to them, helping them any way I can. People call me at all hours. I share my testimony. Working as the Texas coordinator of Feherty's Troops First Foundation, I've been blessed with a lot of opportunities to help people. I've talked people off the ledge. I've just listened, and seen how powerful that is.

And I've discovered that my wounds aren't the sum total of me. I've skydived, learned to play golf, even honed my sense of humor over my injuries: my nickname these days is "Crispy." You have to push everything to the limit. Everything.

Recently I wrote a poem about Chris:

> *Driving*
> *my truck today*
> *I thought of something funny,*
> *so I picked up*
> *my phone to call you.*
> *As I entered your name*
> *it hit me that*
> *you are no longer here,*
> *my friend.*
> *As tears started running down*
> *my eyes,*
> *all I could do was smile*
> *as I felt you next to me.*
> *I heard you say it's okay.*
> *I'm here.*
> *Keep my memory alive.*
> *Now wipe that tear,*
> *have no fear,*
> *and toast to the ones*
> *that couldn't be here!*

Hooyah, Chris Kyle!

RANDY CUPP
BUSINESSMAN, FRIEND

Blayne Cupp, Chris, and Randy Cupp during a charity event for veterans. Chris's friendship inspired Randy to become even more active in veterans' issues.

I first met Chris Kyle at a Boot Campaign fund-raiser for veterans that I helped to sponsor in May of 2012.

We spent the day shooting sporting clays and seemed to hit it off real well. He told me and my son Blayne that he had never killed a big white-tailed deer. We invited him to our ranch for the upcoming hunting season and told him to bring a couple of friends along.

We stayed in touch, and it seemed like he was on TV all summer long. When the time for our hunting expedition came, the first weekend in November, he arrived with two wounded veterans, Lance Burt and Steve Land. We had several volunteers to guide, clean, cook, and otherwise keep Chris and his friends entertained. Chef Jon Bonnell of Bonnell's Restaurant in Fort Worth cooked a dinner that included elk tenderloin, bison tenderloin, stone crab claws, and grilled quail. Coors Distributing of Fort Worth sent twenty cases of Coors Light, Chris's favorite brew.

Lance joked that he was a bullet catcher. He'd "caught" two bullets in Panama during the Noriega incident. He recovered from that and then caught five more bullets in Mogadishu, Somalia, in the operation made famous by the movie *Black Hawk Down*. It just so happened it was the nineteenth anniversary of the event.

Steve Land was a twenty-seven-year-old double leg amputee. He lost his legs to an IED in Afghanistan. He was the lone survivor when an IED hit his Humvee; six others were killed. Steve was the only soldier in the Humvee who was not a parent and suffers from something I have heard called survivor's remorse.

We sat on my porch on Friday afternoon and had a few beers before the evening hunt. Chris told us a couple of stories that I would be nervous to put down in print.

Steve got a scimitar-horned oryx the next morning. Chris and my son Blayne bow hunted but did not get a buck. I had several friends and area ranchers out for a BBQ lunch. Chris entertained the crowd by telling funny stories and demonstrating how to choke a person out. He also referred to my friend's .338 Lapua as a nice midrange rifle.

Lance got a big seven-point management buck Saturday evening. Chris and Blayne were still waiting to get a big whitetail within bow range and did not have any luck.

We took our veteran friends out to dinner at Mary's Cafe in Strawn, Texas, which happened to be one of Chris's favorite places to eat when he was at Tarleton College. While we were eating, I had a call from Allan Meyer of the Mingus Lake Ranch inviting the guys out for an evening to try to empty his bar. The guys accepted, and off we went on another adventure! I mainly sipped water and let the boys have fun. When the hosts were worn down, it took me about forty-five minutes to round my crew up and get them back to the ranch so they could hunt the next morning. Needless to say, I now know what it must be like to herd cats.

Chris and Blayne tried bow hunting again on Sunday morning but had no luck. Maybe deer hate the smell of whiskey, tequila, and cigars . . .

Everyone started packing up around noon Sunday, and by 1 P.M. it was just me and Chris at the ranch. We decided that maybe it would be best if he used his rifle to take another crack at getting his deer. We sat in the blind for quite a while that afternoon and talked about our kids, our life goals, and things that we could do together and separately to help our returning veterans. Chris talked a lot about PTSD and how it is mostly overlooked in society. He explained to me that it was a ticking time bomb. We discussed how to include Chris in some of the charity benefits that I am involved in, combining some of our fund-raising efforts.

I remember a couple of my friends asking Chris if he had considered politics. He told them that in order to be involved in politics, his children would be photographed and their names published. He wanted his children to remain shielded from the public and never mentioned their names in the book for that reason. Chris was very devoted to his family. You could see it in his eyes when he talked about them.

A short time later, a mature eleven-point buck came walking out of the brush in front of us. Chris touched off his .308 rifle and the old buck went down. It was a great day for both of us. Chris had killed his biggest white-tailed deer and I was his guide.

While taking pictures of Chris and the buck, I glanced off the side of the hill we were on and saw a few scimitar oryx feeding in a field. Twenty minutes later, we had stalked up on the herd. Chris selected a big one and got his second trophy for the day.

IN MEMORIAM

On Saturday, February 2, 2013, I was out at my ranch by myself. I'd been at one of my blinds taking photos of some of my deer and had left my phone at the ranch house. At sunset, I went up to the house and made dinner. I kept hearing my phone vibrate, but didn't bother checking it. When I did pick it up, I was shocked by all the missed calls and text messages on the screen. Before I had even checked a message, it dawned on me that there was only one common thread between all the names that I was looking at. I knew that something had happened to Chris.

I tried my best to keep up with the news and hoped the reports were wrong. There were reminders all around, including a bottle of whiskey we'd opened but would never finish together. When I opened the freezer to get ice cubes, I saw the two cans of Copenhagen that Chris had left in case he ran out the next time he was down—he didn't like my Skoal.

Besides being one of the most lethal military individuals in history, Chris was probably one of the most compassionate and respectful men I've ever met. He never failed to thank a former military man or woman for their service. He treated all veterans as equals and was genuinely interested in hearing their stories more than telling them his own.

Chris may be gone, but those of us who got to know him will never forget him. Being a businessman, I found it hard at first to believe that he gave away all of the money from his book; after spending time with him, I believed it. His big black Ford truck looked pretty cool, but it also had around 150,000 miles and he could not afford to replace it. He was a true American hero.

RICH EMBERLIN
DALLAS POLICE DEPARTMENT, FRIEND

Rich Emberlin checks the flank as he follows Chris through a training exercise. At war and at peace, Chris was always ready to lead.

I have a lot of stories about Chris—almost all of them are not what most people would expect about the person they have read about or seen on television.

There was the time a guy ran his mouth at Chris outside of a restroom at a really nice hotel bar in Texas—we'll withhold the name to protect the guilty. We had been at the SWAT range all day and we were tired, dirty, banged up, and just trying to relax. I guess this particular guy didn't think that the BDUs (battle dress uniforms) we were wearing were the appropriate dress for this particular fancy place and voiced his opinion rather obnoxiously.

In a flash, Chris put the guy up against the wall and was about two seconds from choking him out. Fortunately, he stopped at the last moment, realizing the guy wasn't a real threat. So he took it easy on him.

"You're gone when I come out," Chris growled. Then he gave him a gentle squeeze and went inside to do his business.

The guy made it across the street before the restroom door even closed.

I got on Chris about the confrontation. We got into a discussion about what could and couldn't be done now that he was back from the big "sandbox." Like a lot of other SEALs, Chris didn't tolerate a lot of BS from guys like this and occasionally he would choke these types of people out, usually though not always in jest. The guy we'd just dealt with would have been a prime candidate, he suggested.

I told him that back home, the ROEs—"rules of engagement"—precluded choking people out.

"It's assault," I told him.

"Assault? No bro, that was just a little warning." He gave me one of his innocent looks. He was being sincere. For Chris, a choke-out was the equivalent of a big wet kiss on the forehead.

"Look, I'm a cop, and what you just did is *assault*," I told him.

Well, he wouldn't let me hear the end of that. Weeks later, he and I ran into a chaplain who'd been in the Marines and had a mature outlook on life. Chris decided to put the matter to him.

"Is choking someone out assault?" he asked the chaplain.

I rolled my eyes in the background as he recounted the situation. The chaplain considered it carefully.

"It is assault," he said finally. "It's assault with the intent to educate. So you're good to go."

I just shook my head while Chris grinned at me.

Chris could be such a jokester, just a big kid. Then suddenly, if the occasion called for it, he'd be very serious, completely different. He'd be all business. He was the guy you wanted on your team, whether it was a dignitary protection job or playing touch football. He had one speed—full.

And that was the way he took on friendship. As a friend, there were no questions asked: if you called him up in the middle of the night and asked for a change of clothing, five hundred bucks, and a car, you'd get them all.

He was wise beyond his years in some ways, and still a little kid in others. He was the only guy I know who could sit in a room with you for two hours, not say anything, and yet cure whatever had been ailing you when you came in.

I want people to know what a good and nice man he was. What a great husband, father, and friend he was. I want people to know that he never, ever acted like a celebrity—I'm not sure he knew he was one. I want people to know he was a hell of a practical joker. I want people to know he was a true friend and the one true friend of everyone who ever got close to him. I really miss him.

IN MEMORIAM

SARAH AND ELLYSE DYER
FRIENDS

After we learned the terrible news of Chris's death, my four-year-old daughter Ellyse wrote the following prayer:

Dear God,
Thank you for Mr. Chris and for making him better and that he's with you now. Thank you that he got to play with me a lot and for being with him at that very moment.

You see, Elly didn't know her "Mr. Chris" as an American hero—she knew him as one of *her* heroes. She knew him as a friend's daddy who had an inviting smile, twinkly eyes, a huge heart, and wide-open arms. Chris's large presence demanded attention, but his fun-loving and gentle spirit invited laughter and playfulness. Every soccer or basketball practice and game, Elly sought Chris out, knowing he would welcome her up in that big ol' lap of his.

The morning of Chris's death, we were all at the kids' basketball game. We were getting the boys ready to go home to play for the afternoon and we couldn't find Elly anywhere. I looked up at my husband and said, "I don't see Chris, what do you want to bet that she's still in the gym on his lap?" Sure enough, that's where she was, and where she had been for the previous hour and a half—laughing and giggling and playing. If that doesn't tell you about the endless patience and heart of Chris Kyle, I don't know a story that would.

Nearly four months later, Elly's prayers still include the words, "Please be with my friends and Mrs. Taya and give them peace and be with their hearts." She may not understand everything there is to understand about death and heaven, but she understands the void that Chris's death leaves. She knows that Mr. Chris was a hero to his kids and to his wife, and she understands that their hearts all need the comfort only God can provide.

To say that Chris loved kids is an understatement. The fact that he happened to love mine is a bonus that gives his status of "legend" an even greater meaning to us. I would never want to downplay Chris's military achievements, but the legacy that he leaves is so much more than his brilliant and amazing military records. The records would stand on their own, but how much more amazing to have the depth of love and compassion for others that Chris had.

IN MEMORIAM

SCOTT BROWN
MUSICIAN, MARINE, FRIEND

Scott "Scooter" Brown and Chris share a laugh during a hunting trip. Their friendship was a song—literally—as they collaborated on a tune Scooter included on a recent album.

I met Chris for the first time at Base Camp 40—Warriors in the Wild, an organization that takes combat veterans on elk hunts in western Colorado. A mutual friend, Base Camp 40 director Paul Bristol, introduced us on the mountain. Our first conversation went like this:

"Scott Brown? I heard there was some jarhead up here that thinks he can sing," said Chris.

455

"Yup. I heard there was some squid up here that thought he could write books. I hope you brought some in case we need to start a fire."

"I think we're gonna be friends," said Chris, laughing.

I am a U.S. Marine. I served in Iraq in 2003. Now I'm the lead singer of the Scooter Brown Band. When I met Chris, we discovered that we had a lot in common besides serving the country we love. We talked family, kids, music, baseball, rodeo, and hunting. When we met, I hadn't read his book and honestly didn't really know much about him. After reading *American Sniper,* I realized we were in Nasiriyah, Iraq, around the same time in 2003.

Two nights in a row the weekend we were at Base Camp 40, we came down from the mountain to hang out at a little bar in Grand Junction. Both nights we somehow found ourselves in some minor scraps. It seemed like guys just had something to prove and gravitated toward us.

One guy looked like he was gonna hit us with a beer bottle. Chris looked at him and said, "You always hold a beer bottle like you're gonna break it over somebody's head?" While the man was trying to formulate an answer, the bouncer came over to calm things down. He proceeded to tell out antagonists they were trying to start a fight with a Marine and a Navy SEAL, then explained who Chris was. They lost some color in their skin tone and kissed our asses for the rest of the night. It was pretty damn funny to witness.

For some reason, the bar owner thought we were a couple of big shots with lots of money and started talking to us about buying his bar. We'd been putting back some Coors Light, so we entertained the conversation for our own amusement, knowing damn well we couldn't buy any bar.

I turned to Chris and said, "So, what are we gonna name our bar?" We tossed around a bunch of joke names, coming up with the crudest names we could think of.

IN MEMORIAM

Then Chris got quiet. "Valor," he said. "We should name it valor. To pay respects to everyone who's fought and sacrificed for our country. No matter if you got a medal for it or not, we all fought with valor."

It stuck with me.

Back in Texas, we continued our friendship. As a songwriter, the word "valor" kept running through my head. I told Chris I was gonna write a song about it and tossed some ideas around with him. Once the song was finished, Chris said he didn't want any credit for helping to write it. That was typical Chris Kyle style. I told him to go fly a kite.

I only got to play it for him twice. Once while visiting him and Taya, and once at his memorial service at Cowboys Stadium in Arlington, Texas. It was the most honorable thing I've ever been asked to do—and one that I wish I never had to do.

I can honestly say that Chris has had a huge impact on my life. I love everything he stood for, his love for his amazing family, his love for his fellow brothers in arms, and his will to want to give back and help others.

Was Chris a hero to me? Yes. Not just because of his military service but because he was a great father, husband, family man, and friend. It was an honor to call Chris a friend.

Semper fidelis, brother.

SERGEANT VINCE LEE
DALLAS POLICE DEPARTMENT, FRIEND

Vincent and Jennifer Lee at their wedding with Chris and Taya. The couple became fast friends after Chris resettled in Texas.

When you were in Chris's presence, you couldn't help but notice his physical stature. He had wide shoulders, big arms, and a strong handshake. But the really impressive thing about the guy was his personality. His energy filled the room when he walked into it.

I met him a few years back. I'd heard of him before, but what I'd heard seemed almost mythological. It was hard to gauge what was real and what was not. Frankly, I expected to meet a gruff, maybe even mean-spirited man. I did not. Oh, his physical bearing and stance were exactly as advertised: he was a bad-ass. But then, as I watched him interact with the people around him, I saw that he was amazingly humble and kindhearted. He even seemed a little naive: he saw good things in everyone.

I was honored when he selected me to work security for him

during his book tour—although I found it ironic and even humorous that I'd be providing security for a guy who could easily kick my ass. I felt a deep sense of pride as I traveled the country with a man I truly respected and admired.

I remember his very first book signing in Dallas. I arrived at the Barnes & Noble bookstore hours early to conduct a site advance. There was a crowd of two hundred people. I called back to the detail and told them the numbers. We all braced for what would be the beginning of an incredible journey.

Over eight hundred people showed up to get books signed and shake hands with "The Legend" that night. After it was over, we all knew that Chris Kyle was now a rock star. Yet he remained a humble soul. Later on the book tour, we found ourselves booked into a fleabag hotel. We all laughed because we *knew* no one had bothered to research the hotel: Why on earth would they put Chris Kyle in such a dump? It wasn't until weeks later that I found out Chris had a suite at the finest hotel in town but refused to stay there because his security people did not have a room there.

I have a lot of good memories from that tour. No matter where else we were due, Chris was clear that he wasn't leaving until everyone who wanted to take a photo, get a copy of *American Sniper* signed, or just talk was satisfied. It didn't matter how long it took or how little sleep he'd gotten. He would stand there the entire time and thank every veteran for their service. He made sure that every elderly person would not have to stand too long. And through it all, he was more concerned for Taya's safety than he was for his own.

In my line of work I've had an opportunity to meet many great leaders of this nation. I say with no hesitation and absolutely no hyperbole, Chris was as good a man as I've ever had the honor to shake hands with. He is the "rough man" George Orwell speaks of. He stood ready in the night to visit violence upon those who would do us harm. I will miss my friend.

AMERICAN SNIPER: MEMORIAL EDITION

JIM DEFELICE
COAUTHOR OF *AMERICAN SNIPER*

I knew from the start that people would relate to Chris and Taya's story, but I didn't understand how successful we had been telling it until the night of the very first book signing in Dallas.

I was up in New York, and had been talking to Chris via text or phone—they seem to blur together these days—earlier in the day. He claimed to need some sort of encouragement. Chris wasn't a public person and surely didn't like crowds. I can't remember what I said exactly, though I'm sure it was something along the lines of *Just be yourself.*

And: *Don't worry. There'll only be a hundred people or so there. You'll be out of there and back home pretty quick.*

It didn't quite go that way. People started lining up in the afternoon. I've heard estimates that over eight hundred showed up to sign books and meet Chris. He and Taya were there well past midnight. Chris shook every hand and signed every book. I'm thankful they didn't stick me with the babysitter's bill.

In case you don't know, a hundred people at a book signing is actually a lot. A thousand people is unheard of, unless you're already a movie star. In fact, I've been at book signings for movie stars and their crowds were half what Chris's was that night.

I joined Chris and Taya a few weeks later as they swung through mid- and eastern Texas for a number of events. The crowds were just as massive. Hundreds of people showed up in small towns in the middle of the day to buy books, have them signed, and most of all, thank Chris for his service. The publication of the book had made him the brother, son, friend, neighbor they hadn't been able to personally thank for the sacrifices of serving our country.

IN MEMORIAM

American Sniper *has been translated into seventeen languages since its publication in 2012.*

In commercial terms, *American Sniper* has had undreamed of success. At the date I'm writing this, *American Sniper* has been translated into sixteen languages. Well over a million copies have been sold in formats ranging from hardcover to audiobook to e-book. It will soon be made into a major motion picture starring one of the country's biggest

461

box-office attractions. By any measure, the book is in a very unique category.

But I don't think anyone, and certainly not Chris, really gauged the book's success in terms of numbers. For Chris, the smiles, the handshakes, and the thank-yous were the true measure of achievement. He was happy for the success, since it meant more money for the families he was helping—Chris didn't take money for the book—but I strongly suspect he never once looked at a sales tally, let alone a bestseller list.

Chris always gave me a lot of credit for the success of the book, but I think from the beginning to the end he and Taya are the ones responsible. It's their story. Their decision to tell *everything* without feel-good gloss is really the core of the book. It's what people can relate to on a gut level. I think people meeting them in person realized that Chris was just a regular guy, a young man exactly the same as that son or daughter, friend or neighbor who'd gone and enlisted a few years back. He was a man you could have a beer with. And he was a hero to boot.

I've told a lot of stories for the media since Chris died, mostly in an attempt to illustrate that he was a lot more than "just" the highly skilled SEAL that news reports inevitably portray him as. I've talked about the hunting trips he took disabled vets on, and tried to get beyond even that. At different times I've mentioned the snowball fights with my son (Chris lost); his texting me after Hurricane Sandy to see if he could help; the talks we had about how to coach Little League. I've even admitted how completely he whipped my ass at Madden. But none of these stories really get to the totality of who he was. Even alongside the book, they present a limited vision of the complex, generous, and humble human being that was Chris Kyle.

One story I've never told happened in New York City, during a short break in one of the early publicity tours. There was a lull one afternoon and I asked Chris what he wanted to do. I was

IN MEMORIAM

thinking he'd want to take a nap, since he hadn't had much sleep; I wouldn't have minded one myself. Instead he said he wanted to visit the site of the World Trade Center. Though he'd never been there, the destruction of the towers had had an immense impact on his life, and he wanted to pay silent homage to the people who had died there.

Truth is, I hadn't been at the site since September 12, 2001, the day after the bombing. Like most New Yorkers, I knew people who died and families who lost loved ones there. Other people were much more closely affected, certainly, but the place nonetheless filled me with dread. I'd been down in the Wall Street area plenty of times during the decade since the attack, but always managed to avoid the site.

I thought of making an excuse to either beg out of the visit or deflect Chris's request; there were plenty of interviews he had to do, and really, he should have gotten some rest. But 9/11 was the reason he had done so much for our country, and it wouldn't have been right to keep him from the site.

So we went.

The area thronged with people. I don't know that I'd ever felt claustrophobic before, especially in New York where I mostly grew up, but I certainly did there. Inside the temporary museum, Chris walked slowly through the exhibits, examining everything, every picture, every artifact.

All I could do was remember the way the debris still choked the air on 9/12, and the odd way the skyline looked as I walked down from Canal Street. After about two minutes, I went outside for fresh air, my coat open even though it was a cold January day.

Chris came out about a half hour later. He was pensive after he finished. He glanced at me and suggested we have a beer.

"Absolutely," I told him, and I led him a few blocks away to a small place I knew.

He didn't ask me about 9/11 or what I felt. That wasn't his way. He just sat there, unobtrusive, ready to help if needed but otherwise just being a presence—kind of on emotional overwatch, I guess, to use a metaphor from his days as a SEAL sniper.

My claustrophobia passed pretty quickly. In fact, I can't say that I felt it again until the early Sunday morning when I heard he'd died.

The visit to the World Trade Center site affected Chris as well as me. He didn't say anything about it. He didn't have to—it was written in capital letters on his face. I don't think he knew one person who died there, but he somehow felt for each one. He loved making jokes about us "Yankees," even after I pointed out that, properly speaking, New Yorkers are not Yankees at all. But he lived that famous line from Donne about no man being an island. On some level he wanted to save all humanity, or at least all of his fellow countrymen.

That's an odd thing to say about a warrior, let alone one whose renown comes from the number of kills he made. But it's the truth, and it's the odd paradox that defines Chris Kyle and his so-called legend. It's the same paradox at the heart of all wars. In order to save people, Chris had to kill others. He had to turn his world black and white so he could make a difference. In the process, he temporarily lost part of himself.

Maybe not lost. Definitely not lost. But he stowed it behind so many walls that it was hard to reach.

Taya and his children helped him rediscover it. You can read about some of the process in the book. The one thing I would add is that it was still an ongoing struggle when we were working. In fact, the book made things a hell of a lot harder for him. It took him back, and not in a good way.

IN MEMORIAM

Sometimes I didn't realize quite how hard the whole process was for him. I wish I could have made remembering easier. We spent a lot of time together and I got used to reading his moods, but there were points when I was just oblivious to his pain, when I wasn't observant enough to just hang back and sit there on quiet overwatch. Maybe I needed to push to get it all out, to get the book done. Maybe I just wasn't paying enough attention.

Chris never complained. Not once. And when the crowds started coming for the signings, he stayed and shook every hand. He had a kind word and often a joke for everyone. Privately, he hated the fuss. I know for a fact he would have preferred being out hunting or playing with the kids. But he still had a smile for every man, woman, and child who met him on the tours, and a thank-you for every fellow veteran, whether he saw them in the bookstore or the local CVS.

I'll let the others talk about Chris's good works and his impact on their lives. There's plenty to talk about. He's left a big hole in all our lives. I'm not sure why or even how a Texas cowboy and a guy from New York ever got along, but somehow we did. I blame it on Chris: I don't think there's a person alive he couldn't get along with.

Chris's funeral was one of the saddest days of my life. But somehow, looking back on it, I don't remember the sadness that much. What I remember are the crowds I saw on the way down in my car from his hometown to the state cemetery. I expected there would be plenty of people along the roads near Dallas where he lived. There were. But the crowds were just as strong the whole way down, for some two hundred or so miles. People bunched up on the overpasses, gathered on the highway shoulders, held flags on the side roads.

That's what I remember of that sad day, and when I think about it, I smile—thousands of people really understood who Chris was even if they never met him, and paid tribute to that. It was an extraordinary thing.

And in the same way, the most enduring image from the burial service isn't the moving march of bagpipers, the pounding of the SEALs' Tridents on his coffin, or even the final moment at the end when his coffin stood by itself in the deserted cemetery. As moving as these images were, the sight that is burned into my memory is the long line of faces peering over the fence behind us, people from around the city, the state, and the country, regular folks offering one last thank-you to a man who gave his all to his country, his God, and his family.

There was not a space left on the fence line. It was as if all Texas, and all America, had come out to perform one last silent, emotional overwatch for a regular guy, a neighbor, a friend, who just happened to be a hero.

FOR MORE INFORMATION

Taya Kyle has been carrying on her husband Chris's legacy in a variety of ways, from speaking on behalf of veterans, to guiding completion of his posthumous bestseller *American Gun: A History of the U.S. in Ten Firearms,* to continuing his work with a host of charitable organizations. She has established the Web site www.ChrisKyleFrog.com and maintains the official Chris Kyle Facebook page, www.Facebook.com/ChrisKyleFrog. Please visit these sites to learn how you can help Chris's spirit of service live on—as well as for news on charity events, veterans' organizations, *American Sniper* movie updates, Taya's speaking schedule, new projects, and much more. Thank you for your ongoing support. God bless!